T0311563

Space, Taste and Affect

This book is an exploration of how time, space and social atmospheres contribute to the experience of taste. It demonstrates complex combinations of material, sensual and symbolic atmospheres and social encounters that shape this experience.

Space, Taste and Affect brings together case studies from the fields of sociology, geography, history, psycho-social studies and anthropology to examine debates around how urban designers, architects and market producers manipulate the experience of taste through creating certain atmospheres. The book also explores how the experience of taste varies throughout life, or even during fleeting social encounters, challenging the sense of taste as static. This book moves beyond common narratives that taste is 'acquired' or developed, to emphasize the role of psycho-social histories of nostalgia, memories of childhood, migration, trauma and displacement in the experience of what we eat and drink. It focuses on entrenched social dimensions of class, value and distinction instead of psychological and neuroscientific conceptualisations of taste and sensuous practices of consumption to be intrinsically linked to the experience of taste in complex ways.

This book will appeal to undergraduate and postgraduate students of sociology, human geography, tourism and leisure studies, anthropology, psychology, arts and literature, architecture and urban design.

Emily Falconer is a lecturer in Sociology at the University of Westminster. Her research focuses on the politics of affect, emotion and embodied encounters in everyday life. Emily has featured on BBC Radio 4: *Thinking Allowed* (October 2013) to discuss the transformations of food tourism.

Routledge Research in Culture, Space and Identity

Series editor: Dr. Jon Anderson, *School of Planning and Geography, Cardiff University, UK*

The *Routledge Research in Culture, Space and Identity* Series offers a forum for original and innovative research within cultural geography and connected fields. Titles within the series are empirically and theoretically informed and explore a range of dynamic and captivating topics. This series provides a forum for cutting edge research and new theoretical perspectives that reflect the wealth of research currently being undertaken. This series is aimed at upper-level undergraduates, research students and academics, appealing to geographers as well as the broader social sciences, arts and humanities.

For more information about this series, please visit: www.routledge.com/ Routledge-Research-in-Culture-Space-and-Identity/book-series/CSI.

Space, Taste and Affect

Atmospheres That Shape the Way We Eat

Edited by
Emily Falconer

Routledge
Taylor & Francis Group

LONDON AND NEW YORK

First published 2021
by Routledge
2 Park Square, Milton Park, Abingdon, Oxon OX14 4RN

and by Routledge
52 Vanderbilt Avenue, New York, NY 10017

Routledge is an imprint of the Taylor & Francis Group, an informa business

British Library Cataloguing in Publication Data
A catalogue record for this book is available from the British Library

Library of Congress Cataloging-in-Publication Data
A catalog record has been requested for this book

ISBN: 978-1-138-23426-0 (hbk)
ISBN: 978-1-315-30747-3 (ebk)

Typeset in Times New Roman
by Taylor & Francis Books

For Iona

Contents

Illustrations

Figures

Tables

Contributors

Karen Agutter is a historian of migration with a particular interest in migrant identity and receiving society/migrant relations. She is currently a Visiting Research Fellow at the University of Adelaide.

Rachel A. Ankeny is Professor of History and Philosophy and Deputy Dean Research in the Faculty of Arts at the University of Adelaide, and Honorary Visiting Professor in the College of Social Science and International Studies (Philosophy) at the University of Exeter. Her research crosses several fields including food studies, migration history and history and philosophy of the biological and biomedical sciences. in food studies, her research interests include food ethics, food habits of women and children, food habits in the Italian diaspora and the relationship of science to food habits; she leads the Food Values Research Group at the University of Adelaide.

Paz Concha is Adjunct Assistant Professor at the Institute of Urban and Territorial Studies (Pontificia Universidad Católica de Chile) and Postdoctoral Researcher at the Centre for Social Conflict and Cohesion Studies (COES). She is an ethnographer interested in urban and economic sociology. Paz holds a doctorate in Sociology from the London School of Economics (LSE); her thesis was an ethnography of the curation of the street food scene in London, exploring the relationship between cultural economies and placemaking. Paz is currently researching placemaking in commercial districts in Santiago de Chile.

Mukta Das is a Research Associate at the SOAS Food Studies Centre at SOAS University of London. She completed her PhD research on the changing nature of what makes food ordinary in the cities of Guangzhou, Macau and Hong Kong. In particular she examined how South Asian professional and community cooks, grocers and restaurateurs have identified, interpreted and lived their role in extending the boundaries of ordinary Cantonese food and how this impacts on their sense of belonging. With Celia Plender, Mukta completed an oral history project about Neal's Yard Dairy in 2014 supported by the University of Sheffield's ERC-funded Food Futures project. The oral history recordings are housed at the British Library.

Ericka Duffy works in scent and taste. Her interests lie in experiential art looking at different modalities of sensory engagement. She has worked with some of the world's top bars on creative cocktails. She has worked with the Edinburgh Film Festival and the Milan Film Festival presenting multi-sensory cinematic experiences. She has curated events and is a frequent panel member with the Edinburgh International Science Festival. She also works in perfume, coffee, tea and water, most notably, presenting a sensory water experience alongside Tania Kovats' exhibit at the Fruitmarket Gallery in Edinburgh, 2014.

Giolo Fele is Professor of Culture and Communication Studies and teaches graduate courses in Qualitative Methods for Social Research at the University of Trento (Italy). His research interests include communication in emergency situations, sport and social actions and professional tasting. He has published in *Human Studies, Qualitative Research, Forum: Qualitative Social Research, Revue Française de Linguistique Appliquée, European Journal of Public Health, Pragmatics, Empiria: Revista de Metodología de Ciencias Sociales, Etnografia e Ricerca Qualitativa.*

Beth M. Forrest is a food historian, and teaches at the Culinary Institute of America in Hyde Park, NY. Currently President of the Association for the Study of Food and Society, she is currently working on an edited volume on sauce and identity in the western world as well as an edited text on intersections of food, memory and imagination. She has guest edited a special issue on chocolate for *Food and Foodways*, published in *Global Food History* and contributed to the *Routledge Handbook for Food Studies, Gastronomica, The Sage Encyclopedia of Food Issues* in addition to several others. She has been quoted by CNN, *QRS Magazine, The Boston Globe, The Chicago Tribune*, Forbes.com and WAMC radio.

Pier Paolo Giglioli is Professor Emeritus of Sociology of Culture at the University of Bologna (Italy). In his career he has taught or lectured at the University of Washington, University of California (Berkeley and San Diego), Brown University, Swarthmore College, University of Edinburgh, University of Exeter, Université Paris VIII, University of Joensuu (Finland) and the European University Institute (Florence). He is the author of seven books and several articles. He edited *Language and Social Context* (Penguin 1990). His main research interests concern theories of culture, rituals and ceremonies, language and social practices, comparative studies of university systems.

Suzanne Hocknell is a geographer whose work seeks to explore and rehearse practices of understanding, solidarity, care and belonging, within and between more-than human communities. The chapter, "A sticky situation?" draws, in part, on her PhD work. This research engaged 'CoPSE', a novel play-centred methodology, to explore who and what are entangled with the stuff of margarine, why margarine is known and done the way it is, and to investigate how such mundane knowledges and practices shape and are shaped by the ways it appears sensible or possible for human and nonhuman communities to live together.

Eric Laurier is Reader in Geography and Interaction at the University of Edinburgh. Through working with Sally Wiggins he became interested in family mealtimes as settings for the production, maintenance and transformation of appetites and tastes. Drawing on ongoing work on the embodied organisation of practices he has pursued how the handling of the cutlery, plates and the various portions of food provide resources for eating together as intimates. As a child he didn't like onions and would test his parents' patience by picking each sliver out of his food.

Vania Ling is a creative food specialist with a BSc in Nutrition and Food Science and a MSc in Food Policy from the Centre of Food Policy in London. She also has extensive training in violin and piano, and music theory and history. Ling's knowledge and education has led to her fascination in sensory experiences that hone the skills of the palate by incorporating music. In Dublin, Ling created a multi-sensory experience – guests were introduced to food ingredients that thrive in the dark, where the tastes and smells were enhanced and accompanied by the performance of musical works. Additionally, she has also curated coffee and cocktail events across Canada for Coffee Potluck, a community-based collective formed to foster taste discovery.

Louise MacAllister is a geographer whose work addresses the intersection of everyday practices with the practices and discourses of governance; in particular, practices of the body and care, where Louise has focused on body size and fatty materialities. The chapter 'A sticky situation' draws on PhD research undertaken at the University of Exeter with her thesis entitled 'Shaping the family; anti-obesity discourses and family life'. Louise now works for a community development charity in rural Devon, where she manages a range of projects and carries out non-academic research. Tying together both her academic and community development work is Louise's commitment to knowledge politics; in which she foregrounds everyday place based and embodied knowledges within systems of governance.

Nina J. Morris is a Senior Lecturer in Human Geography in the School of GeoSciences at the University of Edinburgh. Her thematic research interests fall into three interrelated areas: cultural geographies of landscape; sensory perception; and human – non-human nature relationships with a focus on health and well-being. She is also interested in experiential learning and research ethics.

Katerina Nussdorfer is currently enrolled at the University of Vienna, in the Department of English and American Studies as a PhD student of American Studies, where she works on her PhD thesis 'Food as cultural and ethnic identity in American twentieth-century literature. She also teaches English and Macedonian, and conducts culinary tours as a food anthropologist docent for Context Travel and her own company Culinary Tours Vienna. Her research focus is on Balkan street food, Habsburg cuisine, immigrant foods in America, Jewish foodways and food on film.

Julie Parsons is an Associate Professor in Sociology. She recently completed an Independent Social Research Foundation (ISRF) mid-career fellowship (2016–2017), working on a Photographic electronic Narrative (PeN) project with men released on temporary licence from the local prison and others serving community sentences on placement at a local resettlement scheme (RS), which is ongoing. This followed a Sociology of Health and Illness (SHI) Foundation Mildred Blaxter Fellowship (2015–2016) exploring commensality (eating together) as a tool for health, well-being, social inclusion and community resilience at the same RS. Her book *Gender, Class and Food, Families, Bodies and Health* (Palgrave Macmillan 2015) was shortlisted for the Foundation of Health and Illness (FHI) book prize in 2016. She has research interests in auto/biography, class, culture, embodiment, emotion, families, fat, feminism, food, gender, health and illness, maternal identities, stigma and the lived experience of prison and punishment. Her preferred methods of research are collaborative and participatory, although she has experience of both qualitative and quantitative approaches. To date her research has made use of asynchronous online interviews; auto/biography (auto-ethnography); computer mediated communication (CMC); in-depth interviewing; participant observation; photo-voice as well as other visual and creative research methods. She was programme lead for the MSc in Social Research from 2010–2014 and is currently programme lead for the BSc (Hons) in Sociology. She is convener of the British Sociological Association (BSA) Food Study Group, and a member of the BSA Auto/Biography study group, the BSA Medical Sociology study group and the British Society of Criminology.

Celia Plender is a lecturer in Social Anthropology at the University of Exeter. Her research engages with experiences of social, political and economic change in Britain. Her PhD focused on two grassroots, retail food co-ops in London and the ways in which each negotiated different visions and values relating to food-based politics, models of aids, practices of care and community building in an era of austerity. With Mukta Das, Celia completed an oral history project about Neal's Yard Dairy in 2014. The research was supported by the University of Sheffield's ERC-funded Food Futures project, and resultant recordings are housed at the British Library.

Thomas Thurnell-Read is a Senior Lecturer in Cultural Sociology in the School of Social Science at Loughborough University, UK. He has over a decade of experience researching alcohol consumption and drinking culture and is internationally recognised as a leading scholar of sociological approaches to the study of alcohol, drinking and drunkenness. He is the editor of *Drinking Dilemmas: Space, Culture and Identity* (Routledge 2015) and a founding member of the British Sociological Association's Alcohol Study Group and, more recently, Consumption Study Group. Beyond his work on the social and cultural aspects of alcohol, drinking and drunkenness, his other research interests include material culture, leisure and tourism, the sociology of the body and emotions and qualitative research methods.

Sally Wiggins is an Associate Professor in Psychology at Linköping University, Sweden. Her primary research focus is on the social aspects of eating, particularly during everyday family mealtimes, and on the ways in which psychological concepts such as food preferences, appetite and disgust are made relevant and consequential within social interaction. This body of research uses both discursive psychology and conversation analysis to offer turn-by-turn analyses of mealtime interaction. As such, it provides an analytical approach that examines the everyday details of eating practices while still addressing issues of relevance for psychology and social interaction. She is author of the methods textbook *Discursive Psychology* (Sage 2016), and co-editor of both *Discursive Research in Practice* (Palgrave 2007) and *Critical Bodies* (Palgrave 2007), as well as author of numerous journal articles and book chapters.

Acknowledgements

I would like to express heartfelt thanks to all authors who contributed to this edited collection on *Space, Taste and Affect*. This collection was a long time in the making, and encountered numerous and unforeseen setbacks along the way. The authors responded with great patience, and continued to work towards improving the revised collection long after we all originally envisaged. I thank them for their compassion and thoughtful cooperation, as much as their innovative and highly interdisciplinary contributions to this fascinating topic.

I extend my thanks to my partner and assistant David Sanchez Tatay, to Nayyar Hussain for proofreading each chapter, to my brother Ruairidh Alexander Falconer for additional proofs, and to the editors at Routledge for their understanding and assistance. Finally, special thanks to author Katerina Nussdorfer for posting an original packet of Macedonian *Stobi Flips* (see Chapter 5) to my University office in the final stages of the editing process, so I could experience first-hand the smoky, nutty taste of a (highly symbolic) food product I had read so extensively about on paper. I ate them all at my desk that very same day.

Preface

Emily Falconer

During my doctorate fieldwork into the embodied cultural capital inherent in backpacking tourism (2009), I was interviewing a research participant in a backpacking beach café over a cold, unappetising and slightly stale bowl of chips. Perhaps our dehydrated bodies were craving salt, or we were tired from our relentless search for 'authentic' experiences, but they tasted wonderful. My participant whispered her confession; that after 10 months 'on the road' in India and South East Asia she had stopped eating the 'local' street food and now snuck into the tourist spots aimed at young, western tourists for 'rubbish bowls of chips and bad pizza'. A year later, I was conducting ethnographic research into tourism consumption in Blackpool: *Coastal regeneration, taste and affect* (2010). Shivering on the bracing North Pier in late October, bright illuminations flashing above our heads, wafts of vinegar in the wind and repetitive pings from the arcade slot machines, a visitor and I shared a bag of hot, oily, deep-fried sugared donuts. The stall holder insisted we get our money's worth: five donuts for a pound- even though we had only asked for three. My interviewee had never visited Blackpool before, and confessed she wouldn't dream of eating 'such junk' at home, but here, and right now, they 'tasted perfect'.

Five years later, my long-standing interest in the multisensory complexities of food and eating drew to me to attend a 'curated experimental dinner' at Westminster Kingsway College on the 28th April 2015, run by the London Gastronomy Seminars. This event was designed by Charles Spence, Professor of experimental psychology at Oxford University, and co-author of *The Perfect Meal: The Multisensory science of food and eating* (2014, with Betina Piqueras-Fiszman). Spence and Piqueras-Fiszman engage in the science of 'neurogastronomy', where the brain adapts to the sense of taste through numerous, multisensorial factors such as visual presentation (colours, size, shapes, familiarity), language, smell, touch and texture, sound and music, light, dark and the weight and colour of the cutlery. Taste, the scientists argue, is not simply a matter of 'the neuroscience of flavor, but rather on all the other (non-food) factors that influence our overall multisensory experience of food' (2014: xvii). The curated experimental dinner felt like a (highly enjoyable) laboratory, and guests as lab-mice, as we were served ingredients in different formats, laid out on plates of varying sizes and colours, with carefully designed linguistic descriptors. Half the participating guests were given spoons twice as heavy as the remaining half. We scribbled down our tastes and feelings on questionnaires ('sweeter'; 'bitter'; 'more/less full'); research data to be collected, experiment results to be calculated. The science was clear: multi-sensual atmospheres and non-human variables were directly connected to our experience and perception of taste. These findings, argue Spence and Piqueras-Fiszman, were indispensable to the dining industry and experience economy; the art of gastronomy could be enhanced through a carefully considered restaurant design. In addition, the authors claimed such techniques could impact on the 'current global obesity crisis' as 'the diner's mind can be tricked into thinking that more food has been consumed that is actually the case' (2014: xviii).

As a social scientist developing my increasing infatuation with the sociology of taste and geographies of affect and what they can tell us about social life, dynamics and inequalities (Falconer 2013, Edensor and Falconer 2015, Taylor and Falconer 2015), I had a pressing sense there was much more to be said about the encounters with 'junk' food on Blackpool pier, and that an entire world of meaningful context was lacking from the curated experimental dinner that evening. Could our embodied experience of taste really be universally calculated by the metal weightiness of the fork? What other predetermined social histories and were unfolding on the seaside pier that night in 2009, alongside the comfort of sugar and hot fat as the sea breeze whipped our cheeks in the dark? Can our appreciation of cold chips in a backpacking café be fully understood without an understanding of embodied cosmopolitanism, a fetishization for the 'Other' and a post-colonial critique of long-term tourism? (see Falconer 2013). Since the hugely influential work of Pierre Bourdieu's *Distinction: A Social Critique of the Judgement of Taste* (1984) it has been widely accepted that taste is not just sensually and environmentally determined, but a highly symbolic signifier of classed distinctions, power and capital, and in its most extreme: symbolic violence. The moral panics surrounding the apparent obesity crisis and cultural 'fatphobia' have long been critiqued by social scientists (Monaghan, Colls and Evans 2014), who question the authority of medical discourse. How might our relationship with that low-cost, piping hot fatty donut oil be enmeshed with discourses of health, deviance, classed value and disgust? Who can fully enjoy a temporary dip into cheap fat as part of a 'tourist experience' and remain free from the moral stigmas it so often evokes? Geographies of affect, which have exploded rapidly over the past decade, detangle the relationship between the non-human and atmospheric, the spatial and temporal, and the 'Ordinary affects' (Stewart 2007) and fleeting encounters that tap into changing political landscapes. I am inclined to agree with Spence and Piqueras-Fiszma and their neurogastronomic theory, yet a true analysis of the numerous multisensual determinants of taste must incorporate the relationship with the social, spatial, affective and political in order to even begin to near completion.

This book follows an ongoing thought process, asking how the experience of taste is significantly shaped by complex combinations of material, sensual and socially symbolic atmospheres and encounters. *Space, Taste and Affect* is an interdisciplinary and international exploration of how the temporal and sensual nature of space, place and mobility can affect taste. This collection combines an analysis of affective atmospheres with embodied social histories, to inform our understanding of taste. Some chapters key into thought-provoking debates about how urban designers, architects and market producers can 'manipulate' the affect of taste through creating certain atmospheres. Other themes in this collection explore how the experience of taste can change throughout the life course, challenging the sense of taste as static and fixed. The research collected in this book looks beyond common narratives that something is an 'acquired' or developed taste, to incorporate phycho-social histories of nostalgia, embodied memories of childhood, migration, trauma and displacement. Yet most importantly, this book moves beyond the psychological and neuroscientific conceptualizations of taste and sensual practices of consumption, to allow for deep-rooted social dimensions of class, value and distinction to be intrinsically linked to the experience of taste in complex ways.

References

Bourdieu, P. (1984) *Distinction: A Social Critique of the Judgement of Taste.*

Edensor, T., and Falconer, E. (2015) Dans Le Noir? Eating in the dark: sensation and conviviality in a lightless place. *Cultural Geographies*, 22 (4), 601–618.

Falconer, E. (2013) Transformations of the backpacking food tourist: Emotions and conflicts. *Tourist Studies*, 13 (1), 21–35.

Monaghan, L., Colls, R., and Evans, B. (2014) *Obesity Discourse and Fat Politics: Research, Critiques and Interventions* Oxon: Routledge.

Spence, C., and Piqueras-Fiszman, B. (2014) *The Perfect Meal: The Multisensory Science of Food and Dining* Oxford: Wiley Blackwell.

Stewart, K. (2007) *Ordinary Affects* USA: Duke University Press.

Taylor, Y., and Falconer, E. (2014) 'Seedy bars and grotty pints': close encounters in queer leisure spaces. *Social and Cultural Geography* 16 (1), 43–57.

Space, taste and affect

An introduction

Emily Falconer

Developing earlier insights into the affective turn and the role of food and emotion in tourist studies (Falconer 2013) and the atmospheric, sensual 'experience economies' of London's dining scenes (Edensor and Falconer 2014), this book focuses on moments where embodied experiences of taste and place are significantly shaped by complex combinations of material, sensual and symbolic affective atmospheres. Scientific and psychological research into taste has exemplified the experimental nature of our senses, where taste aversion is deeply connected to the visual appearance of food (colour, shape), texture, price of food and wine (Almenberg and Dreber 2011) and even the feel and weight of the cutlery and crockery used to consume our food (Harrar and Spence 2013). The science of taste, although deeply influential and with potential to shape the design and production of gastronomy and culinary consumption, remains divorced from how these very visceral and sensual experiences are also deeply embedded in social, spatial, temporal and cultural dynamics. There is significant scope to marry these disciplines to reveal a nuanced complex analysis of how taste is affected in multiple ways. This book approaches taste from a social, cultural and geographic perspective, incorporating the emergent interest in the 'affective turn' within the social sciences. In doing so, this book moves beyond psychoanalytical approaches to taste, association and memory to reveal how atmospheres are integral to the deeply classed, social and cultural aspect of 'taste' as a form of distinction. This approach develops the well-known works of Bourdieu on taste and distinction (Bourdieu 1984). By focusing on an affective, atmospheric and deeply embodied experience of taste and smell, in conjunction with the ways in which taste promotes 'culinary capital' (LeBesco and Naccarato 2008, 2012) and acts as a symbolic marker of distinction, this book draws together multiple areas of disciplinary knowledge to analyse the impact of affect, design and atmospheres on the way we eat and drink. The diverse contributions to this collection make this book particularly distinct, in that they take an international approach to taste across the disciplines of sociology, human geography, tourism and leisure studies, anthropology, psychology, history, architecture and urban design and the arts.

Taste

This book is an examination of taste; the gustatory perception of imbibing food, liquids and edible textures, and the socio-cultural markers of taste as a subject of judgement, aesthetics and distinction. While inherently connected, this focus differs somewhat from the large body of food and consumption studies more generally, which span across sociology, psychology, anthropology, geography, food science, gastronomy and the humanities. Food and consumption investigate an enormity of topics, including the macro politics of the global food system, agricultural production, the global food crisis, food insecurity and health and nutrition outcomes, fair trade and the slow food movement and the hospitality industry. The study of taste, and *Space, Taste and Affect* in particular, attempts to capture the embodied moments, affective encounters and socio-politics that solely surround practices of consumption. In *Making Taste Public: Ethnographies of Food and the Senses* (2018) Counihan and Hojlund claim that the sensorial dimensions of taste – whether it be pleasure or repulsion – is the 'space between people and their food and how they lead to different definitions of quality, and to shared social platforms for performance lifestyle and identity' (2018: 2). This book starts with the premise taste is a reflective activity that is always relational, and builds upon anthropological traditions to incorporate social theories of affect and place-making from cultural geographies, sociology and beyond.

A social study of taste owes a great deal to Pierre Bourdieu's hugely instrumental work *Distinction: A Social Critique of the Judgment of Taste* (trans 1984), which contends that those in the highest positions of power in society determine the dominant aesthetic. Almost without exception, all subsequent writings on taste within the social sciences engage with Bourdieu. Taste and habitus as a marker of social stratification, symbolic (cultural, social) capital and symbolic violence have become a stable apparatus on which to build multiple readings of taste. Bourdieu's theories are employed in relation to food, consumption, art, music and culture, and range to the sociology of education, family relationships and social mobility (Vincent and Ball 2007, Thatcher et al. 2016). At its heart, a critical reading of the sociology of taste is conceptualised as a mode of attachment to the world and others, a shared appreciation (or aversion) that holds us together (Hennion 2007), an interest in how goods and practices create social bonds or divisions (Featherstone 1990, Warde 1997, Gronow 1997), and as a study of how taste can create an *appearance* of innate values and preferences which are deeply determined by social histories and environments (Stewart 2014). More recently, readings of food practices and taste across the social class divide have sought to take a more nuanced approach to Bourdieu, challenging his portrayal of working-class food tastes as primarily determined by insecure access to money and time (Maguire 2017). Others, such as Ray (2017), have asserted greater agency of taste-making, and bring the immigrant body – primarily viewed as labour in critiques of the food industry – into the forefront of a sociology of taste. Arguing for a reversal of thinking that taste is marginal to the lives of marginal people, Ray (2017: 42) observes:

> In this conception, poor, hard-working people can teach us about poverty and suffering, hierarchy and symbolic violence, but never about taste. That might be one of the unfortunate consequences of the overwhelming dominance of Pierre Bourdieu's framework of analysis in sociology.

Perhaps the most useful expansion of Bourdieu's theories to emerge in the study of food is 'culinary capital', a term coined by cultural sociologists LeBesco and Naccarato (2008, 2012). Knowing, buying, consuming, writing about (food blogging) and serving food are all 'acts of signification through which people construct and sustain their identities' (LeBesco and Naccarato 2008: 1). Culinary capital draws on how food is implicated in the accumulation of multiple forms of Bourdieu's capital – economic, social, cultural, symbolic – to acquire and retain status and power. Importantly, and as we shall return to time and again in the course of this book, LeBesco and Naccarato problematise the notion that some foods and practices hold capital while others do not. Rather, value is assigned on a continually changing basis and functions in multiple, often unpredictable ways. In other words, it is not just *what* you eat, but when, how and, most certainly, where. They do not separate culinary capital from multidimensional spaces but rather seek

> to understand how it circulates across this cultural landscape and how it interacts with any number of prevailing values and ideologies … how and why certain foods and food related practices connote, and by extension, confer status and power on those who know about them and enjoy them.
> (2012: 16)

Like Bourdieu, the authors consider resistance to culinary capital that disrupts social norms of middle-class values and status through eating, yet more often than not culinary capital is awarded to some and denied to others, based on a slippery interplay of knowledge and power, which –as this book will argue – become entangled within space, time and affective atmospheres.

Space, Taste and Affect furthers the study of culinary capital by tuning into an affective embodiment of taste practices. As Gronow (1997: 1) observes, 'the more reflexive the concept of taste and the more refined the sense of taste, the more it was separated from immediate sensual pleasure'. Through a close reading of the visceral, material sensations of food and drink, and their fizzy, fatty, bitter or sloppy properties, *Space, Taste and Affect* places these acts of consumption within a wider analysis of socio-cultural histories and political milieus.

To do this, it is necessary to engage with sociologies of disgust as well as pleasure. Tyler (2013) extends Kristeva's influential theories of abjection, to see how social abjection and disgust become attached to some stigmatised societal figures who are seen as 'revolting' (unemployed 'chavs', gypsies, asylum seekers). Specifically relating to food, Rhys-Taylor (2013) takes the case of East London's jellied eel to create sociological connections between 'gut' aversions to slimy fish jelly and the production of class, ethnic and generational forms of distinction. Connecting embodied, affective disgust to social abjection can further help us understand what these aversions can make bodies *do* in particular spaces, and how identities are formed and maintained (Taylor and Falconer 2015).

Part I of this book: 'Distinctive tastes: class, consumption and distaste' explores this through three case studies: beer, fat and wine. This opening section continues Bourdieu's analysis of taste as a form of distinction, demonstrating that the experience of taste is also deeply impacted by spatial encounters and materialities, and the degree to which some subjects can be damaged by classed stigma for embodying the 'wrong' tastes (in the wrong space, and time). Thomas Thurnall-Read, a sociologist who researches the Campaign for Real Ale (CAMRA), provides a detailed account of how drinking real ale has become an intimate embodied engagement with consumer culture, pleasure and disgust with multifaceted meanings. Chapter 1: 'Beer consumption, embodied distaste and anticorporate consumer identities' demonstrates that the significance of distaste is tied to wider changes in social and cultural life and consumption practices. The rejection of mass produced lager, and what it makes the body *do* (burp) and *feel* (disgustingly hungover), becomes a collective process of identity-making, and thus the physical aversion to 'gas and fizz' aligns closely to concepts of locality, heritage, the perceived loss of a particular, masculine 'pub culture' and British national identity. Through an analysis of affective spaces (the changing landscape of the 'local pub') Thurnell-Read argues 'the embodied rejection of mass-produced beer, most vividly seen in expressions of revulsion and disgust, serves to illustrate the socio-political nature of consumption and of consumer bodies' (p. 21).

Space and time, as this book will demonstrate, are key determinants to the experience of taste, but equally as important is questioning who is able to freely travel through these spaces and which bodies get 'stuck' (Ahmed 2000). To travel freely can be a literal privilege of movement, mobility and leisure, and also metaphorical for those who can move through 'foodways' (Parsons 2015) without getting weighed down by the 'wrong' tastes, symbolic violence and social disgust (Tyler 2013, Rhys-Taylor 2013, 2017). In 2011, as the trend for salted caramel was appearing in every dessert and confectionary product in the UK, celebratory chef Nigella Lawson wrote about her passionate 'love affair' with the 'Holy Trinity' of sugar, saturated fat and salt in *Stylist* magazine.[1] The article features a photo of a blissful Nigella, eyes coated in smoky black eyeshadow, with liquid salted caramel seductively dripping down her face. Nigella Lawson, famed for her post-feminist play on the role of the 'domestic goddess' and 'food porn' innuendos (Dejmanee 2016), reveals her wealth – both economic affluence and of culinary capital – as she traces the origins of French caramel au beurre salé, her knowledge of luxury salt and elite chocolatiers 'L'artisan du chocolat'. Fat, salt and sugar are celebrated as exquisite pleasures rather than associated with poor health. In a fleeting line of the article, Nigella recalls curling up in bed with her children 'with a white chocolate Magnum in one hand and a packet of tangy salt and vinegar crisps in the other'. This deliberate nod to what is understood to be mass produced 'junk' food, distanced from the sophistication of fine patisserie, and consumed in bed in front of the TV (and fed to children no less), is teased with momentarily by Nigella, who no sooner having travelled to the land of junk food is back again in an instant, relaying her recipes for finer delicacies. Bourdieu (2005: 72) claims that to 'possess good taste – for the bourgeois – is to have absolute freedom of choice'. For Nigella, her 'shameless and slovenly' (Bourdieu 2005: 78) encounters with the 'wrong' kind of tasty fat and sugar does little to shake our confidence in her authoritative good taste, and she remains safely distanced from social abjection.

Fat is powerfully affective. In Chapter 2: 'A sticky situation? Fatty distaste and the performance of class', geographers Louise MacAllister and Suzanne Hocknell continue the theme of distaste and disgust through 'mapping the moments' in which (some) bodies are likely to get 'stuck' in discourses of 'good' and 'bad' fat. Distaste emerges not through the enjoyment (or otherwise) of fatty tastes, but through tensions in classed habitus and public health narratives. MacAllister and Hocknell argue that 'visceral sensations of fat against lips and tongue are not in themselves sufficient to engender distaste' (p. 30), but rather a 'push-pull of desire-revulsion' of what is known to be healthy or disgusting, (ir)responsible (white, middle-class) parenting practices, a naughty treat or a process of social shaming and othering. The visceral materiality of greasy fats can be both delicious and revolting, depending on who is consuming them, where and when. The authors draw on Ahmed's conception of 'stickiness' (2000) of the 'wrong' fat to the stigmatised other, while it 'slips' more easily off those with privileged culinary capital and middle-class credentials:

> By demonstrating that fatty materialities are not inherently distasteful but become so with and in the classed atmosphere of the encounter, distaste can be conceptualised as slippery, entangled with attempting to protect the situated self from the stickiness of discursive as well as material contamination.
>
> (p. 41)

Returning to the example of Nigella Lawson and Bourdieu's theories of absolute choice, those who embody privilege can travel freely. They can occasionally enjoy the pleasurable tastes of cheap, 'dirty' fatty food as 'experience tourism' (Falconer 2013) without these components 'sticking' or threatening to contaminate their classed identities with social disgust. Part I finishes with what can be argued to be the epitome of culinary capital: the world of wine. Sociologist David Morgan claims snobbery reaches its peak when it comes to choosing, smelling and tasting wine: 'The common feature, of course, is the nose. Snobs either look down their noses or walk by with their noses in the air' (Morgan 2019: 59). Chapter 3: 'Performing taste: the Sommelier ceremony' fixes on the proceedings that unfold within spaces of fine dining, where wine sommeliers perform a strict routine loaded with complex power relations. Authors Giolo Fele and Pier Paolo Giglioli relay this practice in great detail, as every tiny, fleeting affective moment of this intense encounter is crucial to the performance of taste. The defiant silences, the nods, the smell of the cork, the thickness of the glass: the material elements of this subtle execution combine the non-human with the deeply cultural interaction of ordering and tasting wine. Wine tasting is saturated with culinary capital. There is no disputing the sommeliers skill; he/she has mastered a discerning taste over many years of training, yet must remain deferent to the customer in a convoluted interplay of knowledge, power and distinction. So delicate is this rhythmic encounter it becomes severely disrupted by the slightest rupture, where the actors are not fully attuned to their roles, and collapses entirely. The study of taste is intimately connected to social dynamics, from subtle exclusions to symbolic violence. A closer reading of affective moments, material culture, embodied knowledge and theories of classed (and raced, gendered) pleasure and disgust can significantly broaden our understanding of the socio-political dimensions of our everyday lived senses.

Space (and time)

This book is primarily influenced by emotional geographies of embodiment, asserting that the experience of taste is socio-cultural, temporal and spatially determined. Space and time are thus major players. Multiple spaces can interfere with social norms, habitus and expectations relating to taste. In their 'affective theory of taste', Ashwood and Bell (2016: 625) argue 'tastes are often created and accumulated based on attachments and situated events that expand beyond the habitus that Bourdieu argues distinguishes the common from the bourgeois'. Their case studies of classical and folk music demonstrate that the *space* in which the music is enjoyed is a factor which influences the predetermined judgements of class and distinction (such as classical music buskers playing Bach in grotty subway stations) (633). Food tourist studies have highlighted the spatial and environmental importance to our enjoyment of food; *where* and *how* we experience tastes are key to narratives of pleasure, imagined authenticity and the experience economy (think of fresh seafood, ocean sunsets and the squawk of seagulls, smoky street food guzzled standing up in lively and bustling 'local' markets).

Central to these discourses are notions of 'eating the other', embedded in postcolonial theory and critiques of cosmopolitanism. bell hooks claims:

The commodification of otherness has been so successful because it is offered as a new delight, more intense, more satisfying than normal ways of doing and feeling. Within commodity culture, ethnicity becomes spice, seasoning that can liven up the dull dish that is mainstream white culture.

(hooks 2012: 366)

'Eating the other' is therefore often an expression of power and privilege, which explains its prominence in wider postcolonial tourist theory, and is inherently connected to space. Drawing on the 'authenticated spaces' of Turkish grill restaurants in London, Karaosmanoğlu argues that 'ethnicity is not the only "spice" or "seasoning" for the consumer' (2014: 227), but so too is class and gender; the masculine bodies of men cooking meat over the hot grills, the 'rough', run down, grotty and exciting areas of the city that have (so far) not been gentrified are equally as fetishised. Here, the taste of the fatty grilled meats is – for the food blogger- significantly shaped by multiple affects; the 'down the dirty alley' location of the grill, the scruffy décor, the male bodies of the grillers. The imaginations of the consumers play 'significant roles in the authentication of bodies and spaces' (2014: 233), and have a direct bearing on the taste of the products. Elsewhere, in travelling spaces of back-packing food tourism (Falconer 2013), I have argued that 'eating the other' is not always about seeking pleasurable tastes, and the search for imagined 'authenticity' also involves participating in food practices that evoke disgust, pain and sickness as an accepted hardship of embodying a 'true' cosmopolitan identity (Molz 2006). Others, such as Duruz (2010) critique the binary between white consumer and ethnic other. This problematises the idea that only privileged bodies are free to enjoy experience tourism, and shakes the assumption that 'cosmopolitan' and 'migrant' (or 'host' culture) are fixed opposing categories. Instead, through a sensual description of both 'exotic' and 'homely' Asian food in diasporic kitchens, Duruz portrays a nuanced picture of multiple attachments to place-making through 'floating food', which (dis)belongs to different spaces at different times: 'Reflecting on "floating food," we all chart the uneven, contradictory ways we float through life, bumping into each other and sometimes, through intimate yearning, reaching places of temporary anchorage' (Duruz 2010: 49). Taste is continually situated and re-situated in space, place and time.

Part II: 'Moving tastes: mobility, displacement and belonging' examines tastes which 'move' through affective and imagined spaces of 'home', migration, displacement and travel. In the context of displacement, a painful longing for home intensifies the memories of taste, smell and loss as 'everyday life and the multiple contexts in which the culturally shaped sensory properties and sensory experiences of food are invested with meaning, emotion, memory and value' (Sutton 2010: 220). Historians Rachel Ankeny and Karen Agutter introduce the sensory landscape of memory and loss in Chapter 4: 'Food, taste and memory in Australian migrant hostels'. Through oral histories with 'New Australians' (migrants, refugees and displaced persons who were part of the rapid assimilation regime of the 1930s–1980s), Chapter 4 provides a powerful account of how re-shaping tastes can be used to suppress cultural diversity and enforce 'Australian values' and 'ways of life'. Migrant hostels denied cooking facilities in favour of communal canteens with little choice of food, imposing tastes upon their newly arrived residents as part of a wider agenda of assimilation. These were known as 'training centers', and it is interesting to examine how the sense of taste can be used to 'train' and modify their cultural identities to be able to 'fit in' to new societies. Unlike the migrants who arrived in the USA to find that 'the flavour and taste of coffee and donuts welcoming immigrants at Ellis Island were pivotal in creating a "sweet" and "filling" impression of the host country' (referring to Hasia Diner 2001, see p. 63), 'New Australians' experienced an affective atmosphere of hostility, creating uncertainty and trepidation about their new lives. Sensual memories are intensely affective; dirty offal, pungent smells 'polluting' and pervading, overcooked pumpkin 'slop', sloppy mush thrown onto plates and a general lack of institutional care which symbolised the dehumanising treatment and 'underlying aversion of forced assimilation for DPs' (p. 66). Following on from Part I, taste is a not only a marker of choice, but of your ability to choose (or have choice denied). Once again, those marginalised are often the most burdened with a pressure to adapt their tastes to suit dominant norms, whether that be in social discourses of health, classed cultural capital or, in this case, forced cultural assimilation for migrants and displaced persons.

Chapter 5: 'Eating *Stobi Flips,* Drinking *Gazoza,* Remembering Macedonia' continues the theme of migration, displacement and embodied sensual longing as Katerina Nussdorfer documents the multi-sensual affects of two iconic Macedonian products (a packaged peanut maize snack, and a luminous carbonated soft drink) when consumed in distant locales. This chapter perfectly reflects the theme of this book; that food consumed in different, often complex spatial and temporal contexts, can lose, gain or significantly change meaning. Standardised 'junk' food becomes a collectively shared marker of national identity, mobility and nostalgia, taking on mythical qualities of imagined traditions and heightened desire, distorting sensual histories of whether these foods were ever originally enjoyed. However, what is arguably the most pertinent feature of this chapter is the affective properties of these products. *Space, Taste and Affect* is acutely concerned with material culture, the 'social life of objects', and how 'the agency of objects – their fibres, textures, patterns and forms – construct and create material affinities' (Holmes 2019: 175). Nussdorfer brings to life *Stobi Flips* in particular; the garish, instantly recognizable colourful packaging, the feel and sound of the foil, the ritualistic sucking of the sticky film that coats fingers, as an affective trigger of national identity and 'things in and out of place' (Edensor 2002: 114). Taste can become a haunting of the past, and these culinary ghosts emerge 'not only in "real" places but in worlds of memory, emotion and virtuality' (Duruz 2010: 47). Beth M. Forrest completes the theme of 'Moving tastes' through her unique historical analysis '"A tealess, beerless, beefless land": sensing and tasting Spain in late eighteenth and nineteenth-century British travelogues' (Chapter 6). Through a close reading of travelogues, Forrest unpacks the language of taste and the affective power of the descriptive page. Powerful language of disgust – the 'rancid' oil, violently offensive smells of garlic breath, hungry and thirsty 'peasants' living in extreme poverty 'half devoured by vermin' offers an offensive and dehumanising account of Spanish people, their 'backwards' land and culture, through the written evocations of (bad) taste and sensual markers of abjection. Forrest demonstrates how historical literature can create an embodied response in the reader; through our imagined senses – sights, smells, tastes – we are purposely led to dangerous, colonial and xenophobic judgements about 'the other'.

Part III: 'Taste, affect and the lifecourse' adds a temporal element to the affective dimension of taste, demonstrating that *Space, Taste and Affect* is also about time. The temporal context of emotions around food has been studied in depth in my research into backpacking tourists, drawing on a rhythmic analysis of how embodiment tastes shift over an extended period of time (Falconer 2013). Chapter 7: 'Tastes of reflection, food memories and the temporal affects of sedimented personal histories on everyday foodways' engages closely with Naccarato and LeBesco to demonstrate that culinary capital is not just about knowing, but spending time continuing to know – and learn – about 'good' food and taste over time. Through rich qualitative data on food memories, narratives of desire and disgust and temporal affects, sociologist Julie Parsons reflects on middle-class values of what 'good' taste has come to mean, and how to acquire such tastes can be a lifetime of transformation, gaining culinary capital over many years. Parsons notes the 'symbolic cultural markers of distinction and taste in a culinary field that values "time" or the temporal affects of personal histories, sedimented, like limescale fixing itself to the bottom of a kettle' (p. 102). In Chapter 8 'Our daily bread and onions: negotiating tastes in family mealtimes interaction' Sally Wiggins and Eric Laurier bring together insights from discursive psychology and geography to provide a snapshot of the family dinner table. The authors become intensely attuned to every movement and discourse of the affective space of family dinners, exploring how tastes become established through embodied social interactions and spaces during the formative years of our lifecourse: 'Taste is therefore understood here as a collaboratively produced social phenomenon, one that emerges in a close reading of shuddering and of forking risotto and how these actions are closely monitored and responded to' (p. 126).

Affect

Theories of affect are, as LeBesco and Naccarato (2008: 2) might say 'one of the ingredients that flavors this book'. This ingredient is a crucial component to stir into analyses of space and taste and (as much as is ever possible) completes this trinity. The 'affective turn' in academic scholarship, whereby becoming sensually attuned we learn 'to negotiate space through a range of sensory and affective registers' (Waitt and Johnson 2013: 145) has extended its Deleuzian roots in philosophy and emotional geographies (Anderson 2009) to almost all areas of the social sciences in recent years. The turn to affect – characterised by Thrift (2009: 88) as a 'set of flows moving through the bodies of human and other beings' – is understood to greatly expand our scope of social investigation, and make sense of the social world beyond the representational. Stewart, who beautifully captures everyday *Ordinary Affects* claims affect is fleeting, when '*something* throws itself together in a moment as an event and a sensation; a something both animated and inhabitable' (2007: 1). Affect is deeply embodied, emotional and relational, but also non-human, incorporating the material world, objects, light, sound, atmosphere, the density of the air; 'Affect now means something like a force or an active relation' (Wetherall 2012: 15). Not all affects, however, are felt equally. Tolia-Kelly (2006) has warned of the dangers of universalising affect theory, reminding geographers that different bodies register different affective capacities. The emancipatory potential for the affective turn has been powerfully captured in feminist and critical race theory, such as the influential works of Lauren Berlant (2019, and Kathleen Stewart) and Sara Ahmed, who demonstrate that our embodied reactions to other bodies, spaces and momentary encounters are deeply embedded in social histories of race, gender, class, politics and oppressive inequalities (such as 'making the skin crawl', see Ahmed on affective racism (2000: 46)). In geography, an explicit focus on affective atmospheres and what they afford is addressed by Edensor (2012) through the thick, rhythmic, temporal, sensual atmospheric flows of the Blackpool illuminations. In sociology, Mason has explored the charged energy and potent connections to place in *Affinities* (2018), socio-atmospheres entangled in *Living the Weather* (2016) and the formal, frantic or sterile atmospheres of family Christmases and the dynamics of relationality, where she asserts 'atmosphere comes across as a situational, multisensory, spatial, temporal and relational phenomenon' (Mason and Muir 2013: 614).

With some notable exceptions (Rhys-Taylor 2013, 2017; Edensor and Falconer 2014), food and consumption studies – a growing area of focus in sociology, geography and the humanities – has not been as attuned to the affective turn as one might have expected given that taste, as we have seen, is highly sensual, deeply cultural, environmentally determined and seeped in social histories, divisions and distinctions. Atmospheres and 'vibes' are a common discourse in the promotion of the hospitality industry and food tourism, but a scholarly critical analysis of how atmospheres relate to taste remains limited. Working as an ethnographic research assistant on Edensor's project into the affective experience of the Blackpool illuminations (2010–2012), I observed numerous encounters with food and drink that remain omitted from the final publication (the principle focus being on geographies of light and darkness). Much of this data relied on examples of food tourism (see Edensor and Falconer (2011) for our earlier analysis of sensual geographies of tourist spaces) as an integral part of the seaside experience and imagined traditions: fish and chips, Soft Serve ice cream, hot battered donuts, alcohol, Blackpool rock, candy floss, potted shrimps, fried English breakfasts and pots of tea. The sensual elements of these foods – the smell of vinegar, the squeak of polystyrene cups, the feel of warm grease soaking through the paper – completes Edensor's snapshot of an atmospheric flow of bored young children crying, the repetitive flash and pulse of light shows, whooshing trams, rhythmic stops and starts in busy walking crowds, and all intermingled with conviviality and excitement. Yet returning to my reflective example in the Preface of deep-fried donuts on Blackpool pier (see p. xvi), affective atmospheres directly impact on the experience of taste (chips taste 'better' by the sea!). Once again, these atmospheres intersect with culinary capital, the experience economy (Edensor and Falconer 2014) and which bodies can enjoy the sweet, fatty 'junk' foods as part of a temporary place-making without getting 'stuck'. Similar findings emerged in later projects: 'Seedy Bars and Grotty Pints: Close Encounters in Queer Leisure Spaces' (see Taylor and Falconer 2015). Culinary affects and symbolic constructions of taste, smell and touch surfaced as a key theme in registering gendered and classed histories, feelings of home and belonging and how these reflected wider socio-political issues:

> Identifying which foodstuffs belong in which time and place opens new critical terrains for exploring the intersectional affects of space; like the descriptions of 'cheap' alcohol or 'real ale', food is used to describe the significantly differently classed affects of atmospheres, divisions and distinctions. Food and drink are contextualised in the environment in which they 'belong' (or not), and how they affect the 'vibe' or feel of a place. Continuing with the themes of affective, embodied encounters, the context in which they are consumed illustrates whether these are comforting, inviting or disgusting and vile.
>
> (Taylor and Falconer 2015: 51)

Rhys-Taylor (2017), whose terminology prefers the 'sensual turn' rather than the affective, also explores food and the multicultural through a sensory ethnography of east London, unearthing racist rationales in 'gut feelings' towards the abject, such as moral panics about horsemeat, slimy jellied eels of the East End and the perceived 'problem' of inner city fried chicken shops. Affect is a way of knowing what lies beneath the visceral senses, of exploring the relationship between bodies, emotions, spaces and things, and *Space, Taste and Affect* is primarily concerned with what *more* we can begin to know from a closer reading of the sensation of taste.

A close(r) reading of affective spaces permeates throughout this book, yet the final section: 'Part 4: Atmospheric tastes: affect, design and creative space' is where the affective, ambient and atmospheric elements of tasting really come into play. The authors in this section provide rich atmospheric descriptions, and invite us to enter spaces of sensual materiality that directly impact on our experience of taste. Paz Concha engages with Anderson's (2009) theories of affective atmospheres as continually changing, and defines atmosphere as the 'in between' of experiences and environments, as the connection between 'people, places and things' (Bille, Bjerregaard and Sørensen, 2015: 33). In Chapter 9: 'Curating pop-up street food markets in London', Concha uses her ethnographic research into street food markets in South London as a site of 'tasted places', which

> examines the sensorial dimension of the culinary experience on offer- the innovative, hybridised and exciting cuisines, the smells and sounds of cooking, and the embodied experience of eating alongside the carefully crafted décor of the market- which amalgamates a romanticised notion of past (often working-class) market traders with a chic, urban aesthetic to create 'character'.
>
> (p. 132)

Becoming attuned to the feel or 'vibe' of the market, Concha argues that the carefully curated aesthetics of the market – the shabby-chic old fittings, the exposed pipes, the retained, faded signs of traders past – enriches the experience of urban cosmopolitanism (Karaosmanoğlu 2014) as (certain) consumers enjoy their street snacks, often a hybridised amalgamation of the old and new, the global and local, the 'old school' and the most recent, exciting culinary fashions (spiced Korean-style mini-burgers). Concha takes this analysis further, to question how the material, aesthetic and sensorial space of the market is designed to

> appeal to a particular cohort of Londoners and visitors, often those young, middle-class professionals who possess a high degree of economic and cultural capital, and who have been the focus of countless critiques of urban gentrification; how the middle classes make use of space, and displacement of working-class communities.
>
> (Benson and Jackson 2013: 135)

These sensual and material atmospheres, as I have argued, affectively pull people in and out of place (Taylor and Falconer 2015), seducing certain bodies through an imagined sense of urban cosmopolitan identity and belonging (or conversely, exclusion). Concha's chapter illustrates how these multiple affects and embodied knowledges are central to the experience of tasting 'exciting' food through a case study of contemporary London street food scenes.

The atmospheric materialities of taste-making continue in Chapter 10: 'Tales from the cheese counter: taskscape and taste at Neal's Yard Dairy' where anthropologists Mukta Das and Celia Plender invite readers to experience an immersive combination of humidity, wood, glistening wet floors, black slate, artisanal knowledge and non-verbal communication as slithers of fine cheese are tasted directly from steel knives without comment. Their ethnographic research into the highly successful diary, Neal's Yard, is an 'interplay between craft, task and taste' and an 'affective retail space in which customers are not just buying cheese, but also engaging in "the adventure and pleasure of taste, the status of connoisseurship, the pride of supporting a local business or the institution of small-scale farming"' (p. 152). The performance of cheese tasting, carried out in near silence, relies on the sensual and material, where 'quirky' humidifiers of old buckets and pans are used to stage powerful symbols of old farmhouses, blended with a high degree of culinary capital associated with fine cheese. Finally, this book closes with a case study of how sensual atmospheres can contribute to the experience of taste in its most explicit sense. Drawing on our earlier exploration of 'Dans le noir? Eating in the dark: sensation and conviviality in a lightless place (Edensor and Falconer 2014), geographer Nina Morris joins food scientist Vania Ling and artist Ericka Duffy to finish with an immensely affective, interdisciplinary account of 'Blackout' – a purposely designed experience to explore the senses of taste, light and music. Arguing that a 'voluptuous' darkness can enable us to not just *see* differently but *be* different as we enter an alternative sensual habitus, Morris, Ling and Duffy unlock the transformative potential of 'affective landscapes' that enable us to better attune to taste and its complex relationship between body and mind: 'a departure from all-encompassing, accepted or habitual concepts and theories of events and experiences' (p. 166). In the words of Hennion (2007: 111), 'Taste effectively depends on everything – another declension of the word "attachment"'. Space can be a place, a feeling, a moment in which some bodies get 'stuck' or pass through freely, and capturing these sensorial moments and their affective capacities can open a new mode of understanding about the ways we eat, drink and taste our ways through social life.

Note

1 https://www.stylist.co.uk/life/my-love-affair-with-salted-caramel/49185.

References

Ahmed, S. (2000) *Strange Encounters: Embodied Others in Post-Coloniality* Abingdon: Routledge.

Almenberg, J. and Dreber, A. (2011) When Does the Price Affect the Taste? Results from a Wine Experiment. *Journal of Wine Economics* 6(1), 111–121.

Anderson, B. (2009) Affective Atmospheres. *Emotion, Space and Society* 2, 77–81.

Ashwood, L. and Bell, M. (2016) Affect and Taste: Bourdieu, Traditional Music, and the Performance of Possibilities. *Sociologia Ruralis* 57(1), 622–640.

Benson, M. and Jackson, E. (2013) Place-making and Place Maintenance: Performativity, Place and Belonging among the Middle Classes. *Sociology* 47(4), 793–809.

Berlant, L. and Stewart, K. (2019) *The Hundreds* Durham, NC: Duke University Press.

Bille, M., Bjerregaard, P. and Sørensen, T. F. (2015) Staging Atmospheres: Materiality, Culture, and the Texture of the In-between. *Emotion, Space and Society* 15, 31–38.

Bourdieu, P. (2005) Taste of Luxury, Taste of Necessity in Korsmeyer, C. (ed.) *The Taste and Culture Reader* (pp. 72–78) Oxford: Berg.

Bourdieu, P. (trans 1984) *Distinction: A Social Critique of the Judgment of Taste* Cambridge, MA: Harvard University Press.

Counihan, C. and Hojlund, S. (2018) *Making Taste Public: Ethnographies of Food and the Senses* London: Bloomsbury.

Dejmanee, T. (2016) "Food Porn" as Postfeminist Play: Digital Femininity and the Female Body on Food Blogs. *Television & New Media* 17(5), 429–448.

Duruz, J. (2010) Floating Food: Eating 'Asia' in Kitchens of the Diaspora. *Emotion, Space and Society* 3(1), 45–49.

Edensor, T. (2002) *National Identity, Popular Culture and Everyday Life* London: Bloomsbury.

Edensor, T. (2012) Illuminated Atmospheres: Anticipating and Reproducing the Flow of Affective Experience in Blackpool. *Environment and Planning D: Society and Space* 30(6), 1103–1122.

Edensor, T. and Falconer, E. (2011) Sensual Geographies of Tourism in Wilson, J. (ed.) *The Routledge Handbook of Tourism Geographies* (pp. 74–81) London: Routledge.

Edensor, T. and Falconer, E. (2014) Dans Le Noir? Eating in the Dark: Sensation and Conviviality in a Lightless Place. *Cultural Geographies* 22(4), 601–618.

Falconer, E. (2013) Transformations of the Backpacking Food Tourist: Emotions and Conflicts. *Tourist Studies* 13(1), 21–35.

Featherstone, M. (1990) Perspectives on Consumer Culture. *Sociology* 24(1), 5–22.

Gronow, J. (1997) *The Sociology of Taste* London: Routledge.

Harrar, V. and Spence, C. (2013) The Taste of Cutlery: How the Taste of Food is Affected by the Weight, Size, Shape, and Colour of the Cutlery Used to Eat It. *Flavour* 2(1), 1–13.

Hennion, A. (2007) Those Things that Hold Us Together: Taste and Sociology. *Cultural Sociology* 1(1), 97–114.

Holmes, H. (2019) Material Affinities: 'Doing' Family through the Practices of Passing On. *Sociology* 53(1), 174–191.

hooks, b. (2012) Eating the Other: Desire and Resistance in Durham, M. G. and Kellner, D. (eds) *Media and Cultural Studies Keyworks, Second Edition* (pp. 308–317) Chichester: Wiley-Blackwell.

Karaosmanoğlu, D. (2014) Authenticated Spaces: Blogging Sensual Experiences in Turkish Grill Restaurants in London. *Space and Culture* 17(3), 224–238.

LeBesco, K. and Naccarato, P. (2008) *Edible Ideologies: Representing Food and Meaning* New York: State University of New York Press.

LeBesco, K. and Naccarato, P. (2012) *Culinary Capital* London: Berg.

Maguire, J. M. (2017) *Food Practices and Social Inequality: Looking at Food Practices and Taste across the Class Divide* London: Routledge.

Molz, J. G. (2006) Cosmopolitan Bodies: Fit to Travel and Travelling to Fit. *Body & Society* 12(3), 1–21.

Mason, J. (2016) *Living the Weather: Voices from the Calder Valley* Manchester: University of Manchester.

Mason, J. (2018) *Affinities: Potent Connections in Personal Life* Cambridge: Polity Press.

Mason, J. and Muir, S. (2013) Conjuring Up Traditions: Atmospheres, Eras and Family Christmases. *The Sociological Review* 61(3), 607–629.

Morgan, D. (2019) *Snobbery* Bristol: Polity Press.

Parsons, J. M. (2015) *Gender, Class and Food: Families, Bodies and Health* London: Profile Books.

Ray, K. (2017) Bringing the Immigrant Back into the Sociology of Taste. *Appetite* 119(1), 41–47.

Rhys-Taylor, A. (2013) Disgust and Distinction: The Case of the Jellied Eel. *The Sociological Review* 61(2), 227–246.

Rhys-Taylor, A. (2017) *Food and Multiculture: A Sensory Ethnography of East London* London: Bloomsbury.

Smith Maguire, J. (2017) *Food Practices and Social Inequality: Looking at Food Practices and Taste across the Class Divide* London: Routledge.

Stewart, K. (2007) *Ordinary Affects* Durham, NC: Duke University Press.

Stewart, S. (2014) *A Sociology of Culture, Taste and Value* Basingstoke: Palgrave Macmillan.

Sutton, D. (2010) Food and the Senses *Annual Review of Anthropology* 39, 209–223.

Taylor, Y. and Falconer, E. (2015) 'Seedy Bars and Grotty Pints': Close Encounters in Queer Leisure Spaces. *Social & Cultural Geography* 16(1), 43–57.

Thatcher, J., Ingram, N., Burke, C. and Abrahams, J. (eds) (2016) *Bourdieu: The Next Generation* London: Routledge.

Thrift, N. (2009) Different Atmospheres: Of Sloterdijk, China, and Site. *Environment and Planning D: Society and Space* 27(1), 119–138.

Tolia-Kelly, D. (2006) *Affect: An Ethnocentric Encounter? Exploring the 'Universalist' Imperative of Emotional/Affectual Geographies Area* 38(2), 213–217.

Tyler, I. (2013) *Revolting Subjects: Social Abjection and Resistance in Neoliberal Britain* London: Zed Books.

Vincent, C. and Ball, S. J. (2007) 'Making Up' the Middle-class Child: Families, Activities and Class Dispositions. *Sociology* 41(6), 1061–1077.

Waitt, G. and Johnson, L. (2013) 'It Doesn't Even Feel like It's Being Processed in Your Head': Lesbian Affective Home Journeys to and within Townsville, Queensland, Australia, in Gorman-Murray, A., Pini, B. and Bryant, L. (eds) *Sexuality, Rurality and Geography* (pp. 143–158) Lanham, MD: Lexington.

Warde, A. (1997) *Consumption, Food and Taste* London: SAGE.

Wetherall, M. (2012) *Affect and Emotion: A New Social Science Understanding* London: SAGE.

Part I
Distinctive tastes
Space, consumption and (dis)taste

1 Beer consumption, embodied distaste and anti-corporate consumer identities

Thomas Thurnell-Read

Processes through which consumers align their identities with specific products and tastes have been well explored by academics (Belk, 1988; Warde, 1994). However, it is only recently that the role of emotional and bodily experiences which play a part in consumption have begun to receive greater attention (Rafferty, 2011; Rhys-Taylor, 2013). While 'good' or 'bad' consumption can be understood in terms of competing expressions of meaning and morality, it can also be acknowledged that consuming 'in the right way' can 'feel good' (Hayes-Conroy and Hayes-Conroy, 2010). Yet, as Wilk (1997) has observed, academic work on consumer choice and taste largely overlooks the significance of *dis*taste to consumption practices. The act of consumption involves both selection and rejection. This is particularly pronounced when considering eating and drinking practices which involve both 'introjection' (taking in) and 'separation' (keeping out) (Falk, 1994). Consumers can and do express revulsion and hatred for particular tastes and, further, these distastes are often articulated in ways which indicate the affective and embodied qualities of consumption.

While these qualities might manifest at the intimate level, residing within or emanating from the individual consumer body, they can also be read as strikingly social and political. The political content of consumer choice has been explored, meaning that there is now a greater understanding of the ways in which consumers can embrace some elements of consumer culture while actively rejecting others. As Simon (2011: 147) observes, 'many have turned to the realm of buying to express their political concerns and desires' meaning that the ways in which consumers interact with brands can be seen as 'one of the most dynamic forms of political expression today' (Simon, 2011: 148). In this sense, consumers can *use* consumption not only as an expression of individual taste but as a means of resisting 'the signs of corporate life, the symbols, services and commodities associated with large multinational corporations' (Smart, 1999: 1).

This chapter explores the case of the Campaign for Real Ale (CAMRA), a consumer group established in the United Kingdom in 1971 in response to changes taking place in the British beer and pubs industry. CAMRA, therefore, might be understood as part of a wider trend towards resisting mass consumer products which are seen as bland, generic and lifeless (Kingsnorth, 2011). Within this, expressions of distaste for particular beer brands allow a means to voice dissatisfaction with corporate ideology and mass consumption practices. Whilst this is an expression of individual taste (*liking* this beer but *hating* that one), it is also an example of the socio-political nature of consumption meaning individual expressions of (dis)taste are part of wider changes in social and cultural life. The chapter suggests that many of the varied functions of contemporary consumption such as performing autonomy through choice, expressing identity and rebelling against changes (Gabriel and Lang, 1995) can be observed in the examples of consumer resistance enacted via distaste and disgust drawn from analysing CAMRA.

Embodying consumer resistance

The figure of the modern consumer, as Slater (1997: 33–34) observes, has long been viewed through a series of dichotomies; between 'rational or irrational, sovereign or manipulated, autonomous or other-determined, active or passive, creative or conformist, individual or mass, subject or object'. On the one hand, over recent decades we have seen the widespread use of the term 'consumer society' to condemn 'what appeared to be a growing and uncontrolled passion for material things' (Sassatelli, 2007: 2) and an associated concern with the apparent ease with which consumers could be manipulated by powerful companies (Schwarzkopf, 2011). On the other hand, we have also seen a more recent emergence of the powerful, yet problematic belief that consumption can be made 'ethical' (Lewis and Potter, 2011) and that 'consumer activism' can foster 'a larger cultural and political conversation about who and what consumers are and should be' (Mukherjee and Banet-Weiser, 2012: 3).

Many consumption practices may be viewed as symbolic behaviour, used to align oneself with a particular social cause (Moore, 2008). However, a recent trend has been to identify and acknowledge the ways in which consumption ought to be understood as practice as well as performance; paying regard to not just meanings and symbols but materials, competencies, emotions and embodiment as constituents of 'good' or 'ethical' consumer practice (Wheeler, 2012). As Sassatelli and Davolio (2010: 219) observe in relation to the Slow Food movement, which bears many similarities to CAMRA in attempting to empower consumers to resist the pernicious influence of 'mass' or 'fast' food production and distribution, individuals need to combine both 'cognitive knowledge' and 'incarnate taste' in enacting the role of ethical or responsible consumer.

As such, recent studies have attuned scholars of consumption to be aware of the role of the body, and of emotions and senses, in consumer practice. Importantly, as the chapter will illustrate, this involves negative as well as positive experiences and is *felt* as much in disgust as in pleasure. For example, in Nixon and Gabriel's (2016: 53) recent study of individuals who actively reject mass consumption, participants expressed how the spaces and objects of mass consumption were felt as invasive, polluting and contagious; as 'a standardized, artificial world of consumerism that is damaging to one's health' (Nixon and Gabriel, 2016: 53).

One area where these concerns have become pronounced is the global spread of 'fast food' business models which prioritise convenience, standardisation and efficiency in the pursuit of profit and market dominance (Reiter, 1991; Lang and Heasman, 2004; Ritzer, 2013) and, in marked contrast, of various attempts to resist such pressures through 'everyday practices of food production, distribution and consumption' (Donald and Blay-Palmer, 2006: 1917). The Slow Food movement, therefore, foregrounds the political nature of food choices and food practices (Sassatelli and Davolio, 2010) by 'transforming quite simple activities, such as eating a bowl of pasta or holding a farmers' market, into politically meaningful acts' (van Bommel and Spicer, 2011: 1728). While we see that food 'sustains identity' (Warde, 1997: 199) and can be deployed as an instrument of identification and division (Ashley et al, 2004), we also need to acknowledge the ways in which, as Wilk (2006, 21) has argued, 'food is a potent symbol of what ails society'. Thus, the juxtaposition of gluttonous, unthinking, fast food consumers and reflexive, critical, ethical consumers who resist mass production and standardisation has now long dominated popular and academic debates of contemporary food and illustrates the intersection of individual, embodied, social and political facets of consumption (Guthman, 2003).

Adding to these debates, this chapter considers the role of CAMRA in resisting the rationalisation of the British beer industry. Following a brief summary of the research methods and context, the chapter will therefore consider the ways in which the embodied rejection of mass-produced beer, most vividly seen in expressions of revulsion and disgust, serves to illustrate the socio-political nature of consumption and of consumer bodies.

Research methods and context

This chapter draws on a wider qualitative research undertaking focusing on CAMRA and, more generally, recent trends in British beer consumption. Founded in 1971, CAMRA now has over 180,000 members and a sizable staff of over 40 at its headquarters in the English city of St Albans. Throughout its existence, the campaign has focused on protecting and promoting 'Real Ale', a traditional form of beer involving secondary fermentation in a cask or bottle and defined as having no extraneous gases added, in opposition to the widespread use of pasteurised, mass-produced beer. Alongside the campaigning activities of the head office team, over 200 local 'branches' spread across the UK and Northern Ireland hold regular meetings, organise beer festivals and 'survey' local pubs to evaluate them for the extent and quality of their offerings of Real Ale. The majority of those who 'work' for CAMRA do so as volunteers, including a National Executive of 12 directors, local branch presidents, secretaries and finance officers, and the numerous members and non-members who serve beer and act as stewards at local and national beer festivals.

A total of 53 semi-structured interviews were conducted with members of CAMRA including directors, salaried operational staff and local branch members and volunteers as well as others such as ale brewers, beer writers and members of a student ale drinking society, many of whom were also current or previous CAMRA members. Further, participant-observation was conducted in a range of contexts including attending two CAMRA AGMs, local branch meetings and a number of beer festivals and brewery tours. Finally, archival research was conducting focusing specifically on CAMRA publications such as the monthly member's newspaper *What's Brewing* and the annual *Good Beer Guide*.

'All that gas and fizz?! No thanks!'

Throughout the research, it was clear that members of CAMRA exhibited a strong attachment to the beer they consumed. This tended to manifest in two ways. First, as I explore in more detail elsewhere (Thurnell-Read, 2016; 2018), participants could demonstrate a passionate and knowledgeable preference forReal Ale and frequently exhibited an exuberant pleasure in its consumption. It was, for example, common for participants to speak of their attraction to the taste of Real Ale, with various references by interviewees to their 'conversion' when they first realised 'just how good *real* beer could taste'. As Lupton (1998: 139) observes, such experiences can be felt as a 'pull' of desire and attraction towards a particular object 'which we ourselves may find difficult to explain or understand'. However, in the second manifestation of the strong attachments exhibited by Real Ale consumers, both implicit and explicit rejections of mass-produced beer and, at times by association, those who drink it represent the importance of distaste in consumer practices (Wilk, 1997). As such, CAMRA publications and interviews were filled with references to 'nasty fizzy lager' invariably described as 'bland', 'gassy' or 'tasteless'.

To further explore the second of these two manifestations of consumer preference, those representing distaste and disgust, it is worth returning to what might be regarded as the foundational narrative of CAMRA. This involved a trip made to Ireland in 1971 by a group of four friends, three of whom would go on to found CAMRA and guide it through its formative years. As one of the founders recalled during an interview:

> The burping was the main thing, when we were on this holiday in Ireland we had so much keg beer, one night in Dublin I went out of the pub we were in and couldn't stop with these hiccups and went outside and the only way I could get rid of them was to hold my nose tight and put my head between my knees and I was in the middle of doing this in Dublin on a Saturday night … the gas in it, stopped me drinking that beer, and I can't drink lager now for the same reason.

This unusual account, striking in its image of a bodily rejection of the overly carbonated 'keg' beers that had gained majority market share by the early 1970s, resurfaced elsewhere in CAMRA publications and in the narrative accounts of branch member interviewees. Ian, a long-time member of the local branch, recalled returning to the UK following several years of living in Latin America by saying:

> When I came back in 1968 I suddenly found I couldn't drink the beer, and I couldn't understand why. What I didn't know was in that period I was away it had gone from Real Ale to keg beer, to me I didn't know any difference but I suddenly found I couldn't drink it, a couple of pints and I'd had enough, it was horrible … gassed up and horrible.

Ian invokes his disgust as being embodied and immediate, his body rejected the new form of beer before he knew that he had been drinking something different from what he was used to before his sojourn in Latin America. Similarly, Donald spoke of his drinking before his conversion to Real Ale which, interestingly, he described as his 'Damascene moment':

> It was probably only 20 years ago in my late 30s and I'd always drunk fizzy lager until then and I used to get *horrendous* bloody hangovers, drinking one of those Germanic sounding ones, can't remember the name now, I try and block it out.

In these and other expressions we see how the body is referenced as the abiding judge of consumer taste and the locus of a form of 'tacit knowledge' whereby the body knows to reject the invasive and unpalatable substance (Polanyi, 1967).

Such episodes would provide fuel and momentum for CAMRA's early campaigning which sought a means to frame the products of an increasingly dominant oligarchy of breweries frequently derided in CAMRA circles as the 'dastardly' or 'hated' 'Big Six'. During the 1970s one company, the London-based Watney Mann, came in for a particularly venomous attack. For example, the May 1973 edition of *What's Brewing* featured an article titled 'Watney's plastic and orange revolution' which wrote of the company with characteristic disdain:

> Weak beer, fizzy beer, orange beer, plastic beer; pubs either shut down or tarted up but never left as they are. This is the record of Watney Mann – a company that deserves to sink rather than swim … WATCH THIS SPACE for details of further atrocities.
>
> (CAMRA, 1973: 2-3)

Elsewhere, CAMRA publications frequently referred to Watney as 'Grotney', the 1974 *Good Beer Guide* was withdrawn from circulation so that a reference to the brewery could be changed from 'avoid like the plague' to a less libellous, but still unequivocally negative, 'avoid at all costs', and the first Great British Beer Festival organised by CAMRA saw a crowded Covent Garden market hall singing a chorus of 'If you hate Watney's, clap your hands'.

Building on Wilk's (1997: 183) observation that 'distaste and rejection is often more important than taste and consumption in making social distinctions', we see how as much as Real Ale is appreciated as being traditional, authentic and flavourful, such descriptions evidently relied upon the positioning of mass-produced and heavily branded beers oppositionally as being synthetic, inferior and distasteful. When an editorial in the 1992 *Good Beer Guide* describes keg beer as 'chilled' to hide the 'stale, metallic flavour' in contrast to Real Ale which was 'not tampered with' and thus remained 'living, breathing and maturing', it serves to illustrate the perhaps inescapable dualism of taste and distaste (CAMRA, 1992).

That members of CAMRA, as individual consumers, and the organisation as a whole have mobilised disgust in their vigorous rejection of certain beer connects with a deeper understanding of how the emotion of disgust functions as both a bodily and a social emotion (Wiggins, 2013). Disgust, therefore, 'plays a motivating and confirming role in moral judgement in a particular way that has little if any connection with ideas of oral incorporation' (Miller, 1998: 2). Central to the foundational narrative of the organisation is the rejection of mass-produced beers which were said to leave drinkers struggling with uncontrollable hiccups or belches and 'chemical' or 'metallic' hangovers. Such sensory distastes are therefore used by consumers to distance themselves from particular developments in consumer culture. Disgust is not only directed at the things that are physically unpalatable but also at those things that are figuratively unpalatable (Prinz, 2006). Disgust 'creates a boundary between one object (or person) and another, and thus implies that these objects or people are qualitatively different and that one is inferior to the other' and in doing so performs the 'evaluative work' of passing moral judgement about the target object (Wiggins, 2013: 492). Keg beer, the 1990 *Good Beer Guide* (1989/1990: 5) declared, is 'pasteurised, filtered and generally has the stuffing knocked out of it before it leaves the brewery gate', not with the taste of the consumer in mind but with the aim of having the beer 'reduced to a condition which is travel-proof, age-proof and landlord-proof' and therefore made easier and more profitable to sell and distribute. The dichotomy of taste/distaste established at CAMRA's inception, then, is one between authentic 'Real Ale' which is desired by the knowing sovereign consumer and inauthentic fake 'bastardised' by 'big brewers' and 'foisted' upon the unwary or uncritical.

While Watney's beer could be dismissed as 'plastic beer' and 'chemical fizz', elsewhere we can see terms such as 'ersatz beer' and 'lagerade' (a word play on the 'ade' suffix used for soda and soft drinks such as lemonade) used to design corporate beer brands as unwelcome invasions of the world of 'real' beer and 'real' pubs by fake, unpleasant beer and the profit-fixated rationalisation and efficiency driven activities of capitalist modernity (Watson and Watson, 2012). In this sense, the slighting of the 'chemical fizz' of the keg beer being heavily promoted by large breweries at the time can also be recognised as a rejection of a range of features symbolic of mass consumer culture in general (Nixon and Gabriel, 2016). Indeed, similar appeals to tradition and authenticity 'in the face of the cult of the new' have been observed in the field of food consumption (Warde, 1997: 61) and whisky consumption as a 'reaction against globalisation and commodification' (Spracklen, 2011: 106).

By starting with the body of the individual consumer, and the evident importance placed by participants and archival documents on the bodily rejection of mass beer, this section has then led into a discussion of how the wider corporate activity in the beer industry was framed as a hostile force to be resisted and, wherever possible, sabotaged and subverted.

"We don't want to be the campaign against anything"

So far the chapter has explored the prominent role played by disgust and distaste in CAMRA's framing of Real Ale consumption as an act of resistance to the changes being wrought upon British beer consumers during the second half of the 20th Century. Further to this, an overlap emerges between proclamations resisting the activities and influence of large corporate entities and a more direct condemnation of those 'other' consumers who are represented as uninitiated beer consumers who were easily 'cajoled by saturation marketing for lager and keg' (CAMRA, 1982). Expressions of incredulity that others could tolerate, let alone desire, the mass-produced beers to which CAMRA stood in opposition to construct an authentic and discerning consumer self in contrast to the perceived uncritical mass consumer. It is therefore important to note how the perceived drinking habits of other drinkers are used to police the boundaries of what is considered to be sensible, civilised ale appreciation and uncouth or antisocial drinking (see also Thurnell-Read, 2013; Thurnell-Read, 2017).

For instance, references to '*Carling* drinkers' were made by numerous participants both during interviews and fieldwork at local branch meetings and beer festivals, with the ubiquity of the lager brand facilitating the linguistic strategy of positioning those who drink it as unthinking and undiscerning consumers. Ralph, an interviewee with extensive experience in the beer and pub trade and at the time of interview engaged in various roles promoting British beer appreciation, commented that 'you could say that *Carling* is like musak, it's something that you consume in the background that doesn't interfere with what you're doing'. Here, Ralph presents the *Carling* lager brand as an example of bland, unremarkable mass consumer culture. This sentiment was similarly expressed by Gus, one of the brewers interviewed, who described the beer he brewed as being 'exciting' and:

Proper beer for people who know their stuff. OK it's not beer that is going to be a national brand, it's not like *Carling* or whatever but you know, I'm proud of that. That's a good thing, that it's not for your average *Carling* drinker ... because being small and local we can take risks, we don't have to make something that everyone will like.

The contrast between 'average' mass-produced beers like *Carling* and the 'exciting' beers made by his small 'risk' taking brewery serves to polarise tastes between mass and niche and draw an evident distinction between consumers positioned squarely on opposite sides of the sovereign/manipulated, active/passive consumer dichotomy (Slater, 1997).

During fieldwork with a local CAMRA branch, one branch member recounted visiting a local pub recently under new management and promoting itself based on its Real Ale selection, describing how 'we went in the other day and the beer was good, it was fine. They had a few [Real Ales] on but will have to build up trade before all the hand pumps are on'. The tone of this anecdote then turns when 'suddenly about fifteen people came in all ordering lager and shots and the gaffer had to run back in and was running around trying to serve them all'. The juxtaposition of discerning drinkers of Real Ale and a mass of unidentified drinkers of 'lager and shots' implies a degree of incompatibility meaning they 'soon left' and sought refuge in a nearby pub long known for its exclusively ale drinking clientele.

Examples such as this illustrate how feelings of (dis)taste can be understood as situational and contingent upon social context. As Rhys-Taylor (2013: 227) said, such 'complex cultural construction of local forms of distaste' can demonstrate how embodied sensations such as disgust operate at the personal level but also at that of the collective social process. Sensory perceptions such as taste, smell, sight and touch, often expressed in emotive terms such as 'grotty', 'rough', 'dingy' or 'smelly', serve to establish and reinforce divisions between consumers and to 'register gendered, classed histories – feelings of home and belonging' (Taylor and Falconer, 2015: 51–52). Thus, periodic expressions of distaste for the youth orientated themed bars or wine bars increasingly appealing to young professional women might be read as the result of feelings of a threat to places such as the local pub as a distinctly male space. The forceful expression of indignation in the face of changes to British pubs and beer, and British drinking culture more generally, can be seen as a reflection of predominantly male drinkers, long privileged in considering British pub culture their own, feeling 'pushed out' by the youth orientated branding and theming of an increasingly segmented market (Chatterton and Hollands, 2002; Hollands, 2002).

Conclusion

The chapter has explored some of the ways in which disgust and distaste are mobilised in the practices and discourses of Real Ale consumers and, more specifically, in the campaigning activities of CAMRA. It has sought to show that distastes have both a literal embodied and an analogous expressive character where the blandness of mass-produced beers are experienced as a tacit, corporeal engagement with wider social changes. The chapter has used the presence of disgust and corporeal rejection of 'keg beer' in the foundation narrative of CAMRA to consider the interplay of individual expressions of taste, collective identity and boundary work and wider socioeconomic changes. Thus, consumers can use their consumption and their, at times, subversive rejection of particular brands 'as a way to talk about their fears of the growing power of multi-nationals and the destruction of local distinctiveness that goes with them' (Simon, 2011: 153). As with the Slow Food movement explored by van Bommel and Spicer (2011), an organisation like CAMRA provides a focal point for the collective expression of consumer resistance in allowing disparate actors and actions to become coordinated in favour of or against certain characteristics of modern consumer society.

By calling out the activities of corporate breweries as attempts to mask the profit-driven rationalisation of the sector, à la Ritzer (2013), with contrived brands and 'themes' (Bryman, 2004), CAMRA sought to invoke indignation to mobilise the British beer consumers who had, according to the 1992 *Good Beer Guide*, 'found themselves drowning in a sea of slogans' (CAMRA, 1992). From its early years, when the campaign first fought the corporate powers of the UK beer industry by, in the words of two of the organisation founders interviewed, 'trying to undermine their expensive marketing plans and at the same time telling people that their products were rubbish' and simply 'really taking the piss out of them', disgust, distaste and rejection can be seen not simply as individual corporeal expressions, but as including notable social and political elements. Analysis of early CAMRA discourses provide an illustration of how disgust can be political and involve the passing of moral judgement (Miller, 1998). As Falk (1994: 13) has outlined, the mouth is a boundary between inside and outside and therefore a 'site of judgement'. Thus, while preferred tastes align to concepts of locality, quality and heritage, the rejection of tastes associated with rationalised, corporate, mass production give meaningful avenues for consumers to narrate their dissatisfaction with mass consumption in late modernity (Warde, 1997). As such, the case explored demonstrates the wider issues relating to consumer (dis)taste that mean the most intimate embodied engagements with consumer culture, be they felt as those of pleasure or disgust, are part of wider resistance to invasive corporate rationalisation and the associated perceived erosion of local culture or consumer sovereignty (Smart, 1999).

References

Ashley, B., Hollows, J., Jones, S. and Taylor, B. (2004). *Food and Cultural Studies*. London: Routledge.

Belk, R. W. (1988). Possessions and the Extended Self. *Journal of Consumer Research*, 15(2), 139–168.

Bryman, A. (2004). *The Disneyization of Society*. London: SAGE.

Campaign for Real Ale (CAMRA) (1973). Watney's Plastic Orange Revolution. *What's Brewing*, May. St Albans, UK: Campaign for Real Ale.

Campaign for Real Ale (CAMRA) (1982). *Good Beer Guide 1982*, edited by Roger Protz. St Albans, UK: Littlehampton Book Services.

Campaign for Real Ale (CAMRA) (1989/1990). *Good Beer Guide 1990*, edited by Andrea Gillies. St Albans, UK: Littlehampton Book Services.

Campaign for Real Ale (CAMRA) (1991/1992). *Good Beer Guide 1992*, edited by Jeff Evans. St Albans, UK: Verulam Publishing.

Chatterton, P. and Hollands, R. (2002). Theorising Urban Playscapes: Producing, regulating and consuming youthful nightlife city spaces. *Urban Studies*, 39(1), 95–116.

Donald, B. and Blay-Palmer, A. (2006). The Urban Creative-Food Economy: Producing food for the urban elite or social inclusion opportunity? *Environment and Planning A*, 38(10), 1901–1920.

Falk, P. (1994). *The Consuming Body*. London: SAGE.

Gabriel, Y. and Lang, T. (1995). *The Unmanageable Consumer: Contemporary Consumption and Its Fragmentations*. London: SAGE.

Guthman, J. (2003). Fast Food/Organic Food: Reflexive tastes and the making of 'yuppie chow'. *Social & Cultural Geography*, 4(1), 45–58.

Hayes-Conroy, A. and Hayes-Conroy, J. (2010). Visceral Difference: Variations in feeling (slow) food. *Environment and Planning A*, 42(12), 2956–2971.

Hollands, R. (2002). Divisions in the Dark: Youth cultures, transitions and segmented consumption spaces in the night-time economy. *Journal of Youth Studies*, 5(2), 153–171.

Kingsnorth, P. (2011). *Real England: The Battle against the Bland*. London: Portobello Books.

Lang, T. and Heasman, M. (2004). *Food Wars: The Global Battle for Mouths, Minds and Markets*. London: Earthscan.

Lewis, T. and Potter, E. (2011). *Ethical Consumption: A Critical Introduction*. Abingdon: Routledge.

Lupton, D. (1998). *The Emotional Self: A Sociocultural Exploration*. London: SAGE.

Miller, W. I. (1998). *The Anatomy of Disgust*. Boston: Harvard University Press.

Moore, S. (2008). *Ribbon Culture: Charity, Compassion and Public Awareness*. Basingstoke: Palgrave Macmillan.

Mukherjee, R. and Banet-Weiser, S. (Eds). (2012). *Commodity Activism: Cultural Resistance in Neoliberal Times*. New York: New York University Press.

Nixon, E. and Gabriel, Y. (2016). 'So Much Choice and No Choice At All': A socio-psychoanalytic interpretation of consumerism as a source of pollution. *Marketing Theory*, 16(1), 39–56.

Polanyi, M. (1967). *The Tacit Dimension*. London: Routledge & Kegan Paul.

Prinz, J. J. (2006). *Gut Reactions: A Perceptual Theory of Emotion*. New York: Oxford University Press.

Rafferty, K. (2011). Class-Based Emotions and the Allure of Fashion Consumption. *Journal of Consumer Culture*, 11(2), 239–260.

Reiter, E. (1991). *Making Fast Food*. Kingston, Ontario: McGill-Queen's University Press.

Rhys-Taylor, A. (2013). Disgust and Distinction: The case of the jellied eel. *The Sociological Review*, 61(2), 227–246.

Ritzer, G. (2013). *The McDonaldization of Society*, 20th Anniversary Edition. London: SAGE.

Sassatelli, R. (2007). *Consumer Culture: History, Theory and Politics.* London: SAGE.

Sassatelli, R. and Davolio, F. (2010). Consumption, Pleasure and Politics: Slow food and the politico-aesthetic problematization of food. *Journal of Consumer Culture,* 10(2), 202–232.

Schwarzkopf, S. (2011). The Political Theology of Consumer Sovereignty towards an Ontology of Consumer Society. *Theory, Culture & Society,* 28(3), 106–129.

Simon, B. (2011). Not Going to Starbucks: Boycotts and the out-scouring of politics in the branded world. *Journal of Consumer Culture,* 11(2), 145–167.

Slater, D. (1997). *Consumer Culture.* Cambridge: Polity.

Smart, B. (1999). *Resisting McDonaldization.* London: SAGE.

Spracklen, K. (2011). Dreaming of Drams: Authenticity in Scottish whisky tourism as an expression of unresolved Habermasian rationalities. *Leisure Studies,* 30(1), 99–116.

Taylor, Y. and Falconer, E. (2015). 'Seedy Bars and Grotty Pints': Close encounters in queer leisure spaces. *Social & Cultural Geography,* 16(1), 43–57.

Thurnell-Read, T. (2013). 'Yobs' and 'Snobs': Embodying drink and the problematic male drinking body. *Sociological Research Online,* 18(2), 103–112.

Thurnell-Read, T. (2016). 'Real Ale' Enthusiasts, Serious Leisure and the Costs of Getting 'Too Serious' about Beer. *Leisure Sciences,* 38(1), 68–84.

Thurnell-Read, T. (2017). 'Did You Ever Hear of Police Being Called to a Beer Festival?': Discourses of merriment, moderation and 'civilized' drinking amongst Real Ale enthusiasts. *The Sociological Review,* 65(1), 83–99.

Thurnell-Read, T. (2018). The Embourgeoisement of Beer: Changing practices of 'Real Ale' consumption. *Journal of Consumer Culture,* 18(4), 539–557.

van Bommel, K. and Spicer, A. (2011). Hail the Snail: Hegemonic struggles in the slow food movement. *Organization Studies,* 32(12), 1717–1744.

Warde, A. (1994). Consumption, Identity-formation and Uncertainty. *Sociology,* 28(4), 877–898.

Warde, A. (1997). *Consumption, Food and Taste.* London: SAGE.

Watson, T. J. and Watson, D. H. (2012). Narratives in Society, Organizations and Individual Identities: An ethnographic study of pubs, identity work and the pursuit of 'the real'. *Human Relations,* 65(6), 683–704.

Wheeler, K. (2012). The Practice of Fairtrade Support. *Sociology,* 46(1): 126–141.

Wiggins, S. (2013). The Social Life of 'Eugh': Disgust as assessment in family mealtimes. *British Journal of Social Psychology,* 52(3), 489–509.

Wilk, R. (1997). A Critique of Desire: Distaste and dislike in consumer behavior. *Consumption, Markets and Culture,* 1(2), 175–196.

Wilk, R. (2006). *Fast Food/Slow Food: The Cultural Economy of the Global Food System.* Plymouth: Rowman Altamira.

2 A sticky situation? Fatty distaste and the embodied performance of class

Louise MacAllister and Suzanne Hocknell

UK consumers have perhaps never had so much choice in fat. Our supermarket shelves, our kitchen cupboards, our bellies and our flesh are inhabited by butter, margarine,[1] olive oil, oilseed rape, sunflower oil, coconut oil, palm oil, dripping, lard, pumpkin oil, avocado oil, corn oil, duck fat and more. Further, within each fat type choices abound. Consumers can choose organic fats, vegan fats, extra-virgin, spray-able, high-oleic, high-omega, low in saturates, high in poly-unsaturates, trans-fat free, palm-free, gm-free, free-from and even low-fat fats. Whilst the fats eaten may be framed as the outcome of a rational consumer choice, fatty tastes are deeply embodied, shaped by a complex interplay of material, sensory and symbolic factors, and entangled with social and cultural norms, and affective environments. Powerful discursive constructions of edible fats and body fat, in public health campaigns, the media and advertisements, attempt to harness fatty materialities with the affective potential of eaters for capacities as diverse as guilt, shame, fear, pleasure, belonging or care. In this way notions of what it means to consume well that are subject to classed, gendered and other normative framings are reproduced. Yet, fatty eating habits can be so mundane, so familiar, that they often go unnoticed.

This chapter draws on empirical work with eaters to analyse their experience of distaste, placing it within their classed habitus and their articulations and experiences of otherness. Firstly, by focusing on edible fats, we show that the visceral sensations of fat against lips and tongue are not in themselves sufficient to engender distaste. Distaste emerges with and through the affective, material and discursive frictions that are convoked by the stuff of fat. Yet, for our participants, their distaste is bound up with social and cultural notions of what it means to consume fat that are so mundane as to be experienced as unchanging and habitual. Secondly, we demonstrate how such seemingly routine consumption practices entangle with distaste to co-create and perpetuate powerful classed performances of belonging and of othering. Thirdly, drawing on Bourdieu's (1984) work on the habitus, Probyn's (2000) exploration of disgust as a pushing-away of the unwelcome other and Ahmed's (2000) investigations of stickiness, we demonstrate that accounting for distaste can help better understand and theorise fatty eating practices and the performance of belonging.

Researching the materiality of fat and how it comes to matter

Abbots and Lavis (2013) have demonstrated how 'unpacking' food practices can begin to make present the ways in which social and cultural imaginaries frame the ways in which food matters can be encountered, understood, represented and enacted. One approach to such 'unpacking' is to engage methodologies that work to reveal some of the labour necessary for the maintenance of these norms. This chapter draws upon two separate research projects carried out by both authors. Hocknell's research 'Fat chance? Eating-well with margarine' (2017) engages six 'planned discussion groups' (PDGs) each with 2–5 participants (O'Reilly, 2005) who were encouraged to explore their shifting practices and tastes with margarine matters; whilst Louise's project 'Shaping the family; anti-obesity discourses and family life' (2016) employed five focus groups and over twenty interviews to investigate the effects of anti-obesity discourses on everyday parenting practices.

In Hocknell's PDGs participants were chosen because of their relationships to each other rather than for their knowledge of a subject. Hocknell used snowballing methods within her established networks to find participants. She contacted six hosts from diverse class backgrounds, one for each group, with each host inviting up to three friends or family members into their home to share the space of their session. Culturally, educationally and economically Hocknell's participants had grown up in a mix of working and middle-class backgrounds across the UK, and the interplay of these factors had shifted throughout their lives. Within this multi-generational group, some middle-class kids had grown up to become single parents in precarious employment under severe financial strain; whilst working-class kids were now educated, securely-employed, homeowners and so on.

Louise's research was carried out with parents in Devon with participants taking part in focus groups or interviews. Participants were self-selecting following letters sent through schools asking parents to participate in research about their experiences of body size for both themselves and their child(ren). Those who took part tended to view themselves as 'good' parents who fed their children well, but were concerned about an imagined group of 'other' parents whose parenting practices were deemed to cause obesity. The majority of Louise's participants were homeowners, educated to degree level and with above average income for Devon.

Class matters in food discourse. In the UK notions of good and bad taste are deeply entwined with class power structures (and resistance to them). 'Class' is a system through which expertise is established and exercised. On the one hand the knowledges of middle-class and state governance become cemented through existing mechanisms of power as the way in which life should be lived (Rose, 1993), while on the other hand the practices and knowledge framed by the establishment as working-class become figuratively understood as lacking (Skeggs, 2005). Yet our participants do not easily 'fit' in such blocky conceptualisations. Here, we understand class as more complex and multiple than is traditionally understood. In this chapter we are informed by Lawson and Elwood's definition of class as a 'social relation or subjective orientation arising from identities, practices, representation and discourses that unite and divide people, in fluid ways across time and space' (2014: 212), and Gibson and Graham's understanding of class as 'a social *process* of exploitation' within which individuals participate 'in multiple class processes at a single moment and over time' (1992: 109, emphasis added). It is in this context that we engage the atmospheres of *distaste* entangled with and in our participants' articulations of their fatty beliefs, knowledge and practices, to explore their performances of class and expertise. Building on the work of Bourdieu (1984) we demonstrate distaste as a visceral response of embodied selves that are situated and classed by dynamic performances of belonging and othering, these performances are simultaneously social, cultural and embodied.

We are informed in our approach to distaste by Probyn's (2000) and Ahmed's (2000) investigations of disgust. For Probyn, a disgust response is a pushing away of an unwelcome other. Whilst for Ahmed disgust objects are materially and discursively sticky. In this chapter, we use data generated within our empirical work to develop these concepts as they apply to our explorations of distaste. Drawing on our data, we argue that distaste is a specific expression of disgust that emerges within tensions between embodied encounters, social and health discourses and a sense of the situated self. Our empirical examples reveal that for our participants, distaste is rooted both in a fear of the stickiness of the lively stuff of fat, and its material and discursive associations. Such fear prompts performances which simultaneously distance the self from distasteful matters, whilst adding to discourses that bind these same matters with distasteful othernesses. Fatty matters can stick by breaching the boundaries of self and attaching to the flesh, but they are also a speech act that binds together the material and the sign. If they are not pushed away distasteful materialities can contaminate all that they touch, yet, as the examples in this chapter will demonstrate, such matters can also be experienced as pleasurably 'naughty'. All fats are not stigmatised equally in all situations. To embrace immediate visceral gratification in this way, however, is to reject the model promoted within UK policy of the autonomous consumer, who makes food choices following an evaluation of the impact on individual health (Evans, 2010).

By focusing on the relational affective encounters by which fats become felt by our participants as distasteful, we determine how fat, a foodstuff necessary for life, can become simultaneously bound up in discourses of health and morality, and performances of class and belonging. Fat is more than an 'exemplary disgust object' (Ahmed, 2000). Fats can be simultaneously desired and pushed away. Engagements with fat are experienced by our participants with and in 'awkward, unequal, unstable, and creative qualities of interconnection across difference' (Tsing, 2011: 4). In order to maintain a coherent sense of self amidst such pressures, our participants engage a performative enactment of distaste. As such, unpacking distaste exposes a series of tensions which challenge the ways our participants' story themselves as eaters, consumers and members of families and communities. In the following two sections we engage our research examples to show that a multiplicity of material and representational factors work to co-create the experience of distaste, thus we establish distaste to be performative, situated and contingent.

Distaste and the storying of self

This section draws on Hocknell's empirical work. First, we demonstrate that her participants' fatty practices cannot be contained within either their visceral experiences or their knowledge and discourses. Secondly, we show that the stuff of fat is experienced as folded with multiple human and nonhuman others. Thirdly, we argue that fats that taste good to Hocknell's participants' are ones that can be rationalised as acting in the world in ways which accord with their sense of self and of classed belonging, distaste is an embodied response to dissonance with the storying of self. In the discussion below, all names have been changed for anonymity.

Hocknell opened each planned discussion group by explaining that she did not believe there to be a single right way to eat for everyone at all times, and that she was interested to know how people make yellow fat choices given all the conflicting information available. At the start of her PDGs, Hocknell's participants typically styled their fatty practices as 'just habit'. What is notable though is that her participants did not hold back in challenging the accuracy of such narratives as were put forward by their fellow group members. Discussion flowed readily as the structure of the groups worked to create a familiar and 'safer' space in which the fatty practices, narratives, beliefs and relationships of Hocknell's participants could be revealed. Across the six PDGs, Hocknell's participants talked over each other, derided the limitations of each other's beliefs, riffed off each other, laughed and disagreed in their recollections of household practices. In this way it emerged that individual habits and tastes had changed substantially over time. Thinking about their shifting fatty practices momentarily made present to Hocknell's participants the striated space between then and now. Awareness of these gaps troubled their descriptions of their fatty practices as merely habitual, prompting them to explore the complex knowledge, beliefs and encounters entangled with them.

In unpacking why their practices had changed, and how their current habits had developed and were maintained, Hocknell's participants became aware of the ways in which they juggle and prioritise multiple conflicting values and situated belongings. For example, Martin, a retired grandfather in his early seventies, responded to his wife Joan's description of sunflower oil as tasting 'a bit manky' by reminiscing about the visceral joy of 'bread dipped in the beef dripping as it came out of the pan, so it was hot'. But Martin no longer eats dripping. He explained that he 'went in to buying' low-fat spreads because they are supposed to be 'quite healthy' and they 'do the job well enough'. Nonetheless, Martin went on to describe how in social situations he prioritises the embodied pleasures of eating butter over the benefits he believes low fat spreads may bring to his cardiovascular health. This situated performance of belonging has striking parallels with Martin's recollection that when he was young his aspirational mother had considered margarine suitable only for use within baking; whilst for the display of the table, the more expensive butter, specifically *Lurpak* butter, was the valued yellow fat of choice. Distaste for Martin is not only visceral but is situated in the tensions and translations between the classed performances of health and the social framings of fats. Distaste as a marker of distinction is situated and contingent.

This class-based social stigma around the use of butter rather than margarine was not something my younger participants recalled. Regardless of their class background they had grown up primarily eating margarine rather than butter. Alice, for example, a butter eating secretary in her early forties who is from a solidly middle-class family did not recall ever 'having butter at home when I was a child':

> We always had *Flora* and those kind of things, which now I find really just greasy and horrible. We had *Flora*, but then we had this *Outline* thing. It was the most disgusting, it used to make me almost gag, it was really revolting. The texture was weird; I think it was like a diet one. Every now and again mum would go on a diet, even though she really didn't need to diet.

Alice felt that in addition to price, her mum was influenced in her fat choices by social norms. Yet, for her, stigma and belonging were entangled with gendered mores about body shape, and social expectations of familial care, that were both subtler and more complex in their articulations of insider-outsider status than the type of fat seen on their kitchen table.

The fatty tastes articulated by Martin, Alice and Alice's mum mirrored shifting discursive constructions of the stuff of margarine. The early years of margarine manufacture saw efforts to attract consumers by producing an economically thrifty foodstuff that mimicked butter not only in appearance and functionality, but also in flavour and nutritional make-up (Riepma, 1970). Nonetheless, transforming fats into margarine created a novel foodstuff that both consumers and societal norms had yet to learn a taste for, and although margarine became a frugal inevitability for some UK households, it carried with it significant social stigma within its greasy presence on the table (Levene, 2014). It wasn't until the late 1970s (a century after margarine was first marketed) and the launch of soft, spreadable margarines with lipid profiles thought to be beneficial for heart-health, that margarine became widely experienced in the UK as a desirable foodstuff in and of itself (Upritchard et al, 2005). The trans-fat revelations of the 1990s troubled this settlement, but margarine has been reformulated, and advertising and nutritional advice from the UK Government continue to present margarine as the responsible yellow fat choice.

Ruth, a single mother and English teacher in her late thirties, was brought up with margarine but has not bought it since the mid-1990s. She recalled first eating butter whilst on holiday in France 'and going bloody hell this is delicious!' When she talked about her knowledges of butter, Ruth was animated and joyful. She gesticulated, and her eyes lit up as she described how it tasted 'like proper food. Absolutely lovely. Nourishment!' She felt that this experience of 'nourishment' roused her visceral self to the distasteful 'unnatural' otherness of the flavours, smells and textures of margarine. Visceral pleasure was nonetheless not the only factor in Ruth's experience of taste, she explained that she desired to exercise her consumer choice to enact care and belonging but felt that she used:

> A lot of double think – I kind of persuade myself, because ... I'm aware of how, the chain of production ... you know ... the way the cows are treated, but ... I can't afford to prioritise it and you know eat the way I want to eat.

Yellow fat practices were experienced by Ruth as a node where self and world fold together in multiple intimate ways, but she found that her income limited her possibilities to enact such relational care, forcing her to work through what her food priorities actually were. Ruth went on to explain that she had:

> Bought value, *Tesco*'s value, because we had an experiment me and the kids, because I mean things aren't quite so tight now, touch wood and I hope they'll stay that way, but they were really tight last year and whenever, erm, I sort of thought I'm going to try some of the value products and just see if they're good.

Ruth explained that she encountered value butter viscerally as 'absolutely lovely... exactly the same, butter and salt, nothing else. It's just a pack of butter'. However, she continued:

> I'm not buying value butter now ... I don't like the value packaging. There is a stigma about it isn't there ... it's that cultural thing, it's like there's a stigma about those value products.

Distaste for Ruth was described as much more than a straightforward reaction to flavour and texture, it was entangled with her understandings of care, status and belonging which have developed over her lifecourse and come to form her habitus (Bourdieu, 1984). Ruth experienced the classed stigma of value products as sticky and felt a need to enact a separation of herself from them in ways that other participants who were in less financially precarious situations did not. Indeed, Catherine and John, a retired middle-class couple in their sixties, were enthusiastic about supermarket own brands:

So you know a lot of people might think, oh you know that's the brand to go for and this is a cheap alternative. But when you actually read the ingredients you sort of think, well there doesn't seem to be any difference between these two. Buy the cheap one!

Ruth's belief that the experience of nourishment reveals the stuff of fat as acting with and in her body in ways that are healthful, created space in which the liveliness of the stuff of fat became known to her. However, in her assessment of how value butter can be stigmatising, Ruth illuminated how such liveliness can, in part, be captured within other knowledge frameworks and sold to consumers as discrete packages subject to 'lifestyle choice'. She did not just buy any brand of butter, no matter that it tastes 'exactly the same'. Ruth's experiences of the tastefulness of butter were entangled with her material knowledge, cultural positionality and regimes of value (Bourdieu, 1984; Hayes-Conroy and Hayes-Conroy, 2008). Ruth did not just taste the stuff of fat but bodies, processes, relationships, knowledge and beliefs touched by it (Ahmed, 2004), yet the extent of this relationality overwhelmed her and there were multiple others which she felt she must, through necessity of time and money, disregard. As such, Ruth's performances of distaste both co-created and perpetuated exploitative othernesses (Ahmed, 2004; Probyn, 1996).

As the above examples demonstrate, food practices are shaped by a complex interplay of material, sensory and symbolic factors and entangled with the construction and presentation of self. Eaters, are not passive recipients for messages about food matters, subjects are perpetually co-constituted through embodied encounters with others (Ahmed, 2000). Eating is an intermingling and remaking of bodies (Probyn, 2000) and eating selves are, in smaller and larger ways, responsive to all the relations, whether of connection or detachment, that constitute social, cultural and food systems. In other words, eaters are more than consumers, and there is no such thing as an autonomous consumer. Positioned within multiple communities, Hocknell's participants were parents, neighbours, colleagues, friends, gardeners, companions and more, who were situated, framed, judged and offered potential to act by their social, cultural, political and economic capital (Bourdieu, 1984). Further, they experienced fatty materialities as entangled with, and stuck, to multiple others. Eating simultaneously folds these multiple bodies and relationships inwards, into the eaters' body, and outwards, into the world, potentially contaminating both. As is illustrated in the contrasting responses of Ruth and Catherine to 'value' brands, eaters simultaneously belong to and experience the world, and are re-made with and through the classed norms and expectations of their wider communities. Norms which also become stuck to the matters of food.

Distaste is knotted with the ways in which beliefs and knowledge about the stuff of fat and its relationships are produced, maintained and entangled with practices of identity, belonging and self-care. Distaste cannot be contained in the encounter. Through performances of prioritisation, 'strategic ignorance'

(McGoey, 2012: 4) and situated juggling, multiple distasteful othernesses are distanced from the situated self. However, Hocknell's participants found there to be just too many entangled others to think about, and so felt compelled to disregard multiple bodies and relationships. Such settlements remained stable until disrupted by an 'event' which created friction by overflowing and troubling this classed ordering of bodies and processes. Hocknell's participants experienced distaste, not just when 'things, categories, people' (Probyn, 2000: 133) entangled with fatty materialities 'are just too close for comfort' (Probyn, 2000: 133) but because the impossibility of attending to them all revealed disjunctures in their storying of self.

Performing class and expertise through fatty distaste

Fat is central to anti-obesity discourses,[2] with the energy balance being used to explain size as an outcome of an equation of food consumed and energy expended. Louise used focus groups and one-to-one interviews with parents to research the ways in which anti-obesity discourses affect their parenting practices. Louise did not know the participants beforehand, and with a few exceptions, focus group participants were also unknown to others in the group. Participants volunteered to take part in response to a letter sent out through a number of primary schools in Devon, UK. Participants were therefore self-selecting, with an interest in the topic. They tended to deem themselves as holding 'correct' parenting knowledge and in research discussions this was contrasted with a classed 'other' who was framed as lacking.

Policy documents and campaigns targeted at childhood obesity make possible futures felt in the present which, Evans (2010) argues, generate a feeling of an impending health disaster through affective statements such as 'Childhood obesity is a health–"time bomb"'. The presence of future health in present day consumption practices is one of the multiplicity of factors that create a tension in the experience of consuming fat; a tension experienced as distaste. Louise's participants felt assured of their identity as 'good parents' as their habitual practices matched that espoused as 'correct' within such anti-obesity discourses (Bourdieu, 1984). The performance of 'correct' family consumption practices is linked to the performance of a middle-class identity. Across a range of policies on parenting, health, education and care in the UK, the idealised behaviours are modelled on perceived middle-class practices, while practices associated with a working-class identity are framed as those in need of correction (Rose, 1993; Skeggs, 2005; Rawlins, 2009; Guthman, 2011). However, as Hocknell's research has demonstrated the consumption of fat is not straightforwardly directed, rather it is framed with, and in, multiple forces, knowledge and materialities. For Louise's participants the generation of affect in public health campaigns was understood to be an important and powerful factor.

Whilst Hocknell's participants' encountered specific fatty materialities as distasteful, in the context of obesity discourses it was the material qualities of fatty foods more generally that were pushed away by Louise's participants. One interview participant, Carol, a mother of two, described how she could not:

> Remember the statistic now but I read it somewhere that you know, one bag of crisps a day was like eating a big bottle of oil a year and I said to my sister "you wouldn't feed them that would you?", and she was like, "well, no", "well, that is what you are doing", and she was like, "oh really", and I thought there must be lots of other parents that have no idea that this one packet of crisps is actually, I think I got that information leaflet from my nursery.

Carol's words are revealing of the tension between her own practices and discursive constructions of fat as bad, and her sister's parenting practices of allowing her children to consume crisps. Carol expresses disgust towards the material properties of 'a bottle of oil', but the viscous, unctuous and insensate (Forth, 2013) properties of liquid fat alone do not account for the way Carol expressed her feelings about crisps. By considering the interplay of material and discursive tensions, and differing practices around crisps, Carol's disgust can be better understood as distaste; a tension within the self, between relational others, discourses, affects, and matter. Carol cites an information leaflet from a nursery as the source of her knowledge about oil in crisps. The leaflet 'sticks' (Ahmed, 2000) to her existing imaginings of fat to produce a reaction of avoidance of crisps, the food that she now conceptualises in terms of its fatty components. Carol expresses distaste which is rooted in the particular materialities of fat's greasy and viscous texture and linked to classed discourses of health and eating well. However, Carol's privileging of health discourses and reaction to the material stickiness of fat are experienced as distaste not for her own consumption of fat, but for that of others, in this case those who consume crisps. Carol's distaste is not merely expressed for the foodstuff, but for those who consume it. They have become 'stuck' to the matter they consume and the anti-obesity discourses with which it is entangled.

This entanglement between the material and discursive creates an atmosphere of distaste for crisps that cannot be accounted for by thinking only about taste as merely a 'sense' of the body; it is rooted in a parenting practice that Carol perceives to be irresponsible. The correct way to parent as envisioned in policy falls into line with traditionally white, middle-class practices and knowledge (Gillies, 2008; Rawlins, 2009). Both Gillies (2008) and Rawlins (2009) draw on the contextual factors that shape decision making in the lives of those parents whose practices are stigmatised within policy. However, Carol's quote demonstrates the enduring power of a discourse of a specific and singular version of parenting responsibility in which perceived middle-class practices are valorised. Furthermore, it becomes acceptable to talk of the practices of 'others' in terms of disgust and irresponsibility rather than visceral pleasures and broader social contexts. Fatty consumption practices become enrolled within this affective discourse of classed behaviours, visceral feelings and caring responsibilities and expressions of disgust, distaste and pleasure become expressions of class, expertise and responsible caring practices.

The classed expression of distaste for both fatty foodstuffs, and those who consume them was similarly expressed by Amy, a focus group participant and a mother of two. Amy articulated her distaste for processed foods which she referred to as fatty, unhealthy and consumed by those without the 'correct' knowledge. She explained:

> A documentary has been coming out about what's in these foods and some of them are quite horrific ... they are actually disgusting, you know when you break it down and you think this is what you are putting into this generation.

Amy's expression of distaste for fatty foods is an outcome of an affective discursive construction of fat as harmful, which becomes viscerally felt through the consumption of processed foods. As such, Amy's visceral experiences of consumption are in line with policy constructions of eating well and feeding children well, and leaves her feeling good about her eating habits and how she feeds her children. Amy is performing the role of the middle-class responsible parent; drawing on Bourdieu (1984), Amy's classed 'habitus' which leads her to avoid fatty and processed foods, also matches the 'field', or context, of policy which frames such food as bad. Amy's knowledge that the consumption practices of 'others' is out of tune with her taken-for-granted normative practices of consumption, and with those of health policy is awkward for Amy. Amy's performance of expertise became crystallised in expressions of distaste for the foods that existed in tension with this performance, and those who consumed these foods.

Distaste that passes from foodstuff to the consumer is an example of the discursive 'stickiness' of the stigmatised other (Ahmed, 2000). Furthermore, assumptions about those whose consumption practices are felt as distasteful serve to perpetuate social shaming and contribute to an affective sense of the distasteful other. As Kate, a focus group participant and mother of two lamented:

> Fat is too cheap, junk food is too cheap, it shouldn't be the case that, that, people who have low incomes spend their money on McDonalds and Burger King buying a 99p cheeseburger, they should be spending that pound on a punnet of fruit, but because they can buy a burger, they will, and, and, it, it's got so far now.

The classed performance of the researcher encounter evokes Kate's distaste for fatty and processed foods. The affective atmosphere of good parenting, expertise and the spectral threat of the 'bad' other in the research encounter relied upon the discursive regurgitation of fat as something which is distasteful. These examples illustrate the interconnections between the performance of classed identity and embodied senses that come to appear natural, and which serve to reproduce somatic classed identity.

Conclusion

It is unsurprising that taste is a key mechanism through which our participants encounter the stuff of fat. What is important, however, is that their perceptions of the distastefulness of a fat did not rest in any straightforward way on their visceral disliking of the flavour of that same fat. In eating, 'material relations and immaterial forces all intersect with individuals' sensory grasp of the world, complicating one's visceral experience' (Hayes-Conroy and Hayes-Conroy, 2008: 465). In disgust, those which have already been 'designated as the beyond' (Ahmed, 2000: 3), those othered materialities, relationships, discourses and classed existences become drawn too close for comfort. The experience of distastefulness, however, is not simply an embodied rejection of such perceived topologies of proximity. Our mapping of the moments in which fat or fats were expressed as distasteful in our research encounters demonstrates that distaste differs from disgust in that it can be understood as the push-pull of desire-revulsion arising within situated material, discursive and social tensions.

Caring for the self and proximate others through attentiveness to the embodied experiences of eating fats was articulated by our participants as a matter of concern. Our participants have described how they experienced the stuff of fat as messy performances that traverse, connect and transform bodies (Mol, 2008; Probyn and Evers, 2010), and they expressed unease about the kinds of bodies and relationships with which they might become viscerally entangled. Food 'enters into what we become' (Bennett, 2007: 133). For food to be encountered as tasteful by our participants then it needed to accord with their conceptions of self, community and belonging, and not with those identities with which they did not wish to be associated. Hocknell's participants reported that the experience of distaste, although shaped by visceral encounters, was primarily a product of their attempts to maintain a coherent storying of self and belonging when different regimes of value were in tension. As such, if the social situation dictated, they not only ate fats that in other circumstances they felt to be distasteful, but even experienced joyful 'naughtiness' within these moments of dissent. Conversely, tasty fats that carried situated social stigma could not be savoured but came to be experienced as distasteful.

Louise's research builds upon this to demonstrate that, for her participants, the expression of distaste goes beyond the food itself. A range of somatic markers have come to be discursively associated with eating and notions of body-failure or success (McDowell, 2006; McRobbie, 2009;

Jones, 2012), including consumption practices, metabolic disease and body size. Those that consume food that is experienced as distasteful become 'stuck' to the expression of distaste, however it is also the case that foods which have become culturally associated with lack of food knowledge are amplified in their distastefulness. As Louise's research demonstrated, vocalising and acting on that distaste then becomes a practice by which barriers are drawn between a 'distasteful and unknowledgeable' other. The affective environments of Louise's research encounters enabled an exploration of socio-cultural factors that shape the way in which fats may be framed as distasteful. Fats are often linked in media and policy documents to laziness, obesity and working-class bodies (Guthman, 2011), and so become discursively associated with such meanings. To consume fats for Louise's participants was to come too close to some of these attributes which are negatively perceived. The result of which is not only a pushing away of fatty foods, but, for research participants who were invested in presenting themselves with expertise, a discursive and classed enactment of distancing themselves, and their family, from those whose food practices existed in tension with their own.

The participants' distasteful encounters with the stuff of fats 'cannot be contained in meetings between the stuff of fat and lips, tongue, or guts' (Hocknell, 2016: 18). Their experiences reveal frictions between visceral sensations and classed discourses of health, care, citizenship and belonging as they pertain to past, present and (imagined) future selves. Such tensions demonstrate as much about the social processes entangled with the participants' constructions of self and other as they do about the fatty objects of their distaste. Further, the data generated within our research encounters, pertains not only to the beliefs and practices of the research participants. In considering the complex ways in which fats are known, done and experienced, accounting for distaste helps to better understand and theorise both fatty eating practices and classed performances of belonging. In sum, by demonstrating that fatty materialities are not inherently distasteful but become so with and in the classed atmosphere of the encounter, distaste can be conceptualised as slippery, entangled with attempting to protect the situated self from the stickiness of discursive as well as material contamination. Furthermore, such attempts to safeguard the self are performances of expertise and belonging which act to re-produce social relations of hierarchy, otherness and disgust.

Notes

1 For a product to be labelled as margarine in the UK it must have 'a fat content of not less than 80%' (FSA, 2010). However, throughout this chapter we have used the term to include 'spreadable yellow fats' as is normal in colloquial English.
2 Sugar is also central to anti-obesity discourses, and Louise has written about it in relation to this research project (MacAllister, 2016).

References

Abbots, E., and Lavis, A. (2013). Introduction. In: Abbots, E. and Lavis, A., (Eds.) *Why we eat, how we eat: Contemporary encounters between foods and bodies.* Farnham: Ashgate, 1–12.

Ahmed, S. (2000). *Strange encounters: Embodied others in post-coloniality.* Abingdon: Routledge.

Ahmed, S. (2004). *The cultural politics of emotion.* Abingdon: Routledge.

Bennett, J. (2007). Edible matter. *New Left Review,* 45, 133–145.

Bourdieu, P. (1984). *Distinction: A social critique of the judgement of taste.* Cambridge, MA: Harvard University Press.

Evans, B. (2010). Anticipating fatness: Childhood, affect and the pre-emptive 'war on obesity'. *Transactions of the Institute of British Geographers,* 35(1), 21–38.

Food Standards Agency (FAO) (2010). Yellow fat guidance. Available from https://www w.food.gov.uk/sites/default/files/multimedia/pdfs/yellowfatguidance0610.pdf. [Accessed 23 October 2016].

Forth, C. E. (2013). The qualities of fat: Bodies, history, and materiality. *Journal of Material Culture,* 18(2), 135–154.

Gibson, K., and Graham, J. (1992). Creating space for an alternative politics of class. *Economic Geography,* 68(2), 109–127.

Gillies, V. (2008). Perspectives on parenting responsibility: Contextualizing values and practices. *Journal of Law and Society,* 35(1), 95–112.

Guthman, J. (2011). *Weighing in: Obesity, food justice, and the limits of capitalism.* Oakland: University of California Press.

Hayes-Conroy, A., and Hayes-Conroy, J. (2008). Taking back taste: Feminism, food and visceral politics. *Gender, Place and Culture,* 15(5), 461–473.

Hocknell, S. (2016). Chewing the fat: 'Unpacking' distasteful encounters. *Gastronomica: The Journal of Critical Food Studies,* 16(3), 13–18.

Hocknell, S. (2017). Fat Chance? Eating Well with Margarine. PhD thesis, University of Exeter. http://hdl.handle.net/10871/27794.

Jones, O. (2012). *Chavs: The demonization of the working class.* London: Verso Books.

Lawson, V., and Elwood, S. (2014). Encountering poverty: Space, class, and poverty politics. *Antipode,* 46(1), 209–228.

Levene, A. (2014). The meanings of margarine in England: Class, consumption and material culture from 1918 to 1953. *Contemporary British History,* 28, 145–165.

MacAllister, L. (2016). Intervention – taxing sugar, sweetening inequality: Disrupting George Osborne's 'Sugar Tax' with the agential properties of sugar itself. *Antipode.* http://wp.me/p16RPC-1l0.

MacAllister, L. (2016). Shaping the family; Anti-obesity discourses and family life. PhD thesis, University of Exeter. http://hdl.handle.net/10871/23947.

McDowell, L. (2006). Reconfigurations of gender and class relations: Class differences, class condescension and the changing place of class relations. *Antipode,* 38(4), 825–850.

McGoey, L. (2012). Strategic unknowns: Towards a sociology of ignorance. *Economy and Society,* 41(1), 1–16.

McRobbie, A. (2009). *The aftermath of feminism: Gender, culture and social change.* London: SAGE.

Mol, A. (2008). I eat an apple. On theorizing subjectivities. *Subjectivity,* 22(1), 28–37.

O'Reilly, K. (2005). *Ethnographic methods.* Abingdon: Routledge.

Probyn, E. (1996). *Outside belongings.* New York: Routledge.

Probyn, E. (2000). *Carnal appetites: Foodsexidentities.* New York: Routledge.

Probyn, E., and Evers, C. (2010). Introduction: Researching intimate spaces. *Emotion, Space and Society,* 3(1), 1–3.

Rawlins, E. (2009). Choosing health? Exploring children's eating practices at home and at school. *Antipode,* 41(5), 1084–1109.

Riepma, S. (1970). *The story of margarine.* New York: Public Affairs Press.

Rose, N. (1993). Government, authority and expertise in advanced liberalism. *Economy and Society,* 22(3), 283–299.

Skeggs, B. (2005). The making of class and gender through visualizing moral subject formation. *Sociology,* 39(5), 965–982.

Tsing, A. (2011). *Friction: An ethnography of global connection.* Princeton, NJ: Princeton University Press.

Upritchard, J., Zeelenberg, M., Huizinga, H., Verschuren, P., and Trautwein, E. (2005). Modern fat technology: What is the potential for heart health? *Proceedings of the Nutrition Society,* 64, 379–386.

3 Performing taste

The sommelier ceremony

Giolo Fele and Pier Paolo Giglioli

The atmosphere of wine tasting

In this chapter we explore the cognitive and ceremonial practices whereby sommeliers create a particular gustatory experience. As with the other chapters in this book, we contend that multiple factors affect taste. Some reflect macro sociological forces which shape the tasting experience, such as class, gender, race, life cycle and social and geographical mobility (see, for example: Bourdieu, 1979; Lamont, 1992; Bennett et al., 2009; Walmsley, 2005; Sherman, 2006; 2011). Others concern a close reading of the tasting encounter itself – for instance, the atmosphere and decor of the setting, the interaction among the participants, the ceremony in which tasting is part of a performance — all phenomena which are better examined through a closer micro sociological analysis (see, for example: Hennion, 2004; 2007; Schwartz, 2013). In this chapter we shall focus on both micro (the performance in detail) and macro (class and cultural capital) sociological factors inherent in the sommelier ceremony, as a close reading of this ritualistic and affective encounter can reveal a great deal about class, power and taste (Bourdieu, 1979).

First, through a detailed analysis of the sequential structure of the sommelier's service, we will show how she creates a multifaceted atmospheric scenario in which to experience quality wine. It is by means of this ceremonial work that a particular alcoholic beverage is transformed into a legitimate marker of taste and, more generally, that notions of 'good' and 'bad' taste surrounding wine are taught and reproduced. However, the sommelier's encounter with his client does not only involve a ceremonial dimension: the encounter is further embedded in a service relationship, in which, on the part of the sommelier, there is an intrinsic tension between the authority he has by virtue of his specialised knowledge and the personal deference he needs to give his customer. This tension resides in a delicate and complex power dynamic between the client's wealth and entitlement (economic capital) and his perceived lack of competence and 'proper' knowledge of wine and the customs in which it should be tasted (Bourdieu, 1979; Beckert, Rössel and Schenk, 2017). In the second part of the chapter, we shall discuss how this tension, linked to the different role (and often, classed position) of the sommelier and client, may threaten the ceremonial performance and spoil the tasting experience.

Like other figures of the wine world, the role of sommeliers has changed and differentiated in recent years. Its origin was that of a specialised waiter who gave customers advice about the correct pairing of food and drink in luxurious eating establishments. More recently, many sommeliers engage in related but different activities: they work in wine bars, participate in tasting competitions, teach courses in wine appreciation. However, for the purposes of this chapter, we shall concentrate on their prototypical activity: the serving of wine in upmarket restaurants. Our research, part of a larger study on the world of wine in Italy, is based on 30 interviews with sommeliers in two Italian towns – Florence and Trento – in 2016 and 2017. They were all members of AIS (Associazione Italiana Sommelier, the largest Italian sommelier association): half of them were young men and women at the beginning of their careers; ten were established, middle-aged sommeliers who worked in hotels and restaurants located in the two towns, and five had reached the top of their sommelier career and occupied executive positions in AIS. We also relied on the observation of wine festivals and wine fairs, the study of 'The Best Sommelier' competition on YouTube (see References for list of videos used in our analysis) and participation in introductory courses to the sommelier profession (for an illustration of the sommelier's work when instructing a lay audience on how to perform a wine tasting, see Giglioli and Fele, 2016).

As with all luxury goods, the appreciation of quality wine requires predetermined knowledge and taste: that is to say, it requires: (i) a set of developed expertise concerning the world of wine; and (ii) the capacity to discriminate and select so that one can act appropriately in particular circumstances. At issue is not just the nature of the product that is consumed, but *how* it is consumed, for it is the latter which transforms any product into a symbol of good taste (Bourdieu, 1979). This is particularly the case for luxury goods, which, unlike goods mass-produced for general consumption, are perceived to require the right environment, circumstances and encounters to be fully appreciated (Dion and Borraz, 2017). They have an 'aura' (or frame) which characterises them as such and ensures that the experience of consumption occurs in particular situations and occasions. The notion of 'atmosphere' (Heide and Grønhaug, 2006; Heide, Lærdal and Grønhaug, 2009) is pertinent here, as it refers to a number of features which enhance the experience of consuming food and beverages in luxurious environments (for example, the furnishing, the arrangement of the tables, the lighting, the background music and smells, as well as human presence, interaction and customer treatment). The sommelier plays an integral part in creating the 'right' atmospheric encounter. His function is twofold: on the one hand, it is cognitive because the sommelier provides important information on the origin and characteristics of a wine, as well as on how well it matches the food ordered by the customer; on the other hand, it is ceremonial because the sommelier's presence shapes the experience of eating out, making it special and 'memorable' (Piqueras-Fiszman and Jaeger, 2015).

The task of the sommelier is to offer her customers a *distinctive* taste experience in the dual sense of the word, that is, serving a quality wine that is *distinct* from other drinks and which, in turn, *distinguishes* its consumers from others who do not have the cognitive and social resources to appreciate it (Bourdieu, 1979; Bennett and Silva, 2011; de Morais Sato et al., 2016). Bourdieu's work (1979) is crucial in understanding how distinction through taste (and, more generally, through lifestyle) shapes and is shaped by social stratification. *Distinction* is the way in which people differentiate themselves from other people through the possession of cultural capital, i.e., both objectified cultural goods and manners, behaviour and practices learned from early socialisation. What is relevant here is that the economic means necessary to purchase luxury goods (economic capital) do not automatically translate into the cultural capital necessary to choose them and enjoy them in the 'appropriate' way. We focus here not on the ways signs of distinction locate its bearer in an abstract social structure, but on the ways they are concretely displayed and managed within social interaction (Sauder, 2005). The following section gives a closer reading of the ceremonial practice (Quintão and Zamith Brito, 2015; Ratcliffe, Baxter and Martin, 2019) of serving wines by a sommelier. The 'right' atmospheric encounter is accomplished when the sommelier shows how the tasting of wine should be properly performed and the customer actively participate in this ceremony.

The four phases of the ceremonial practice of sommellerie

We first attempt to describe in detail the service provided by the sommelier as a ceremonial practice and performance which facilitates the theatre of wine tasting, and mediates the customer's selection, consumption and modes of degustation. These ceremonial practices contribute to creating the 'right' atmosphere for a memorable meal and, ultimately, impact on the visceral sense of taste itself. As in all service encounters, the relationship between the sommelier and the customer is characterised by a delicate balance between the knowledge, hence the authority, of the service provider, the sommelier, and his deference towards the customer. Four phases of this practice can be identified: offer; presentation; control; and closure. This ceremony may be more or less precise depending on the formality of the occasion. Nevertheless, we believe that the situation is structured according to these four phases in every service relationship in which a sommelier is involved.

Offer

The *offer* concerns the customer's wine selection from the variety of options offered. In most cases, a wine list provides the customer with a large array of possibilities; she can consult it and make her own independent choice. In these cases, the customer operates on the basis of her knowledge of wine and the sommelier usually does no more than approve of the customer's choice, often with a positive comment like 'excellent choice', 'a very good vintage', 'perfect pairing'. While the sommelier's positive assessment produces ritual deference, it also acknowledges the client's knowledge and, as it were, ritually ratifies it on the basis of his own expertise. Alternatively, reflecting the clear preference of the sommelier, the customer may recognise the sommelier's authority by asking him for advice:

> The best client is the one who says: 'you tell me', who lets me advise him, who is willing to taste, because there are some people who do not want to. The most difficult client is the one who thinks he knows best, that he's an expert.
>
> (Roberto, middle-aged sommelier, Trento)

This acknowledgement by the customer of the sommelier's knowledge can be performed in multiple ways. The advice requested from the sommelier may relate to a general preference: 'I'd like a good red wine', a choice of wine appropriate for the food chosen: 'We're going to have fillet steak Voronoff, what do you suggest?', but also to a generic concern perhaps linked to the occasion: 'What wine do you suggest to celebrate our anniversary today?' or a more specific request for clarification relative to the wine list: 'What's this wine like?' The way in which the customer's request is expressed defines the way in which she recognises the sommelier's knowledge. When the client makes a generic request for guidance: 'What do you recommend?' or asks for clarification about a wine on the list, the sommelier's expertise is fully acknowledged and he is granted overall control over the client's choices. In some cases, however, his authority is limited by some generic preferences expressed by the client: for instance, if she says: 'I'd like a good red wine', she automatically discards suggestions that include white wines. Sometimes the customer may consider the sommelier's knowledge useless and superfluous: 'I want the most expensive wine you've got', making a choice based on considerations that exclude any mediation.

The sommelier's knowledge of wine is thus revealed immediately in the very first moments of the service. Often, however, such knowledge is 'recipient designed' (Sacks et al, 1974: 696): that is to say, the sommelier modulates his suggestions about the choice of wine according to his perception of the customer's preferences. First of all, it is not uncommon for a sommelier to ask the customer explicitly if she already has a partiality for a particular wine:

> The first thing I ask is: red or white? Some answer me something like 'just a bottle of normal white wine', but there are also those who want to understand, who want a correct pairing with the food they have chosen and then you get more satisfaction. It is more challenging, but much more satisfying.
>
> (Federico, young sommelier, Florence)

This interactional move enables the sommelier not only to understand whether the customer has preferences, but also, and especially, to determine whether the customer knows her way through the world of wine, whether her knowledge is solid and the extent to which she can engage in discussing the wine chosen with the sommelier. Another way in which the sommelier can give advice is to express a limited set of options: 'I have three suggestions for you' and ask the customer to choose from them. This reduction of options is part of the mediation work performed by the sommelier. Finally, when the sommelier chooses the wine for the customer, he can make the choice appear to be a recommendation rather than an imposition: 'I recommend a nice Merlot'.

This first phase of the ceremony is essentially discursive. First the sommelier asks the customer if and what he has chosen; then the customer chooses or asks the sommelier to suggest a wine; finally, the sommelier proposes a particular wine. When the sommelier does this, he always explains the reasons for his choice, usually related to details written on the label: 'it is a very famous wine of this region', 'a very important producer', 'a very good vintage', etc. or to the wine's organoleptic qualities: 'it's got quite a full flavour, with robust tannin'. Also, economic considerations can play a role, sometimes explicitly stated by the customer: 'we'd like a good red, but without spending too much', occasionally inferred by the sommelier:

> Obviously if I see that a customer is very careful about his budget, I am not going to propose a 50 or 60 euro wine, I try to satisfy him without making him spend so much. I must understand the customer, classify him, and offer him the best solution.
>
> (Franco, middle-aged sommelier, Trento)

> If a customer tells me "I don't know much about wine, bring me what you want, even the house wine", I try, without being pushy, to suggest he chooses something better, for instance a Marzemino [a red wine from the Trento area], which costs a couple of euro more and is a little better. Generally, they listen to me and say 'Ok, let's try it' and then they thank me, and this is very satisfying.
>
> (Mauro, young sommelier, Trento)

This first phase may also involve the customer challenging the sommelier's expertise in the world of wine by testing and assessing his knowledge. More often, however, the customer may simply want to share his experiences and lay knowledge with the sommelier: 'I tasted a similar one a few months ago'. In this case, the client considers the sommelier to be an expert and arbiter of taste who can give him precise information about wine or help him learn to make distinctions and pay attention to particular features of a wine.

Presentation

Once the wine has been chosen in accord with the customer, we move to the second phase of the ceremony, what we call the *presentation* of the wine. In contrast with the first phase, this is not discursive. By this we do not mean that the sommelier does not talk to the customer (about generic topics, but also about the wine), but that the discursive dimension is not central to this part of the ceremony. The wine is not simply poured; it requires a presentation that transforms a material object into one which represents significant appreciation and taste. The purpose of this second phase of the service ceremony is to determine whether the wine is drinkable, whether it has defects, whether the choice made from the wine list matches the actual experience of tasting the wine. Only if the wine fulfils certain conditions can it be served. In this phase of the service, the wine becomes alive and 'active': it is not just a bottle, a label or a prestigious product, but must instead demonstrate its quality in practice. Officiating over this operation of transformation is the sommelier. Unlike the backstage of a restaurant kitchen, her actions are not concealed from the customer; on the contrary, they are made visible and public. They are part of a theatrical *mise-en-scène* of a complex celebration. The sommelier becomes a performer and the customers settle into an audience.

It is at this stage that the sommelier takes the bottle and presents it to the customer, showing him the label (proof that the wine ordered corresponds to the wine that will actually be drunk). Then she removes – with skill and care – the cork from the bottle and sniffs it: this is the first actual contact with the wine, enabling the sommelier to give a preliminary evaluation. Then she shows the cork to the customer, placing it on a little dish on the table. Finally, the sommelier makes the second and definitive evaluation when she pours a small quantity of the wine into a glass and tastes it. Usually she does this turning her back on the customer so that the act of tasting is not seen, thus making it clear that she is not a diner and that this is a tasting service. In addition, the act of tasting is very brief: the sommelier must only decide if there are defects in the wine, not relish the wine as the customers do. The wine may also have to be aerated to fully express all its qualities to the full; in this case, if the wine is red, the sommelier must first decant it.

In short, in this phase of the ritual – the *presentation* – the wine is prepared to be served. To become an object worthy of the concentrated attention required by a degustation (Hennion and Teil, 2004; Hennion, 2015), the wine must undergo procedures that let it present itself in the best possible way in order to be appreciated and enjoyed. The sommelier performs this mediation between the object of taste and the taste itself.

Control

The third part of the ceremony, the *control* phase, concerns how the wine is served in the customers' glasses and the first tasting takes place. The wine, as we know, is served first to the person who has ordered it, in a small amount. The customer tastes the wine and decides whether to accept it. Typically, the customer gives a nod of approval and then the wine is served to the other customers at the table. The control phase is the first opportunity to gather the customer's impressions. The sommelier may ask the customer if the choice is appropriate, and if her expectations coincide with what she has tasted. Here a reciprocal exchange ritual may take place: the customer shows that she appreciates the wine (and any suggestion by the sommelier as to its choice), describing her taste experience in appropriate terms; the sommelier shows his deference to the customer by making encouraging remarks, praising her choice, inviting appreciation. The sommelier can enrich the customer's stock of knowledge (cultural capital) and enhance the quality of her sensory experience by accompanying this initial encounter between the customer and wine with additional comments and further specifications. Both actors are thus rewarded: the sommelier has his knowledge reaffirmed and valued; the customer is treated with respect and deference.

For a customer to reject or find some defect in the wine after it has been examined and approved by the sommelier is rare, and strongly undermines the latter's expertise. In this case, the sommelier may request the client to describe what is wrong with the wine, but the request does not entail any rejoinders:

> Sometimes a client may complain about some faults of the wine, for example that the wine is corky. In fact, he's often wrong. I have noticed that many customers do not know what corkiness is. But in such a circumstance, the wine is not served, the glasses are changed, and a new bottle is opened, because it would be unpleasant to start arguing or bickering with a client. Moreover, restaurant owners do not want complaints from the customers, especially if they are rich and important.
>
> (Giovanni, middle-aged sommelier, Florence)

In a service relation, as the old adage states: *the customer is always right.* As the above quote exemplifies, the sommelier's knowledge of wine and its subtle qualities or misgivings are generally far superior to that of the client. Yet what is at stake here is the power relation between customer and sommelier, and the obligation for the latter to be deferent to the former: the entire mood of the occasion depends on this. Using culinary knowledge and an objective understanding of what constitutes a 'corky' taste to develop into a power dispute, no matter how insidious, would disrupt the ceremonial interplay of the wine tasting. Thus no quarrel arises over the quality of wine, and the sommelier accepts the customer's decision.

Closure

Once the wine has been served and 'controlled', the sommelier's work is practically finished. In the *closure* phase – the fourth phase of the ceremonial practice – the sommelier attends to the wine by placing the bottle on the table with ritual care: for example, putting a bottle of white wine in a bucket with ice or preciously wrapping a bottle of red wine in a napkin. She then takes leave of the customer without appearing to abandon him. The wine is put on the table or on a *guéridon* with the label facing the customer; the wine is thus definitively handed over to the customer. Now it is no longer the sommelier who administers the drink: it is the customers (or waiters) who distribute it directly. The sommelier has completed her mediation work. She may however continue to collect her customers' opinions on the wine, commenting on them, correcting them, qualifying them and so on; in this way, the sommelier accompanies the customers' gustatory experience with her own judgement of taste. She may agree with the customers' opinion and encourage it by giving positive feedback on even rudimentary expressions of appreciation: 'Mm, good', thus continuing to show deference and respect to them. On their part, they recognise the sommelier's authority and expertise.

Knowledge, deference and distinction

In the previous section, we have shown how the experience of wine tasting in the luxury restaurant sector is socially constituted. We have described the sequential structure of the ceremonial encounter between a sommelier and client(s) and how all the actors participate in the ritualistic atmosphere in which the tasting takes place (Rook, 1985; Cowan and Spielmann, 2017). It must be added that, at all points in this sequence, the general rules of focused encounters (Goffman, 1961) – a shared focus of attention and a required level of involvement – have to be observed by all participants. Otherwise, the rhythmic encounter becomes disrupted and collapses, as in the following case:

> This guy comes with his girlfriend and is seated by the maître who takes his order for the food. I go to the table, greet him and ask him which wine he would like to drink. 'Tell me what you have', he says to me, without having even glanced at the wine list and continuing to talk to his girlfriend. Of course, we have plenty of wines and I propose him three or four which I thought were well suited to the food he had ordered and start illustrating them to him. But he doesn't pay any attention to what I'm saying and continues chatting with his girlfriend and laughing. I try to keep calm and gracious and say to him: 'What would you like, then, sir?' Without even turning his head towards me, he says 'Whatever you want, man, provided it's good'. I could have killed him.
>
> (Oscar, young sommelier, Trento)

It is interesting here to notice how the ceremony of wine tasting was initially accepted by the customer. He asked for the service of the sommelier in the first place, but immediately diverted his attention from the sommelier's proposals, refusing to engage with his role in the performance. Finally, he answered the pointed sommelier's question by saying he would accept any wine that was served, clearly showing that wine tasting was for him simply peripheral to the occasion. While the sommelier's knowledge had been sought initially: 'Tell me what you have?', it was right away discarded and considered superfluous. The customer ended this preliminary interaction accepting whatever wine the sommelier chose to serve. In this case the tasting of the wine is taken as simply peripheral to the occasion. The knowledge of the sommelier was initially stimulated, sought by the client, as if the initial interrogation: 'Tell me what you have' was a sign of true interest in knowing more regarding the wines. The disappointment of the sommelier is based on this false opening of the ceremony; his expertise is undervalued and he feels humiliation at being so rudely ignored whilst practising his craft. Years of training in wine knowledge remained oblivious to the customer, and the role of the wounded sommelier was downgraded to that of mundane 'service' (there is a hierarchy of front of house staff in the service industry). Wine was not considered an object of taste to be savoured and appreciated, but simply a beverage to be ingested without paying any particular attention – the necessary prerequisite of any act of tasting (Hennion, 2015).

The sommelier-client encounter rests on a delicate balance of knowledge and power. All 'taste workers' (Sherman, 2011; Ocejo, 2012; Dion and Borraz, 2017) have the mastery of specific skills which the client does not usually possess. In the case of luxury goods or services, it often happens that a good portion of customers are newcomers to this opulent world: that is, as we have noticed before, they possess the necessary economic means to purchase the goods, but not the cultural capital necessary to choose them and enjoy them in the appropriate way (Yamauchi, 2019). This is especially the case with quality wines. In the last 30 years, the demand for them has greatly increased and wine consumption has changed from a kind of 'nourishment', which in past centuries contributed significantly to enriching the low-calorie diet of the popular classes, to luxury consumption symbolising status membership (Goffman, 1951; Mortelmans, 2005; Järlehed and Moriarty, 2018). The ability to choose a wine and the knowledge of how to drink it is today indicative of Bourdieu's theory of taste and distinction. Many novice consumers, however, do not feel at ease in this complicated world of vine varieties, first growths, blends and vintages, and need somebody to orient them and mediate between them and the wine. Several new figures have risen in recent years to fulfil this task: wine critics, journalists and bloggers; naturally, the sommelier is one of them, but his role is different as he is the only one to have a direct face-to-face encounter with the customer. His job is not only to sell wine (Smith Maguire, 2010; Rodd et al., 2012), but also, and especially, to motivate its consumption by creating a particular symbolic and cognitive frame for the social occasion. It is this atmospheric encounter which directly impacts on the sensual enjoyment of the wine. Thus, the sommelier becomes a cultural intermediary (Smith Maguire and Matthews, 2012; Rodd, Ellis and Beal, 2012; Ocejo, 2012) who provides his customers with an opportunity to transform class (their increased economic resources) into status (cultural self-assurance) (Bourdieu, 1979; Sherman, 2005, 2006, 2011). The authority the sommelier derives from his knowledge is remarkable. Not only does he influence the actual choice of a wine on a particular occasion, thus mediating between the customer's preferences and the market, but, in a more general way, also contributes to shaping the customer's opinions in the long term: he justifies his suggestions about what to drink on the basis of normative ideas of what constitutes 'good' taste in the matter of wine, and in so doing, demonstrates, especially in the case of 'new wealth', how to exhibit a cultural lifestyle of *good taste* appropriate for someone who has gained the economic capital to have meals in very expensive restaurants.

Most often, in fact, clients do follow the sommelier's suggestions and get accustomed to quality wines by means of his advice. However, unlike the job of other cultural intermediaries working in fields such as media, advertising, fashion, entertainment or tourism (see, for example: McFall, 2002; Mears, 2014; Skov, 2002; Wynn, 2012), that of the sommelier is embedded in a service relationship in which personal deference is a central element, for in domestic and luxury services, the 'recognition' of those to be served involves the personal subordination of workers' own sense of selves (Sherman, 2006). This is very clear in the unfolding of the sommelier's relationship with his customers, which are frequently dotted with 'status rituals' (Goffman, 1967: 57) and 'distinction work' (Hanser, 2007, 2012), that is, with the asymmetrical rituals of deference, recognition of prestige and also honorifics by which unequal social positions are marked in face-to-face interaction. This inherent imbalance in the two roles of the relationship is increased by the different class position of the interactants, the customer generally being far wealthier than the sommelier who waits on him. Indeed, ironically enough, the sommelier could not (or only very rarely) afford to buy the wines she so warmly recommends.

Finally, it is the client who pays and has the last word. At times, his demands or indifference to the wine he is drinking may frustrate the sommelier's specialised knowledge and love for wine. As one of them told us:

> There are some customers who make curious demands. For instance, last night I uncorked a very young Brunello, six years old, and they asked me to decant it. And I did it, in the end it's the customer who pays. It was a business dinner, an important dinner, the customer wanted to show off in front of his guests, he told me:
>
> 'Look, the wine is a bit closed, can you decant it?' 'No problem', I answered. But decantation is more appropriate for other wines .... The new Russian businessmen are very well off and often they open really exceptional and very expensive wines. When I worked in Cortina [*a summer and winter luxurious resort in the Dolomites*], at C*** Hotel, one night we had a table with some Russians, who spent ten thousand euros for the wine, at least ten thousand, we opened some of the top European wines and they ...

– They didn't appreciate them as they should have …

Obviously, their culture is very different from ours, it's not up to me to pass judgment. We know that they do not understand much about wine, don't understand what they are drinking even when they are drinking something sublime … It's nice to open a bottle of Chateaux Margot or an important bottle of Burgundy, a Chambertin, a Montrachet, but many customers do not know how to appreciate it.

(Daniele, young but experienced sommelier, Florence)

The first episode referred to in this quote shows how a customer who wanted to flaunt his knowledge about wine makes a request which reveals his scanty expertise, thus threatening to expose his lack of cultural capital. The sommelier, however, far from highlighting the client's ignorance in front of guests, complies with his demand. His superior knowledge is embedded in a service relationship where the sommelier must politely submit to the need of assisting his client. The second, while showing once more the patient deference of the sommelier to his customer, again demonstrates how economic and cultural capitals differ. Distinction is based on manners and practices which shape the ways in which cultural goods should be legitimately appreciated (Smith Maguire, 2018). This quote further demonstrates the inherent snobbery in the fine wine industry, where sociologists (Morgan, 2018) have critiqued the symbolic violence (Bourdieu, 1979) targeted at 'nouveaux riches' who have the economic resources to buy expensive goods, engage in forms of conspicuous consumption and obtain the signifiers of upper-class membership, but do not possess the 'appropriate' manners and behaviour necessary to enjoy them.

Conclusion

In this chapter we have described how the sommelier contributes to creating an atmosphere which directly shapes the tasting experience of wine in luxurious hotels and restaurants. We have argued that the ceremonial encounter between the sommelier and his customers constitutes a reality in itself, a 'finite province of meaning', to use Alfred Schutz's (1962) words, in which the visceral sense of tasting wine as an attentional and reflective moment takes place. The success of this ceremony and its affective power is however contingent on the actors' collaboration in maintaining the balance between expertise and personal subordination, between a complex interplay of cultural knowledge and classed power. In principle, they conflict with each other: a sommelier who impresses her oenological knowledge too firmly may intimidate customers, souring the creation of the 'right atmosphere' in which to enjoy fine wine. Conversely, a sommelier who passively accepts a customer's order and praises it without providing any guidance or suggestions fails to create the sense of exclusiveness and of a memorable event for the customers (Hanefors and Mossberg, 2003). Continuing with this fine balance of interchange, a client who imposes his choice without following the sommelier's advice or accepts it without showing any interest undermines the concerted construction of wine tasting, exposing his inferior experience of 'good' taste. By focusing on the various phases of the sommelier's ceremonial work, we have tried to provide an initial analysis of this delicate balance, following the artful undertones of snobbery (Morgan, 2018) and distinction. Adopting an interactionist approach to the study of social status (Sauder, 2005), we have examined the micro processes which create, maintain, modify and transmit status relationships, namely those relationships whose object is symbolic and concern the attribution of prestige and deference to actors.

References

Books and articles

Beckert, J., Rössel, J., and Schenk, P. (2017). Wine as a cultural product: Symbolic capital and price formation in the wine field. *Sociological Perspectives*, 60 (1), 206–222.

Bennett, T., Savage, M., Silva, E., Warde, A., Gayo-Col, M., and Wright, D. (2009). *Culture, Class and Distinction*. London: Routledge.

Bennett, T., and Silva, E. (2011). Introduction: Cultural capital – histories, limits, prospects. *Poetics*, 39 (6), 427–443.

Bourdieu, P. (1979). *La distinction. Critique sociale du jugement*. Paris: Éditions de Minuit.

Cowan, K., and Spielmann, N. (2017). The influence of rituals on luxury product consumption: Implications for brands. *Journal of Brand Management*, 24 (5), 391–404.

de Morais Sato, P., Gittelsohn, J., Unsain, R. F., Roble, O. J., and Scagliusi, F. B. (2016). The use of Pierre Bourdieu's distinction concepts in scientific articles studying food and eating: A narrative review. *Appetite*, 96, 174–186.

Dion, D., and Borraz, S. (2017). Managing status: How luxury brands shape class subjectivities in the service encounter. *Journal of Marketing*, 81 (5), 67–85.

Giglioli, P. P., and Fele, G. (2016). Il sapere del sommelier. Verso un'etnografia della degustazione. *Etnografia e ricerca qualitativa*, 9 (1), 53–71.

Goffman, E. (1951). Symbols of class status. *The British Journal of Sociology*, 2 (4), 294–304.

Goffman, E. (1961). *Encounters*. Indianapolis, IN: Bobbs-Merrill.

Goffman, E. (1967). *Interaction Ritual: Essays on Face-to-Face Behavior*. New York: Doubleday.

Hanefors, M., and Mossberg, L. (2003). Searching for the extraordinary meal experience. *Journal of Business and Management*, 9 (3), 249–270.

Hanser, A. (2007). Is the customer always right? Class, service and the production of distinction in Chinese department stores. *Theory and Society*, 36 (5), 415–435.

Hanser, A. (2012). Class and the service encounter: New approaches to inequality in the service work-place. *Sociology Compass*, 6 (4), 293–305.

Heide, M., and Grønhaug, K. (2006). Atmosphere: Conceptual issues and implications for hospitality management. *Scandinavian Journal of Hospitality and Tourism*, 6 (4), 271–286.

Heide, M., Lærdal, K., and Grønhaug, K. (2009). Atmosphere as a tool for enhancing organizational performance: An exploratory study from the hospitality industry. *European Journal of Marketing*, 43 (3/4), 305–319.

Hennion, A. (2004). Pragmatics of taste. In: Jacobs, M. and Hanrahan, N. (Eds) *The Blackwell Companion to the Sociology of Culture*. Oxford and Malden, MA: Palgrave, 131–144.

Hennion, A. (2007). Those things that hold us together: Taste and sociology. *Cultural Sociology*, 1 (1), 97–114.

Hennion, A. (2015). Paying attention: What is tasting wine about? In: Antal, B. A., Hutter, M., and Stark, D. C. (Eds) *Moments of Valuation: Exploring Sites of Dissonance*. Oxford: Oxford University Press, 37–56.

Hennion, A., and Teil, G. (2004). Le goût du vin. Pour une sociologie de l'attention. In: Nahoum-Grappe, V., and Vincent, O. (Eds*)* *Le Goût des «belles» choses. Ethnologie de la relation esthétique*. Paris: Éditions de la Maison des sciences de l'homme, 111–126.

Järlehed, J., and Moriarty, M. (2018). Culture and class in a glass: Scaling the semiofoodscape. *Language and Communication*, 62, 26–38.

Lamont, M. (1992). *Money, Morals and Manners*. Chicago: Chicago University Press.

Maguire, J. S. (2018). Taste, legitimacy, and the organization of consumption. In: Wherry, F. F., and Woodward, I. (Eds) *The Oxford Handbook of Consumption*. New York: Oxford University Press, 1–18.

McFall, L. (2002). What about the old cultural intermediaries? An historical review of advertising producers. *Cultural Studies*, 16, 532–552.

Mears, A. (2014). Seeing culture through the eye of the beholder: Four methods in the pursuit of taste. *Theory and Society*, 43 (3), 291–309.

Morgan, D. (2018). *Snobbery: The Practices of Distinction*. Bristol: Policy Press.

Mortelmans, D. (2005). Sign values in processes of distinction: The concept of luxury. *Semiotica*, 157, 497–520.

Ocejo, R. E. (2012). At your service: The meanings and practices of contemporary bartenders. *European Journal of Cultural Studies*, 15 (5), 642–658.

Piqueras-Fiszman, B., and Jaeger, S. R. (2015). What makes meals 'memorable'? A consumer-centric exploration. *Food Research International*, 76, 233–242.

Quintão, R. T., and Zamith Brito, E. P. (2015). Connoisseurship taste ritual. *Consumer Culture Theory*, 17, 255–273.

Ratcliffe, E., Baxter, W. L., and Martin, N. (2019). Consumption rituals relating to food and drink: A review and research agenda. *Appetite*, 134, 86–93.

Rodd, M., Ellis, N., and Beal, T. (2012). Discursive constructions of the role of cultural intermediaries in the wine markets of Japan and Singapore. *Qualitative Market Research: An International Journal*, 15 (2), 128–147.

Rook, D. W. (1985). The ritual dimension of consumer behavior. *Journal of Consumer Research*, 12 (3), 251–264.

Sacks, H., Schegloff, E. A., and Jefferson, G. (1974). A simplest systematics for the organization of turn-taking for conversation. *Language*, 50 (4), 696–735.

Sauder, M. (2005). Symbols and contexts: An interactionist approach to the study of social status. *The Sociological Quarterly*, 46 (2), 279–298.

Schutz, A. (1962). On multiple realities. In: Natanson, M. (Ed.) *Collected Papers. Vol. I: The Problem of Social Reality*. The Hague: Nijhoff, 207–259.

Schwartz, O. (2013). Bending forward, one step backward: On the sociology of tasting techniques. *Cultural Sociology*, 7 (4), 415–430.

Sherman, R. E. (2005). Producing the superior self. Strategic comparison and symbolic boundaries among luxury hotel workers. *Ethnography*, 6 (2), 131–158.

Sherman, R. E. (2006). *Class Acts*. Berkeley: University of California Press.

Sherman, R. E. (2011). The production of distinctions: Class, gender, and taste work in the lifestyle management industry. *Qualitative Sociology*, 34 (1), 201–219.

Skov, L. (2002). Hong Kong fashion designers as cultural intermediaries: Out of global garment production. *Cultural Studies*, 16, 553–569.

Smith Maguire, J. (2010). Provenance and the liminality of production and consumption: The case of wine promoters. *Marketing Theory*, 10 (3), 269–282.

Smith Maguire, J. (2018). The taste for the particular: A logic of discernment in an age of omnivorousness. *Journal of Consumer Culture*, 18(1), 3–20.

Smith Maguire, J., and Matthews, J. (2012). Are we all cultural intermediaries now? An introduction to cultural intermediaries in context. *European Journal of Cultural Studies*, 15 (5), 551–562.

Walmsley, E. (2005). Race, place and taste. Making identities through sensory experience in Ecuador. *Etnofoor*, 15 (1), 43–60.

Wynn, J. R. (2012). Guides through cultural work: A methodological framework for the study of cultural intermediaries. *Cultural Sociology*, 6 (3), 336–350.

Yamauchi, Y. (2019). Service as intersubjective struggle. In: Maglio, P., Kieliszewski, C., Spohrer, J., Lyons, K., Patrício, L., and Sawatani, Y. (Eds) *Handbook of Service Science, Volume II*. Cham: Springer, 811–837.

Archival

Websites (last accessed 13 August 2019).

Best Sommelier of the World Mendoza 2016 https://www.youtube.com/watch?v=fm1Q7sYHtz8.

Meilleur Sommelier de France 2006 part2 https://www.youtube.com/watch?v=jzsrCkebjDg.

Prise de commande MSF 08 https://www.youtube.com/watch?v=Ee-eCR7Dn_8.

Sommelier Christopher Bates https://www.youtube.com/watch?v=OU_W-gMqLCo.

Sommelier Francesco Azzarone https://www.youtube.com/watch?v=nFjv6R7C2JE.

Sommelier Stefaan Camerlinck https://www.youtube.com/watch?v=q3aHWhM1D5g.

Sommelier Veronique Rivest https://www.youtube.com/watch?v=YzGh0D6e2oU.

Vins de Provence - – Finale du concours du Meilleur Sommelier de France 2012: Romain ILTIS - –27/11/2012https://www.youtube.com/watch?v=jhil4WLF-NU.

WOSA 2013 Sommelier Cup Final Will Predhomme presentinghttps://www.youtube.com/watch?v=kgp-0gScXmg.

Part II
Moving tastes, mobility, displacement and belonging

4   Food, taste, and memory in Australian migrant hostels

Rachel A. Ankeny and Karen Agutter

Food has increasingly become a focus of reflection and scholarship, yet much less attention has been paid to how 'negative' tastes are formed, and in particular how adverse food reactions can come to be associated with memory and place and have deeper connotations and meanings. 'In the multiple sensory properties of food—sight, smell, texture, and taste—lay multiple ways of conveying meanings and memories' (Counihan, 2004: 25). In our Hostel Stories project, which explores the government-run hostels that served as temporary accommodation for large numbers of migrants who came to Australia between the late 1940s and the late 1980s, we have been struck by the vivid memories that many migrants have of the food served upon arrival in Australia, especially their descriptions of particular tastes as unappetising, unpalatable or even revolting, which frequently dominate their accounts of their experiences.

The Australian Research Council-funded Linkage project Hostel Stories: Toward a Richer Narrative of the Lived Experiences of Migrants was carried out at the University of Adelaide in conjunction with community and government partners. Hostel Stories has received over 600 registrations of interest and conducted over 90 oral history interviews with former migrants who went through the post-World War II South Australian hostels,[1] as well as sourcing voluminous archival material on the hostel system across Australia. The first wave of migrants included not only those from the United Kingdom (the traditional and preferred source for migrants to Australia) but also the so-called Displaced Persons (DPs) from post-World War II Europe, and then a second wave closely followed from all over Europe as well as globally, as Australia sought to increase its population and foster economic prosperity. Waves of refugees arrived in later years as the result of unrest in a variety of locations including Eastern Europe, South America and Southeast Asia, often generating extremely diverse populations within the migrant hostels. Despite differences in background and experiences among these migrants, and in what was provided in various hostels over what is admittedly a relatively long period, the clear point of commonality among these migrants was the food: although plentiful and nutritious, the food is typically described by most as 'horrible'. This chapter uses oral histories, contemporary popular press coverage, archival materials and scholarly work to explore migrants' reactions relating to food during their time residing in the hostels, showing how critical tastes were to the construction of these locales and migrants' memories of them as well as to their settlement in Australia.

This chapter further highlights how the affective qualities of food and taste became a way of expressing discontent and asserting identity within the transitional space of the hostel, cutting across cultures and nationalities to provide a bargaining chip. Even in later years when hostel management became more conscious of needing to serve culturally appropriate food, in part by employing so-called 'New Australians'[2] in hostel kitchens, food, and especially its lack of palatability, was still a source of constant complaint and conflict between migrants and hostel management, and between migrant groups. Our research documents how the smell, texture and taste of foods such as mutton and pumpkin still affect migrants today, leading to continued refusal to eat these foods, and trigger (typically negative) memories of hostel life. Hostel food clearly contrasted with what had been eaten in places and spaces left behind for those who had migrated, and the new, unfamiliar and oftentimes uncomfortable space of the hostel negatively affected perceptions of the food and tastes served within it.

Life in the hostels

The arrival of large numbers of refugees and migrants in the post-World War II period, in particular those of non-British origin, marked a significant shift in Australian immigration policy, and key to the acceptance of these new arrivals by the general population was the promise of their rapid assimilation. Australians were assured by the then Minister for Immigration, Arthur Calwell, that everything possible would be done to assimilate them into the so-called 'Australian way of life'.[3] Key to this assimilation process was education in the English language and in important aspects of Australian culture, including Australian foodways, provided in the hostels (notably sometimes called 'training centres').[4] All hostels had some common characteristics: communal living with shared bathrooms, toilets and laundries as well as central kitchens and large dining rooms where meals were served, and board included in the rent (which was charged after the first week of residence), with no option for opting out of eating within the hostel. Officially, private cooking for one's family was not allowed and therefore there were no provisions for it.[5] To participate in communal mealtimes, and consume what was offered, appeared to be a mandatory part of this assimilation 'training'.

Previous scholarly literature has analysed various aspects of this history: Panich (1988) describes the difficulties faced by DPs in the hostels associated with food, as do Sluga (1988) writing about the Bonegilla Hostel in Victoria and Peters (2001) about hostel life in Western Australia. Hassam (2009) explores the food experiences of and formalised protests by British migrants as portrayed in popular media; elsewhere we (Agutter and Ankeny, 2017) have documented the disempowerment of DP women and families via food habits within the hostels using archival documentation and oral histories; and Postiglione (2010) examines migrant food experiences in the 1950s, comparing British and Italian accounts, particularly what she terms 'food dispossession' (Pennay, 2012: 49). However these accounts do not tend to stress the affective memories created via the sensual elements of taste, smell and texture and their underlying meanings. As Diner (2001) notes in her account of the experiences of migrants who came to America, the flavour and taste of coffee and donuts welcoming immigrants at Ellis Island were pivotal in creating a 'sweet' and 'filling' impression of the host country (Diner, 2001: 16–17). In contrast, those who came through the hostels in Australia had much more negative impressions that to this day have created strongly affective reactions and deeply important meanings among many former migrants.

Taste memories

Certain foods and tastes were shown to trigger particular shared memories for Australian migrants (Langfield and Maclean, 2002): pumpkin, the Australian term for the broad category of winter squashes used as starchy vegetables, is frequently mentioned as particularly problematic by those who migrated from a variety of locales and spent time in one or more of the hostels. As pumpkin was easily available and relatively inexpensive, it often was served within the hostels as a filling and nutritious vegetable option. But many hostel residents found it not only foreign but distasteful. As described by a Dutch migrant who came to Australia as a ten-year-old child:

> I will not eat pumpkin ... even today I don't eat pumpkin of any description. There we got pumpkin for breakfast, pumpkin for lunch, pumpkin for tea and I now hate pumpkin ... I have vivid memories of it, oh God not this again ... Bloody pumpkins ... it will go to my grave with me [laughing].
>
> (JV, 17 May 2013)

His memories of his hostel experiences are vividly connected with having to eat pumpkin frequently (whether or not it actually was served at every meal, which seems unlikely given the archival evidence). Once he left the hostel, he never wanted to return again, enacting these desires not only literally but also symbolically by avoiding the food that he was forced to tolerate in that context.

A couple who migrated from England to gain better work opportunities generally thought the hostel food was acceptable but nonetheless also noted issues with pumpkin:

> Of course they gave us pumpkin; well, we'd never had pumpkin in our lives before and so that was a bit of a learning curve having this orange stuff, very sloppily, very sloppy mixture thrown on our things.
>
> (R and GS, 18 July 2014)

In this description, it is notable that it is not only the lack of familiarity of the food that is off-putting; as the wording underscores, the way in which the pumpkin came to symbolise lack of care, a sort of 'sloppiness' often associated with institutional food and perhaps more generally with the hostel and life in it, is critical. Such attitudes also were noticed by European migrants, for instance when they went on a food strike at the Mayfield West (New South Wales) migrant hostel. According to media reports:

> They said the food was not fit to eat ... The men complained ... that the food was not fit for human consumption and was thrown on their plates ... the men realised that, coming from different countries, their tastes were different, but Australians would not eat what was served up to them.
>
> (Newcastle Morning Herald and Miners' Advocate, 1952)

Jones, In his study of food symbolism and identity Jones claims:

> Understanding how messages are conveyed through culinary behaviour requires an examination not only of victuals but also of the preparation, service, and consumption of food—for all are grist for the mill of symbolization.
>
> (2007: 129)

Thus in these examples we see that food, and how it is presented, can serve as a signal of more general attitudes: good cooking can be welcoming, and providing good food can communicate respect, affection and comfort, poor or 'sloppy' cooking has powerful opposite effects. The lack of care symbolised in the overcooked watery pumpkin, and the unappealing slop that was 'thrown' onto plates, induced powerful affective memories in the migrants who became adverse to eating pumpkin. In addition, these migrants note that pumpkin was 'of course' served, pointing to the fact that it is well-recognised as a frequent source of complaint among former hostel residents, and also intimating that they were not picky or demanding but that these affective responses were commonly shared by others.

The serving of pumpkin was insulting to some migrants who noted that in Europe it was used to feed cattle, not humans (Morris, 2001: 72). Some former hostel residents, such as the chef Stefano Manfredi who arrived with his family in 1961 and lived at Bonegilla (Victoria), was perplexed and disgusted by the food that was served. Remembering the vegetables offered in the hostel, Manfredi questions if they were indeed vegetables, describing the:

> [P]allid pastel-coloured cubes ... Some were vaguely carrot-coloured; others, by their absence of colour, were probably potatoes – but who knew? They had no taste. And what was even worse, no texture. None of the food had texture.
>
> (Manfredi and Newton, 1993: 11)

Other conflicts in taste occurred in association with the style of cooking in the hostels to even how food was prepared there and in Australia more generally: a migrant from Uruguay in the mid-1970s noted that her husband did not like the food because of the 'gravy' that tended to be put over everything. Further:

> He didn't like [it] because it wasn't cooked in the way we used to cook ... we [do] barbecue, and barbecuing a different way too ... here they cut the ribs like that a long side while we cut in this way [motioning]; it's different and we do the barbecue with charcoal not in the gas ... it's different ....
>
> (NG, 16 July 2013)

Hence differences in food preparation continued to underscore not only the migrants' physical but also their symbolic displacement from their original locales.

An even more notorious source of migrant hostel residents' complaints was lamb or mutton, which has come to be closely associated with, and almost iconic of the low quality of hostel food. A newspaper article noted that:

> [o]ne of the most popular dishes among the children is a special meat loaf made from liver, kidneys, heart and other delicacies. New Australians have yet to gain a taste for mutton and lamb.
>
> (The West Australian, 1950b)

As a resident of the Woodside Hostel (South Australia) comments, the mutton had a 'foul game like odour and taste to it. We were not brought up on sheep meat' (WB, 1957). As a migrant from Germany also noted:

> 'The food was mainly, you know, it was always mutton and it put my husband, my late husband, off for the rest of his life ever eating lamb. Lamb is nice, you know; that's how bad it was.'
>
> (BR, 6 February 2013)

Here we see how the experiences in the hostel directly related to food, as well as the negative associations between the time spent in the hostel and particular foods, came to affect and even alter these migrants' tastes: even those who had been used to eating lamb (and whose children were game enough to eat offal!) found lamb and mutton off-putting and distasteful after spending time in the hostel. In our research and elsewhere, former migrant hostel residents frequently mention mutton and lamb, especially the smell of it pervading not only the dining rooms but also the living quarters and other parts of the hostel complex. During interviews and discussions even some 50 or more years later, their reactions typically are physical, the revulsion visible on their faces and in their body language. In their work into sensing spaces of consumption and disgust, Taylor and Falconer refer to Tyler's (2013) theory of 'social abjection', where the: 'dirty, polluting, filthy imaginaries are tied up with the immoral, disgusting bodies and saturated with socially stigmatised meanings and values' (Taylor and Falconer, 2015: 48). The 'foul' odour of lamb as it pervades and 'pollutes' the unwelcoming transitional space of the hostel can symbolise the underlying aversion of forced assimilation for DPs.

In another interview, a migrant from Lithuania emphasised how repulsive the lamb in the hostel was:

> Australian men they call us bloody New Australian ... And food, they think we don't know nothing, he bring like lambs or so, still with poo in, I found. When you eat you can find manure in there. So dirty, so everything dirty ... European people, nobody eat because can't eat this food.
>
> (JK, 26 February 2015)

She associates provision of unclean food by those working in or running the hostel as indicating that they thought they could fool migrants by giving them a much lower standard of food than they themselves would be willing to eat, whereas in fact she asserts Europeans simply would not tolerate unclean food, despite having come from war-torn and economically depressed locales. As another Lithuanian migrant indicated, the food:

> Was terrible and they probably thought all these hungry people coming from Europe, you know ... I think we had mutton for breakfast, lunch and dinner ...
>
> (AL, 26 February 2015)

Lamb thus came to be associated with the negative attitudes of the receiving (largely Anglo-Celtic) culture towards the newly settled migrants, at an extreme as a symbol of their contempt and disdain and assumption that these migrants were lower-class and desperate. Ironically, lamb more generally has high status as a key symbol of Australian culture due to the history of its production and relationship with the country's pastoral origins, and more recently its association with patriotism and nationalism (Ankeny, 2007; Santich, 2012), but in the context of the hostels it came to be seen as a force of hostility and oppression. Here, the disgust at the poor quality of the 'dirty' lamb becomes entangled with ill feeling about the host culture, and a form of affective resistance to their dehumanising treatment of recent migrants.

Meat was generally problematic for many: part of the problem was its preparation and the lack of culinary knowledge, including among migrants who began to work in the hostel kitchens in later years. As described by an Austrian migrant who arrived in his twenties:

> The lunch was too much mutton ... I don't think they cooked it the right way either, I wasn't impressed with it ... when I left, I said to myself I'll never eat any sheep, because I never ate any sheep meat before I came

here and I'll never eat it again, although nowadays I really like a leg of lamb or something like that.

(WH, 19 June 2013)

Even in the 1970s–1980s during which the food improved and more attention was paid to providing multicultural offerings, Vietnamese refugees still tend to mention the meat in negative terms, especially the lamb:

At first some food was good but I didn't get used to lamb, it was harder to eat, but later on I got used to it.

(DN, 11 September 2012)

For some new arrivals, the food that was served left lasting impressions because it was unfamiliar, was served out of context or even worse. A migrant at Uranquinty Hostel (New South Wales), for example, firmly believed that eating the inside of a pineapple would kill you (Morris, 2001: 72), and hence found it troubling that they were served pineapples. Remembering the food at Woodside, WB (1957) comments on the fact that Australians served 'large wedges of plain cake with a layer of icing on top' for dessert. Not only was this 'gross', to use the migrants' own words, it was also out of place and in turn was viewed as disrespectful, as cake was 'always something special that you could have at special celebrations'.

Thus for former hostel residents, certain foods remain strongly associated with their impressions and memories of their time spent within these institutions. Even if food was plentiful and oftentimes of decent quality, those foods that were unfamiliar, prepared in ways that were different from those to which they were accustomed or simply seemed to be prepared or served in a disrespectful manner provide shared ground among these migrants for negative associations in relation to hostel life.

Conflicting tastes

Migrants' tastes which were in conflict with the dominant culture occasionally proved to be advantageous. As noted in a newspaper article, sour milk was preferred to fresh by migrants at one of the hostels, a fact that emerged when a consignment of 300 gallons of milk was delivered to the centre and proved to be sour. It was stressed that the migrants 'like to drink it that way and they also like to prepare numerous special dishes from milk in that state ...' (The West Australian, 1950a). Commonwealth Hostels Ltd (the governmental entity that oversaw the migrant hotels) recognised quite early on that these taste conflicts warranted attention:

The different food tastes of 10 nationalities in one hostel is a poser [an Australian term for a problem or dilemma] waiting the visit here next week of a dietitian ... a dietitian investigating food and catering

arrangements in hostels would arrive in Adelaide on March 10 ...
Migrants at Glenelg Hostel this week criticised food supplied there. Mr.
Connole [a regional operations officer] said the cosmopolitan nature of
the group at Glenelg created catering difficulties. Every effort was made
to suit the tastes of at least 10 nationalities there.

(News, 1953)

In this case, different tastes and food habits were viewed as a problem, and
migrants as overly demanding and perhaps even ungrateful. One migrant
noted that the food was better at a second hostel where she resided:

Food was better there, yes. Because I think some of the people working in
the kitchen there, I think some of them were also New Australians, so I
mean you know preparing the same food but you prepare it in a different
way and it tastes different, which is good.

(AL, 26 February 2015)

Here we see that not forcing migrants to assimilate into Australian eating
habits but providing some variety of options often was received positively.

Elsewhere discontent with the food caused 'riots': Italian men threw their
trays of food on the dining-room floor at the Maribyrnong Hostel in Victoria
in a notable incident in 1952, smashing plates and scattering cutlery; according
to media coverage:

[T]hey complained loudly that the food was not palatable to them ...
Camp menus include some Continental foods but officials say that it is
impossible to cater for all tastes.

(The West Australian, 1952)

This theme recurs throughout popular media coverage, sometimes even
portraying migrant tastes as odd or inappropriate:

Most men at the hostel were satisfied with meals served, but the difficulty
was to suit every taste. Most Italians would eat spaghetti indefinitely, but
others would not touch it. Recently three Poles ate a dog because they
thought it would be good for throat and lung trouble ... The menus were
designed to give migrants a taste for Australian food.

(Newcastle Morning Herald and Miners' Advocate, 1952)

Surviving hostel menus (NAA: D1917, D19/49, for example) support this
statement, with a dominance of quintessential Australian foods such as white
bread, meat and boiled vegetables. The expectation was that migrants, and
DPs in particular, would be thankful for the food that was provided and
quickly adopt Australian foodways. The hostels clearly had a mandate to
change migrants' tastes as a part of assimilating them to their new home,

which was largely attempted through complete control over what and how residents ate. Set menus, served en masse in communal dining rooms, and the prohibition of cooking for oneself or one's family resulted in the dominance of a typical Australian diet and way of eating, removing the important and central role food traditionally had played in the cultural and commensal circle of the migrant family (Agutter and Ankeny, 2017). In many ways food arguably was a more powerful force for assimilation than language or other cultural norms. What tastes people came to have were taken as evidence of their efforts to fit in and accept the dominant Anglo-Celtic culture.

It is notable that the British disliked 'continental' European food as much as European migrants disliked British and Australian food. Conflicts emerged between various groups of migrants and intensified in later years as hostel kitchens came to be staffed with those from Europe, many of whom had previously lived in the hostels in the immediate post-war period. A frequent complaint in contemporaneous official reports was that 'New Australians' spoiled the food:

> Our first meal at Bathurst was breakfast. We got into a queue and at last reached the serving hatch. Middle Europeans slapped a dollop of semolina pudding on one plate and some meat floating around in a lot of grease on another. Few could eat it.
>
> (Sunday Herald, 1951)

A British migrant who stayed in a hostel in the mid-1950s noted in an interview with us that she disliked the food because of 'all the olives in it' (JS, 7 February 2013). In one hostel, vigorous protests by British migrants against food prepared by European migrant cooks at the hostel focused on the lack of variety of food and heavy seasoning used by the cooks; after the complaints were investigated, one of the protest leaders noted that 'there has been a vast improvement in the food. It is now cooked more to *our taste*' (Goulburn Evening Post, 1951, emphasis added).

Through these examples, we see that taste is relative but also serves as a collective norm. It emerges from past experiences and familiarities, but also provides a way of marking out one's own group as different from others, for instance in connection to food habits associated with particular religions or sects. As noted by Counihan and Van Esterik: 'Food marks social differences, boundaries, bonds and contradictions' (2008: 3). Food also clearly represents a way of asserting control, particularly in situations such as institutions where there are few other ways to exert it (see Agutter and Ankeny, 2017 for other uses of food in the hostels to exert control, such as cooking on illegal camp stoves). In the case of the hostels where residents usually could not choose what they ate, complaining about the food became a way of protesting or resisting assimilation attempts, in contrast, for instance, to retaining food traditions from the homeland as has been documented with other migrant groups (for example, see Dusselier (2002) on Japanese-Americans in concentration camps during World War II).

Attempts were made to employ British migrants especially in the hostel kitchens to help produce and serve food that was more to the taste of those in that group, but it was noted that these migrants did not want this type of work: 'if it were not for the available New Australian staffs at hostels ... we would be in a serious plight so far as staffing was concerned' (NAA: SP446/1, 502/13/3, 1951–1952). In the meantime, attempts were made to 'adjust' the catering to meet British 'tastes', including reducing the amount of meat served at breakfast time, and the introduction of kippers. However, as some of our interviewees have noted, these types of menus often reflected stereotyping of tastes according to very generalised ethnic lines: in fact, the tastes of those from different regions in Great Britain often conflicted radically, as of course did individual tastes. So, for instance, one British migrant noted that:

> One thing that sticks in my mind, you used to get beautiful kippers, they used to bring in and they were huge things, proper Aberdeen kippers, beautiful things ...
>
> (JR, 8 February 2013)

While a couple who also came from England but who were from a Scottish background noted repeatedly that they hated the kippers (M and CM 26 March 2013).

According to some, the solution to this conflict was clear: Robert Borteux (1952), who had been in Europe at the end of the war, wrote to the *Advertiser* (Adelaide, South Australia) to emphasise the importance of allowing all to fulfil their own tastes:

> We all have different tastes. How can it be possible to satisfy everyone, especially people of different nationalities, as we found out in Germany in the displaced persons camps. There the DPs having no money, were given the food and allowed to cook it as and when they liked. Even then we had complaints about the quality of the food, although the quality and quantity was the same as the Germans themselves got. The only way to make the people happy is for them to be able to buy what they like and cook it as they like.
>
> (Borteux, 1952; see also Hassam, 2009 on this letter)

However for various pragmatic and logistical reasons including food and fire safety as well as cost, migrants at most hostels for the duration of their stay were not permitted to cook for themselves.

As this chapter asserts, issues of taste were far more deep-rooted than personal preference, but represented a lack of control, autonomy and perhaps even disrespect; in a Parliamentary debate about installing individual kitchens at the Gepps Cross (South Australia) Hostel in 1953 (a proposal which eventually was enacted at this hostel but did not become widespread even in hostels with large numbers of British migrants), Oxford-educated lawyer, I. B. Wilson (Liberal SA) argued that:

[E]very Englishman and every Australian regards his home as his castle. He wants to feel that he has a place where he and his family can be alone if they so desire. He wishes to eat meals of his own choice. If he likes his eggs soft boiled he expects them to be prepared in that way. He does not want to be served up in a community kitchen with eggs that the community cook says are correctly cooked, and which probably are according to the taste of some people, but which are wrongly cooked according to his taste.

(CPDHR 19 February 1953, as quoted in Jordens, 1995: 52–53)

Tastes conflict, but more importantly tastes are markers not only of choice but of the ability to choose. Hostels typically denied migrants these choices (and many others), though in this case the British migrants were able to cook their own food and hence choose for themselves.

Conclusion

In the migrant hostels in Australia between the late 1940s and the 1990s, food became an 'enduring artefact of resistance, social change and placemaking' (Dusselier, 2002: 139). The control inflicted on refugees and migrants through what and how they ate within the liminal space of the hostel system meant new arrivals were deprived of any opportunity to participate in their traditional foodways or to make decisions about their consumption habits more generally, as well as having important cultural values associated with preparing and consuming food go unsupported. Therefore, we contend that food served as an artefact of resistance and change less because of conflict over what precisely was served and more because of the ways in which migrants' taste preferences were undermined and attempts made to reshape these tastes as part of a process of assimilation. Food also served as a major point of conflict between groups of migrants, and hence became a way of expressing discontent as well as identity claims that were much less about food than they might first appear. The hostel thus served as a transitional space where attempts were made to shape migrants' tastes to fit within standard Anglo-Celtic norms in order to assimilate them, but which instead resulted in strong negative reactions and created uncertainties about the new place to which they had come. When migrants complain vigorously about the pumpkin, gravy and mutton that they were served decades ago in the hostel systems, they are recalling a time when they were not permitted to exercise their tastes, and when they were no longer home but had not yet arrived.

Notes

1 University of Adelaide Human Research Ethics Committee approval H-2012–120.
2 The term 'New Australian' was first coined by the Minister for Immigration, Arthur Calwell, in the late 1940s. Use of the term was encouraged in the wider

Australian society in order to replace the pejorative terms commonly in use such as 'reffo' (short for 'refugee') and 'Balt' (short name for those from the Baltic states including Lithuania, Latvia or Estonia) and as a symbol of assimilation. However, the term itself quickly took on a derogatory meaning although some of our interviewees continue to use it to this day in a neutral sense.

3 The 'Australian way of life' was a rarely defined but frequently used term in official, public and even advertising vernacular in the late 1940s–1950s and referred to the idea of a quintessential and specific Australian spirit or character which was associated with certain ideals and values (see White 1981: 158–160). At this time Australians were associated with certain characteristics such as being generous, sport-loving and egalitarian and living a suburban life centred around the nuclear family (see Eggleston, 1953: 13).

4 Note that we are using the generic term 'hostel' to cover all forms of government-provided refugee or migrant accommodation. In reality, the accommodation centres operated in subtly different ways, they were interconnected in terms of policies and practices and had many common characteristics, with flow of migrants often occurring between them. For example, at reception and training centres (such as Bonegilla in Victoria), active assimilation occurred; new arrivals were then sent to other centres such as workers' hostels (Glenelg in South Australia, for example) or in the case of dependant women and children to holding centres (such as Wacol in Queensland). A third tier of centre, the migrant hostel, predominantly accommodated family groups.

5 As discussed later, one exception in the early period was the British-only Gepps Cross Hostel in South Australia, where kitchenettes were added due to migrant demands.

References

Books and articles

Agutter, K., and Ankeny, R. A. (2017). Food and the challenge to identity for post-war refugee women in Australia. *History of the Family*, 22, 531–553.

Ankeny, R. A. (2007). The moral economy of red meat in Australia. In: Friedland, S. (Ed.) *Food and Morality: Proceedings of the Oxford Symposium on Food and Cookery.* Totnes: Prospect Books, 20–28.

Bourdieu, P. (1984). *Distinction: A Social Critique of the Judgment of Taste.* Cambridge, MA: Harvard University Press.

Counihan, C. M. (2004). *Around the Tuscan Table: Food, Family, and Gender in Twentieth-Century Florence.* New York: Routledge.

Counihan, C. M., and Van Esterik, P. (2008). *Food and Culture: A Reader, 2nd edition.* New York: Routledge.

Diner, H. (2001). *Hungering for America: Italian, Irish, and Jewish Foodways in the Age of Migration.* Cambridge, MA: Harvard University Press.

Dusselier, J. (2002). Does food make place? Food protests in Japanese American concentration camps. *Food and Foodways*, 10, 137–165.

Eggleston, F. W. (1953). *The Australian Nation.* In: Caiger, G. (Ed.) *The Australian Way of Life.* Melbourne: William Heinemann Ltd, 1–22.

Hassam, A. (2009). Hostels and communal feeding are not the British way of life. *Food, Culture and Society*, 12, 313–334.

Jones, M. (2007). Food choice, symbolism, and identity: Bread-and-butter issues for folkloristics and nutrition studies. *The Journal of American Folklore*, 120 (476): 129–177.

Jordens, A. M. (1995). *Redefining Australians: Immigration, Citizenship and National Identity*. Sydney: Hale and Iremonger.

Langfield, M., and Maclean, P. (2002). "But pineapple I'm still a bit wary of": Sensory memories of Jewish women who migrated to Australia as children. In: Hammerton, A. J., and Richards, E. (Eds) *Speaking to Immigrants: Oral Testimony and the History of Australian Migration*. Canberra: Australian National University, 83–110.

Manfredi, S., and Newton, J. (1993). *Fresh from Italy*. Rydalmere, NSW: Hodder and Stoughton, Rydalmere.

Morris, S. (2001). *Uranquinty Remembers: A Migrant Experience 1848–1952*. Wagga Wagga, NSW: Uranquinty Progress Association.

Panich, C. (1988). *Sanctuary? Remembering Post-War Immigration*. Sydney: Allen & Unwin.

Pennay, B. (2012). "But no one can say he was hungry": Memories and representations of Bonegilla Reception and Training Centre. *History Australia*, 9, 43–63.

Peters, N. (2001). *Milk and Honey but No Gold: Postwar Migration to Western Australia*. Nedlands: University of Western Australia Press.

Postiglione, N. (2010). "It was just horrible": The food experience of immigrants in 1950s Australia. *History Australia*, 7, 901–916.

Santich, B. (2012). *Bold Palates: Australia's Gastronomic Heritage*. Adelaide: Wakefield Press.

Sluga, G. (1988). *Bonegilla: 'A Place of No Hope'*. Parkville, Victoria: The University of Melbourne.

Taylor, Y., and Falconer, E. (2015). "Seedy bars and grotty pints": Close encounters in queer leisure spaces. *Social and Cultural Geography*, 16, 43–57.

Tyler, I. (2013). *Revolting Subjects: Social Abjection and Resistance in Neoliberal Britain*. London: Zed Books.

White, R. (1981). *Inventing Australia: Images and Identity*. Sydney: Allen & Unwin.

Archival

Borteux, R. (1952). 'Letter to the editor', *Advertiser* (Adelaide), 19 May, p. 4.

Goulburn Evening Post. (1951). Hostel food improves. 30 May, p. 1.

NAA (National Archives Australia): D1917, D19/49; MWAD Organisation, 1948–50, Adelaide.

NAA (National Archives Australia): SP446/1, 502/13/3 Commonwealth Hostels Ltd, Finsbury Residents' Complaints file [box 14], 1951–52, Sydney.

Newcastle Morning Herald and Miners' Advocate (NSW) (1952). 'Migrants end meal strike', 24 March, p. 2.

News (Adelaide, SA) (1953). 'Problem for food expert', 4 March, p. 2.

Sunday Herald (1951). 'Do we want migrants?: The migrant's point of view', 1 July, p. 9.

The West Australian (1950a). 'Sour milk preferred by migrants at Northam', 11 January, p. 2.

The West Australian (1950b). '4,500 for meals at Northam Migrant Camp', 15 August, p. 13.

The West Australian (1952). 'Stir in camp over food for migrants', 29 July, p. 3.

WB, (1957). *Memories of Woodside Migrant Reception Centre*, written submission to Hostel Stories Project, University of Adelaide.

5 Eating *Stobi Flips*, drinking *Gazoza*, remembering Macedonia

Katerina Nussdorfer

The Macedonian cultural centre, part of the Macedonian Orthodox Church 'St. Naum Ohridski' in Vienna, is located in a quiet suburban street in Vienna's 21st District. Everything about the building is inconspicuous, and only when one enters the yard leading to the community room do signs of Macedonia start to appear: notices on the board written in Macedonian Cyrillic script, pictures of two Macedonian presidents, the Macedonian flag.

I am here to meet the secretary of the Macedonian club, hand out questionnaires and interview people. Once inside, I sit down on a wooden bench, a TV to my right blasting off news in Macedonian at full volume. As I begin to rummage through my bag looking for the stack of questionnaires, a cardboard box – half ripped-open, propped on a shelf high up behind the makeshift kitchenette – catches my attention. Red-and-yellow foil bags peek out, ready to be sold for one euro, a pop to the regular visitors of the community centre: family-size packs of Vitaminka *Stobi Flips*.

Stobi Flips, a national peanut-maize based snack otherwise known as *Smoki*, are as given for Macedonians as white bread. Bright orangey-yellow, crunchy and salty, they are so distinctive in flavour – perhaps because of the peanut-maize combination – that comparing them to any other peanut flips instantly results in fierce defence of their uniqueness and the superiority of *Stobi Flips* over any other similar snack. Eating *Stobi Flips* is a ritual: the more you have, the thicker the grainy sticky film on your fingers is; and though it builds, and clumps, and grows, and layers with each new helping, licking it off the fingers is only allowed at the very end, when there are no more *Stobi Flips* left in the bag/bowl.

Then, just as I am about to start explaining about the questionnaires, a middle-aged Macedonian woman who tends the bar brings me a drink: a cold, perspiring 0.5-litre bottle of *Gazoza*, the bright-yellow, pear-flavoured cult soda made by Prilepska Pivara, the second largest brewery in Macedonia. Though I have come here to talk about food, and food from Macedonia in particular, I had not expected to engage with any foodstuffs at all, let alone these very two iconic products. To be met with these instantly recognisable products – the garish colours of the *Stobi Flips* branding and the luminous sugary liquid – was an instantly affective experience of national identity

(Edensor, 2002). Even if there were no signs in Macedonian Cyrillic script, no Macedonian flags, no pictures of President Ivanov, I would still know this was a Macedonian space just by having the *Stobi Flips* and the *Gazoza* in front of me.

Introduction

Multiple factors, often at times co-dependent, can be crucial in the determination of a person's particular food choice(s) and experience of taste. One may find the same food (product) appetising or repulsive, based on time, how it is prepared/presented/sold, the affective atmosphere in which it is (to be) consumed and, above all, location. Often, foods and food items consumed in a different spatial and temporal context may lose or change their meaning and purpose, or become inappropriate, obsolete or detestable. This chapter aims to explore the intricate ways in which the consumption of certain 'home foods' (*Stobi Flips* and *Gazoza*) can generate feelings of homesickness, nostalgia and national identity for members of the Macedonian diasporic community in Austria's capital of Vienna, while at the same time acting as a remedial tonic for these yearnings for the past, and what was once was considered 'home'.

The historical and political context of this case study is central to the significance of these 'home foods'. Geographically, Macedonia is not far from Austria, and to travel 'back home' is generally more frequent than in the case of Macedonian immigrants in more far-off countries. Be that as it may, the majority of Macedonian immigrants came to Austria fleeing from war. While many Macedonians came to Austria during the 1970s, when Austria had a bilateral agreement with Yugoslavia for skilled workforce import, especially in the building and construction sectors, two other waves of immigration can be especially noted: the years during and after the war in Yugoslavia 1991–1995, and the period from 2001 to the present day. As a result of the civil war in ex-Yugoslavia, about two-thirds of all immigrants to Austria from 1991–2001 – which saw a general rise of 37.3 per cent – were immigrants from the ex-Yugoslavian countries. Of those, 13,696 are recorded to be with Macedonian citizenship. The second large wave of immigration from Macedonia came shortly after the armed conflict in 2001, and albeit slowing down at intermittently, this wave is still ongoing, with more and more Macedonians coming over the last decade, and an observable continuous increase in the immigration of Macedonians to Austria since 2011. Based on official statistics, at the beginning of 2016, 28,091 people of Macedonian origin lived in Austria, almost half of which – 9,892 or 46 per cent – residing in Vienna.[1]

Since Macedonian products are generally scarce in Austria (there is no Macedonian shop and Macedonian products which *are* available are sold alongside products from other Balkan countries, in select Austrian supermarkets, Turkish and other ethnic stores), the aim of this ethnographic research was to determine if Macedonians in Vienna buy any 'home' foods, and, if so, which ones in particular. Subsequently, based on the outcome of that research, it was to be determined why those products are preferred, as well as whether or not they induce any meaningful affective experiences of nationhood and belonging. The objective of the research was to primarily identify which 'home' products, if any, yield (such) feelings of nostalgia and yearning, and to further explore the varied aspects of how that nostalgia is being manifested within the context of displacement due to conflict. This chapter attempts therefore to show how consuming these particular products outside their 'natural habitat' of the Macedonian table/kitchen/home/festivity/ market, and in the new environment of their Austrian counterparts, leads to the creation of culturally constructed tastes, influenced by Macedonian immigrants' new lived realities. They are transported to this host location because of their unique affective properties (colourful packaging, collective national taste) and, in turn, when consumed their meaning appears to acquire a new dimension: they become artefacts of Macedonia.

Methodology

This research was carried out independently in 2016. From early May 2016, a total of 938 questionnaires were sent out to Macedonian immigrants living in Austria using social media groups, private contacts, the Macedonian Embassy in Vienna and the Macedonian Orthodox Church in Vienna as well as the Macedonian Social Club. Some parties I approached were members of several groups, thus lowering the total number of potential participants. The total number of valid, correctly completed, returned questionnaires was 63. The anonymous questionnaire consisted of 20 questions and was divided into 3 parts: general demographic data (age, gender, year of arrival and place of residence in Austria); 12 questions regarding shopping habits, particularly concerning Macedonian or ex-Yugoslavian/Balkan foods, with 3 questions regarding the participant's child(ren)'s familiarity with these foods; and 4 questions regarding Macedonian/Balkan restaurants in Austria.

The questionnaire helped distinguish between two groups: those who emigrated before the fall of Yugoslavia, i.e. 1991, and those who came subsequently, as immigrants from the Republic of Macedonia. While it was initially planned that the scope of the survey should include Macedonians living all over Austria, feedback came exclusively from people residing in Vienna, in spite of questionnaires also being sent out to Macedonian communities in Graz and Linz. This resulted in data that only covered Vienna, and consequently, the research continued with a sole focus on Vienna.

Out of the total of 63 completed questionnaires, all of which were anonymous, 41 participants fell into the group of people who have lived in Vienna since before Macedonia's independence in 1991, and 15 into the group of people who have lived in Vienna since after Macedonia's independence in 1991. Seven participants were born in Vienna. The gender/age division was such that 28 participants identified as male and 35 as female, with the youngest participant being 16 and the oldest 72 years of age. There were 35 participants with children and 26 without, while 2 had not provided data regarding their children status. Of the food products listed in the questionnaires as being purchased in Austria, more than half are industrially made products that were also produced in ex-Yugoslavia. The other mentioned products can be classified under Macedonian (*Stobi Flips, Resana, Strumka, Gazoza*), generic, unbranded products (ground coffee for making Turkish coffee, filo pastry for making *baklava* and *pita,* cured meats, canned meats, dry pasta, wine, *alva,* white cheese) and agricultural produce (beans, rice, cabbage).

Although there are much larger Bosnian/Croatian/Serbian communities in Vienna (21,119, 20,138 and 72,518 respectively, as opposed to 9,490 Macedonians),[2] and a much more accessible and wider scope of products from these countries on the shelves of Austrian (including Turkish) supermarkets, the premise of the research was that Macedonians living in Vienna in 2016 would tend to include ex-Yugoslavian products as a regular part of their shopping and eating habits. It was also presupposed that, as a result of the inclusion of such products in their daily diets, a certain level of Yugo-nostalgia would be reported as present while consuming said products. Ten products in particular – available in Viennese supermarkets – were expected to fall into this Yugo-nostalgia-inducing group: *Eurokrem* (sweet spread), *Cockta* (soda), *Medela štrudle* (cookies), *Domaćica Kraš* (cookies), *Plazma keks* (biscuits*),* *Crvenka Munchmallow* (cakes), *Argeta pašteta* (meat/liver spread), *Cedevita* (vitamin powder drink), *Životinjsko carstvo* (chocolate for children), *Podravka kokošja supa* (instant chicken soup). However, though mentioned in some questionnaires, these products were considerably less popular than the more often featured Macedonian products, especially *Stobi Flips* and *Gazoza.* These two products were quoted to be the most bought/sought after in Vienna.[3] They were also quoted to be most regularly brought back in suitcases from Macedonia, with 32 out of 63 people reporting regularly bringing these and other special foods back from their trips to Macedonia. *Stobi Flips* and, to a lesser extent *Gazoza* (since it is liquid, bulkier and more difficult to transport) can therefore be viewed as foods that create 'local identiti[es] on a global stage' (Wilk, 2008: 324). Both products are considered to be foods that trigger an affective, culinary nostalgia for Macedonia and are overall mentioned far more often than any other product or dish (37 and 29 times respectively, with 12 people quoting *Strumka,* the other pear-flavoured Macedonian soda).

Taste, affect and national identity

Edensor (2002), in his study of national identity and everyday life, argues that the intimate relationship between people and the everyday 'things' that evoke a sense of national or regional identity is key to our sense of belonging. With regard to food items, the taste, smell and packaging of familiar, iconic food items can produce multiple sensual affects. *Stobi Flips* and *Gazoza* are industrially mass produced, low cost and low nutrition convenience snack foods. Though neither product is an agricultural produce or home-made dish, I argue their flavours can still be considered 'traditional' and 'national' in the sense that they both have been on the market for several decades, and their widely consumed, unique tastes are innately inseparable from the taste depository of Macedonians in the sense in which Rozin and Rozin speak of 'Traditional flavors [that] serve the same function as traditional costume or traditional religious practice … as means of defining a culture group, of identifying an individual with it, and of separating that group from others' (2005: 37). These two products serve as a means of reconfirming belonging to the given immigrant group. Similarly, much as Manalansan (2013: 292) highlights '[f]ood … is a sensory, emotional, and pneumonic trigger for remembering the homeland and the past, as well as evaluating one's present situation or future predicament', home foodstuffs, such as these, often give rise to nostalgic and nationalistic feelings as an obvious and unavoidable element on immigrant tables. However, according to Bourdieu (Korsmeyer, 2005: 74), '[e]ating habits, especially when represented solely by the produce consumed, cannot … be considered independently of the whole lifestyle' and, in that sense, when people living in Macedonia buy these products, they make their choice based on a variety of factors: availability, health, taste and price. Importantly, most participants made the point that they did not buy these products on a regular basis, as these fall in the category of 'junk', 'leisure' or 'occasion foods'. They are laden with fat, salt, artificial colouring and sugar and are poor in nutritional value, but they are at the same time a popular choice for family outings, birthday or other parties and as travel, TV or cinema snacks. Shoppers in Macedonia also have the opportunity to make their choice between these two products and other similar-in-taste-and-purpose products, but in the absence of other such Macedonian products *Stobi Flips* and *Gazoza* have become the most popular treat of choice for Macedonians in Vienna.

Participants in the survey mentioned, unprompted, that they 'know that these products are not the healthiest', that they 'try to not give them to [our] children', or that they 'don't eat them every day', but almost all of them (95.2 per cent) said they buy them because of the taste. If, as pointed out by Manalansan (2013: 292): '[t]he sensual experiences of food often become events of both imagined and real diasporic homecomings' and 'the taste and smell of food can be a way to travel back "home"', then taste, as the primary reason why these particular products are being consumed, should also be the primary trigger of nostalgia. This is indeed confirmed by the results of the survey, with 60 out of the total 63 participants choosing taste over the other possible given reasons, such as smell (23), package and design (12), colour (6) and form/texture (5). Similarly, asked why they buy/consume/cook with Macedonian/ex-Yugoslavian/Balkan products, 49 of the 63 participants reported taste to be of primary importance, choosing it over answers such as 'no appropriate replacement', 'quality of the products' and/or 'habit'. For these products, taste seems to override (any) nutritional value; taken out of their usual context, they seem to serve more than their original purpose. Being factory made, ready to eat, prepacked, easy to transport, non-perishable – they prevail over other, more 'ethnic', more 'authentic' foods. In the case of Macedonia, nothing should be more 'Macedonian' than *ajvar* (red pepper spread), *burek* (filo dough pastry) and *tavče gravče* (baked white beans casserole), and yet, *Stobi Flips* and *Gazoza* – because of the above-mentioned features, or perhaps in spite of them – seem to triumph them over as markers of Macedonian belonging.

Yet it is not just the taste which evokes this sense of Macedonian identity, but the multitude of sensual affects associated with these two items, such as the brightly coloured packaging, the way the foil feels and the countless memories of taste and consumption from childhood. Edensor claims that experiences of national identity are felt in numerous ways and triggered by a collective familiarity. He states 'there are different ways of knowing besides the cognitive and it is important to acknowledge the embodied, habitual, unreflexive way of knowing one's place and the things which belong within it' (2002: 106). Many food products and brands have become synonymous with a collective national nostalgia – from the USA confectionary *Twinkies* to the sparkling red and silver foil of Scottish *Tunnocks Tea Cakes.*

According to Warde (Ashley et al., 2004: 72), '[w]hen we make our food choices, novelty is seductive'; Ashley et al. assert that 'Yet, here is simultaneously, and apparently paradoxically, an appeal to the traditional, to the old-fashioned ways of eating the "safe", comforting foods inscribed in the well-tried practices of household and families' (2004: 72). Hence, in addition to embracing 'home' food for comfort, this sort of culinary reminiscence appears to have a nostalgic facet to it. Participants in the survey expressed both nostalgia and an emotional connection to these products, even if with rather subtle notions in sentences such as 'feeling like home', 'reminds me of my childhood', 'I am used to their taste', 'I like the familiar taste', 'out of habit', etc. The lead of *Stobi Flips* and *Gazoza,* as well as other Macedonian products points to a stronger-than-expected correlation between consuming these foods and nostalgic feelings towards Macedonia, rather than towards ex-Yugoslavia (more than 6 per cent of participants). According to Ruvio and colleagues, '[N]ostalgia establishes a symbolic connection with people or events from the past and consumption objects are significant evidence of the past ... consumption objects, such as family recipes or specific food products, can stir up nostalgic emotions and memories' (2013: 220).

Furthermore, as Baumeister and Leary (cited in Vignolles and Pichon, 2014: 4) explain, '[b]oth nostalgia and food practices tend to increase people's feeling of belonging to a culture'. So, the act of endorsing consumption of these particular products can be seen as both a means of satisfying the needs of to belong to a group and to make a statement about that very belonging.

Taste and belonging

While bringing 'home' foods to a new country is one of the most typical recorded migrant behaviours (Anderson, 2005), less obvious, and yet just as significant to note, is the spatial role of place and how this impacts on the idealisation of the taste(s) of (these two) products. How does consumption of these products in the locality of Vienna, Austria, foster the feeling of 'being home', especially since, as Anderson (2005: 162) emphasises, 'foodways change' and 'are created by dynamic processes'. The emotional and intimate attachments to these products appears to be collectively strong, overriding any concerns over the lack of nutrition. Their consumption is consciously condoned, with statements such as 'we don't eat them every day', 'back home we wouldn't eat them', 'we don't eat them regularly', 'they are special to us even though we may be idealising them'. Thus, in the new urban 'terroir' of Vienna, *Stobi Flips* and *Gazoza* begin to stand as a very 'obvious' and tangible link to the Macedonian culture left behind by these immigrants. Much like Ashley et al. (2004: 72) accentuates that tastes are not static and constant, and that 'our tastes for certain foods are shaped within specific historical formations', we can add that they are also shaped within or rather by and from specific location formations. Consequently, space and location appear as factors just as powerful as taste in the evaluation, perception and (dis)enjoyment of food.

Drinking a glass of *Gazoza* becomes more than an experience of refreshment and taste, and transcends into an affective experience of memory and national identity for immigrant Macedonians. We can call this an *emotional-cognitive-gustatory spiral*. Subjective feelings of nostalgia are thus triggered by the consumption of certain products (but also by looking at, touching, smelling and even hearing them) and, in turn, those feelings of nostalgia induce remembering those tastes in a different setting (both in place and time), craving them anew, even developing an imagined sense of nostalgia for a taste that in actuality may never have been enjoyed with the same intensity in the past (as evidenced in the statement *'back home we wouldn't eat them'*). In that sense, the sensory experiences or memories of such experiences appear to play a vital role in the self-perception and the process of (self-) identification of some Macedonians living in Vienna.

Haden (Korsmeyer, 2005: 349) speaks of an 'archive of taste' (as a witty analogy or juxtaposition to the Slow Food Movement's 'Ark of Taste') and, in that sense, by consuming *Stobi Flips* and *Gazoza,* Macedonians living in Vienna call forth from a collective 'archive of taste' that recreates comfort through confirmation and an almost fictionalised familiarity. Equally important here is what Sutton (Korsmeyer, 2005: 305) identifies as 'the concept of *xentia*, or absence from home', and says 'the terrible emotional overload of *xentia* – living in a foreign land – is temporarily relived in the experience' of consuming familiar, 'home' food. Food, thus, stands to serve as that 'physical object as a tangible site for memory which can facilitate a "return to the whole"', the 'whole' being a 'point of [cultural] identification for people displaced by migrations caused by larger global processes' (Sutton, 2005: 305).

Novelty of the familiar: the taste of 'home'

These global processes of which Sutton (2005) refers – in the shape of war, displacement, economic and cultural globalisation – work in complex and paradoxical ways when it comes to food and taste. The more people world-wide 'eat' other cultures, the more (some of) those cultures cling to their most prominent and distinguishing idiosyncrasies with the purpose of cultural identity survival, preservation and continuity. This is where the availability of home and familiar foods in a new place contributes to the alleviating feeling of it (not) being 'home'. James (2005) stresses that '[t]he globalization of food is not ... just a matter of the movement of foodstuffs between nations; nor is it simply the amalgamation or accommodation of cuisines', but rather '[a] complex interplay of meanings and intentions which individuals employ subjectively to make statements about who they are, and where and how their Selves are to be located in the world' (James, 2005: 383). Haden (2005: 350) also speaks of the '[w]ell synchronized' and intricate process of 'invention, processing, packaging, transportation and retailing of food products', which in turn 'also *produce* taste'. Certain places in particular facilitate this process of 'producing' and affecting taste: the ethnic supermarket/restaurant, the home and, on a microlevel, the kitchen and the dining area. These places are crucial in the process of maintaining the sense of 'home' for Macedonian immigrants in Vienna. Sutton (2005: 304) speaks of the 'power of tangible everyday experiences' – eating *Stobi Flips* as a TV or picnic snack, for exam-ple – '[in evoking] the memories on which identities are formed', thus high-lighting the significance of food practices, including cooking and the way of consuming food, in relation to maintaining (a sense of) a 'home identity'.

One significant parameter in determining and/or maintaining this nostalgic consumption is the place(s) where these products can be/are consumed and procured. Here, the supermarket chain Merkur, part of the Re-We group, seems to be in the lead, with 23 people mentioning it as the place where they buy such products, and with 36 out of 63 people claiming they buy the special Macedonian and Balkan products in Austrian supermarkets. Thus, Merkur, but also other supermarkets in Vienna, seems to aid the creation of many imagined tastes and contribute to the re-construction of those very tastes in the rather liminal sense of the spatial reality that they offer to this group of shoppers. These spaces evoke feelings of nostalgia and recognition that pro-vide comfort and reassurance, that soothe and satisfy at the same time. There are various Bosnian, Croatian, Macedonian, Serbian and Slovene products, most of which are 'old' products, i.e. ones that were produced during the existence of Yugoslavia, and which have survived the test of time until today. This combination of selected products is almost like an array of curated exhibits that would normally not necessarily be grouped together on shelves

in supermarkets in their respective home-producing countries. Placed together, however, so different in their nutritional and culinary content, they form
a collective body of 'familiar foods', 'foods from home', foods that come to
mean more than the sum of their nutritional and gustatory purposes.
According to Bell and Valentine (2006: 2), 'food practices code and demarcate cultural boundaries, even in the most mundane ways'. Supermarket
shelves are one such location where those cultural boundaries are not only
being set but also altered, juxtaposed and modified.

Other such places in Vienna, where the demand of Macedonians for 'home
foods' is met, are the branches of the chain of Turkish supermarkets Etsan.
Unlike Merkur and the other 'Austrian' supermarkets in Vienna (Re-We
group, SPAR group, the recently bankrupted Zielpunkt) where shoppers can
find these ethnic products alongside others, the Etsan are strictly ethnic shops,
which, in addition to a large selection of Turkish products, also offer a wide
array of products from many Balkan countries, including Macedonia.
Twenty-three out of 63 people said they buy Macedonian and Balkan food in
'Turkish supermarkets', and 20 out of 51 that they buy them in both Turkish
and Austrian supermarkets. Here, Macedonians buy (some of) their food
(including *Stobi Flips* and *Gazoza*), but above all, experience 'home' on a
unique level – via the multi-sensual affects of food. As Anderson (2005: 125)
says, '[e]verywhere, food is associated with home, family, and security', and
these supermarkets and the foods exhibited offer exactly that: the aspect of
the 'purchase of food [as a] form of self-expression', long argued as immensely
important for an immigrant faced with the unfamiliarity of a new
environment.

Conclusion

For the Macedonian immigrant community in Austria (ca. 21,000 out of
which almost half live in Vienna),[4] the procurement and consumption of
specific 'home' foods and alimentary products have come to stand as vehicles
for nostalgic travel, tools for gustatory reminiscence and affective markers of
national identity. One of the products – the pear-flavoured carbonated non-
alcoholic drink *Gazoza*, which some Macedonians consider a national beverage rarity – may never have been an important feature in the diet and daily
eating habits of a person's life while still residing in Macedonia, yet is among
the first things to be collectively craved when living in Vienna. In the questionnaire data, this is quoted to be precisely because of its distinct, irreplace-
able flavour, as is the case with *Stobi Flips,* which likewise are considered to
have a unique and inimitable taste. These once-taken-for-granted flavours,
transported into the mundane reality of daily food life in Vienna, acquire
almost mythic characteristics. These two products repeatedly emerged as the
most coveted and longed for, establishing a traceable relationship between
Macedonia, as the country that they represent, and Vienna, the location in
which they are consumed. *Stobi Flips* and *Gazoza* simultaneously mark a

particular diaspora of Vienna as Macedonian, and are themselves markers of foods and tastes that have an affective and symbolic value wider than the sum of their nutrition and flavours.

Equally, based on both the quantitative and qualitative data arising from the questionnaire and informal interviews, it appears that the *place* in which these products are consumed (outside of Macedonia) affects the process of consumption, impregnating them with new meaning and taking on a greater intensity than when consumed at 'home' (in Macedonia). Thus, the 'new' location, with all of its implications (distance, unfamiliarity, unavailability of food, 'new', unpalatable or 'foreign' food, comfort, nostalgia), influences the way these products are perceived and, in turn, the way that these products taste: acceptable and accepting, comforting, familiar, happy and affirming.

For immigrants, tastes, products, agricultural produce, dishes and desserts that were often taken for granted in Macedonia, take on new meanings and affective qualities when discovered in their new host societies. The reunion between immigrant and childhood products often results in an ordinary, low-quality snack food becoming glorified out of all proportion. A not-so-favourite casserole at home becomes the reason for a small 'culinary pilgrimage' to a certain restaurant in town. Eaten within this contextual change, food becomes more than the sum of its parts, but rather a multifood vehicle of remembering, acknowledging and reconfirming the idiosyncratic identities that come to be; it becomes a crossroads of cultures in the form of 'migratory meals' and revered mythical products. These foods, prepared, served and consumed outside of their usual cultural setting, directly inform nostalgic depositories of taste. As Haden underlines: 'Once nutritional needs are met, the capacity of food to take on a plethora of culinary specific meanings pushes it beyond its role as nutrient and into that of being a "language"' (2007: 344). The function of *Stobi Flips* and *Gazoza,* within the urbanity of Vienna, becomes almost entirely symbolic and affective, overriding any dietary purpose that they may (initially) possess.

Notes

1 Source: http://medienservicestelle.at/migration_bewegt/2016/12/07/mazedonische-co mmunity-rund-28-000-personen/.
2 Source: www.statistik.at/web_de/services/stat_jahrbuch/index.html.
3 *Stobi Flips* and *Gazoza* are actually the two Macedonian products that one can almost certainly find on offer in Etsan, the chain of Turkish supermarkets in Vienna. *Gazoza* was also on offer regularly in the Zielpunkt supermarkets till December 2015 (Zielpunkt announced that it would file for bankruptcy in the summer/autumn of 2015 and closed its last branches in Vienna in January 2016 (https://www.ksv.at/insolvenz-zielpunkt). Other products, while sporadically available, cannot be found on offer regularly in any supermarket in Vienna.
4 According to the Austrian Statistical Bureau (www.statistik.at/web_de/services/stat_ jahrbuch/index.html), the number of people who came from former Yugoslavia (the six republics, excluding Kosovo), as of 1 January 2015 was registered to be 308,793, of which 20,852 were from Macedonia (9,490 in Vienna alone).

References

Anderson, E. N. (2005). *Everyone Eats: Understanding Food and Culture*. London and New York: New York University Press.

Ashley, B., Hollows, J., Taylor, B., and Jones, S. (2004). *Food and Cultural Studies*. London and New York: Routledge.

Bell, D., and Valentine, G. (2006). *Consuming Geographies: We Are Where We Eat*. London and New York: Routledge.

Bourdieu, P. (2005). Taste of Luxury, Taste of Necessity. In Korsmeyer, C. (Ed.) *The Taste and Culture Reader: Experiencing Food and Drink*. Oxford: Berg, 72–78.

Edensor, T. (2002). *National Identity, Popular Culture and Everyday Life*. London: Bloomsbury.

Haden, R. (2005). Taste in an Age of Convenience: From Frozen Food to Meals. In Korsmeyer, C. (Ed.) *The Taste Culture Reader: Experiencing Food and Drink*. Oxford: Bloomsbury, 344–358.

James, A. (2005). Identity and the Global Stew. In Korsmeyer, C. (Ed.) *The Taste Culture Reader: Experiencing Food and Drink*. Oxford: Bloomsbury, 372–383.

Korsmeyer, C. (Ed.) (2005). *The Taste Culture Reader: Experiencing Food and Drink*. Oxford: Bloomsbury.

Manalansan, M. F. (2013). Beyond Authenticity: Rerouting the Filipino Culinary Diaspora. In Ji-Song Ku, R., Manalansan, M. F. and Mannur, A. (Eds.) *Eating Asian America: A Food Studies Reader*. New York and London: New York University Press, 288–292.

Rozin, E., and Rozin, P. (2005). *Culinary Themes and Variations*. In Korsmeyer, C. (Ed.) *The Taste Culture Reader: Experiencing Food and Drink*. Oxford: Bloomsbury, 34–43.

Ruvio, A. A., Russell, W., and Belk, R. W. (2013). *The Routledge Companion to Identity and Consumption*. New York: Routledge.

Sutton, D. E. (2005). Synthesia, Memory and the Taste of Home. In Korsmeyer, C. (Ed.) *The Taste Culture Reader: Experiencing Food and Drink*. Oxford: Bloomsbury, 304–308.

Vignolles, A., and Pichon, P. E. (2014). A Taste of Nostalgia: Links between Nostalgia and Food Consumption. *Qualitative Market Research Journal*, 17(3), 4–5.

Wilk, R. (2008). Real Belizean Food: Building Local Identities in the Transnational Caribbean. In Counihan, C., and Van Esterik, P. (Eds.) *Food and Culture: A Reader*, Second edition. London and New York: Routledge, 308–326.

6 "A tealess, beerless, beefless land"

Sensing and tasting Spain in late eighteenth and nineteenth-century British travelogues

Beth M. Forrest

In her book, *Diary of an Idle Woman in Spain*, English writer Frances Elliott made great use of the senses to convey her experience of travel. In her poetic introduction, she evokes images of an:

> Emerald band, in the cool gorge, I see tents and tilted wagons. The thrum of guitars and castanets drift upwards; the drone of Moorish ballads, the cries of children, men leaping in the wild dances of old Spain, swinging cudgels, and flinging arms in Phyrrhic rounds; large-eyed Gitanas and brown-faced peasants looking on.
>
> (1884: 12)

As she passed through the countryside she saw the 'rugged mountain' made from hard, granite blocks, dotted with juniper trees, oaks that had been tested by gusting wind, all of which gave an effect that she termed 'magical'. Yet, as soon as she arrived at the railway station all of this romantic allurement disappeared. As further testimony to the jolting reality of Spain, she was served a supper with 'dry cakes and drier biscuits ... amazingly dry food' (1884: 201). This was despite her seeing plenty of dried fruits in local shops, all of which she believed would have relieved her suffering. Equally problematic, at the meal:

> Water there was *à discrétion*. (Spanish of all classes are enormous water drinkers. No soon do you enter Spain than you hear them crying out in piteous voices from the railway cars, *Agua, Agua*, for all the world like thirsty chickens).
>
> (1884: 201)

Spain might have appeared to be moving into the industrialised age, but it remained hungry and thirsty, picturesque only in romantic imagery that draws on the pre-industrial as well as the Roma and Arab/Islamic cultures. Her narrative succinctly encompasses many themes of cultural importance in the nineteenth century –gastronomy, nationalism, and concepts of technological, economic and cultural progress all conveyed through an affective discourse.

This chapter offers a case study of how travel narratives, specifically travellers to Spain in the late eighteenth and nineteenth century, evoke sensual affects with greater political implications. By describing a complete sensorial experience within a context of aesthetic taste, which celebrated one's own national evolution and denigrated that of Spain, these texts served to ultimately imprison Spain and the Spanish within a defeated, political past. Dirtiness, offensive smells, hunger, thirst, shame and pride became emotional experiences that shaped perceptions of national character. Preserved and relayed through travel narratives, these affective experiences offered what appeared to be a rational explanation for historical developments: why Spain had lost its empire, why Spain had remained pre-industrial and why Spain remained culturally unrefined. These practices, then, became a way of 'othering' place and people through representations of disgust and disdain. By considering how food and the senses have been tied to cultural constructions of nationalism, Orientalism and imperialism, scholars can better appreciate how food, cuisines, the senses and aesthetics have been used as political and cultural weapons reflecting discourses of power.

Nineteenth-century Europe and the United States experienced the rise of gastronomy and the modern nation-state, both of which converged in an intense consideration of national cuisines and national character. Thus, the topic – and judgement – of diet and the senses embedded and extended the social commentary of the 'other'. Sensorial knowledge contributed to such discussions, by expressing an awareness of aesthetics (traceable to the palate and the use of all of the senses) and a reflective depiction of those who ate and judged such experiences. Indeed, as Ben Highmore has noted, the use of 'aesthetics' (as a catch-all term):

> For heuristic inquiry into affect and its interlacing of sense perception and bodily dispensation … will have to work hard to disconnect itself from the tradition of aesthetic thinking that has remained bound to the moral mission of the artwork and its evaluation.
>
> (2010: 123–4)

Highmore argues that it is in the 'ongoing-ness of process', the daily and the incomplete that aesthetics and affective states manifestly reside (2010: 123). It is for this notable intersection – an acknowledgement of all of the senses, a broad application of aesthetics and the literary evocations of affect (or descriptive passages that trigger such affective responses) – that travel narratives can provide a rich case study to consider the intersection of the physical body, taste and power.

Travelling across difference

The establishment of national borders played a crucial part in travelogues of nineteenth-century Spain, especially when the senses were entangled with concepts of power. For the British and Americans, during the rise of imperialism, spatial sense and temporal sense blanketed one another (Hontanilla, 2008). Such synesthesia of time and space allowed the imagination of the past to shade the present with meaning, and thus became contemporarily relevant. Consequently, it also allowed the construction of a sense of the Spanish 'other' as abiding, continuous traditions that manifested materially in actual behaviours, aesthetics, tastes and even an understood morality. Collectively, everything experienced by the traveller became *sensed* evidence of an emerging cultural and national hierarchy based on observable and comparable developing technology and robust economics, habits and attitudes of people and perceived social progress or inertness.

From 1660–1780, a growing number of wealthy English travellers embarked on the Grand Tour, a practice that extended well into the nineteenth century. This final educational exercise became just one of the many ways in which people crossed trans-national borders. Of course, there had been a longer history of militarists, missionaries and merchants whose profession and calling had taken them overseas. Yet, the motive for the Grand Tour was unique, for it was *to experience* knowledge already learned. Similarly, although not necessarily quite the same, were travel writers, whose goal it was to *record and frame the experience* of knowledge to be learned. Taken together, however, both depend on an understanding of the empirical; for the Grand Tour it was an outward observation while for the travel writer, it inherently included the body and affect. Toward the end of the eighteenth century, even those who might not be able to travel enthusiastically participated through armchair travel by which the reader created a perception of culture and nation. During the years 1773–1784, travelogues circulated at twice the rate of other literary genres (Batten, 1978).

The motives of travellers were quite different from merchants, officials or diplomats in that observation was the means to the end, a great adventure, which by definition ventured into the unknown and possibly dangerous (Hontanilla, 2008). The best-selling and controversial English writer, Richard Twiss, wrote in the introduction to his book, *Travels through Portugal and Spain in 1772 and 1773,* that although he had already travelled to the British Isles, as well as the typical grand tour of France, Switzerland, Italy, Germany and Bohemia, he was determined to visit Spain and Portugal. This was especially true because, in his assessment, he had 'never seen any satisfactory account of those two kingdoms' (1775: i). As such, for the travel writer, Spain offered a unique opportunity to present to readers something that was perceived as entirely different from the rest of Europe. Notions of civilisation and culture were not homogenous in Europe and ideological borders, political and religious, were drawn within Europe (Turner, 2001). Against English and American values of liberty and Protestantism, the romantic, exotic Spain would certainly be considered 'different'. The travelogues, and the experiences documented by the travellers, became yet another vehicle through which such confirmation would be established.

The impetus for the travel writer was to be both receptive, processing sensory and environmental experience by *taking it in*; and active, meaning able to conceptualise perceptions and experiences in ways that conformed to a framework of linear time (the past, present and future). The way to enforce this framework was through the process of recording, or *writing down*. For the traveller and travel writing, both products of their own, particular culture, sensory perceptions and temporally bound conceptualisations are further framed by moral and aesthetic constructs (Kisoo, 2005). William G. Clark wrote in the preface to his book, *Gazpacho or, Summer Months in Spain*, that he set out to tell his readers 'not what Spain *is*, but what it looked like to me', very much suggesting that the traveller became the arbiter of culture (1851: vii). Because the travellers were building knowledge through experience, it is no surprise, then, that the senses became such a rich source through which the reader was also sensuously engaged. In his travelogue, after surveying his night's room in León, Joseph Townsend said that 'I was, however, too much of a traveler to feel disgust' (1791: 67), strongly suggesting that any reader certainly would have done. In societies where citizens were part of a new, modern state, which corresponded to the rise of national boundaries, the sharing of sensory cues – visual, auditory, tactile, olfactory and gustatory – became part of a discourse of state and culture (Howes and Classen, 2013; Corbin, 1986). When other places, other nations, *seemed different*, such a realisation affirmed perceptions and ideas about both the 'us' and the 'other' which would reify colonial constructs.

Richard Ford, known for his popular books on his Spanish travels and his observations on its people and culture, perhaps best conveyed the intersection of the sensed and affective different*ness* between the Spanish and the English, when he described an experience near Alcalá where he happened upon laborers reaping grain:

> The scene never fails to rivet and enchant the stranger, who, coming from the pale north and the commonplace in-door flail, seizes at once all the novelty of such doings. Eye and ear, open and awake, become inlets of new sensations of attention and admiration, and convey to heart and mind the poetry, local color, movement, grouping, action, and attitude. But while the cold-blooded native of leaden skies is full of fire and enthusiasm, his Spanish companion, bred and born under unshorn beams, is chilly as an icicle, indifferent as an Arab: he passes on the other side, not only not admiring, but positively ashamed; he only sees the barbarity, antiquity, and imperfect process; he is sighing for some patent machine made in Birmingham .... his bowels yearn for the appliances of civilization by which 'bread stuffs' are more scientifically manipulated and manufactured, minus the poetry.
>
> (1847: 116)

In this case, travelogues documented physical and emotional reactions of the travel writers and of those they encountered while travelling. Such a

conveyance of abjection fed into the larger context of debasement, the practice of 'othering' and the rhetoric of colonisation. For those who read the
accounts, the embodied experiences became a contagion of cultural attitudes
of Spanish people and towards Spain by non-Spanish on a visceral level.

Sensing differentness

In can be argued that eating and tasting 'foreign' food marks a complete
sensorial immersion in the host countries visited by the travel writer. In the
lead up to this consumption, however, there is a panoply of experiences to
witness and feel, and indeed many travel writers richly noted the sights
(romantic ruins, Oriental imagery), sounds (often harsh guitars and guttural
voices), touch (the linens rough and mattresses lumpy as potatoes). Yet even if
we restrict consideration to olfactory concerns of travel writers, travel writers
had plenty to say that could evoke an affective reaction in their reader; these
aromas signified larger issues about the Spanish themselves, which could then
be viscerally understood.

One common observance of Spain seems to be the smell of garlic that
wafted through the country. In *Scenes in Spain* (1837) an anonymous writer
who observed a rabble wearing dirty clothes and 'whose breaths issued flames
of garlic strong enough to stagger the nerves of any one but a Spaniard'
(Anon, 1837: 258). Charles Dickens remarked that it was rancid oil 'mingled
with the smell and taste of garlic' that ruined every Spanish meal (1863: 262).
Edward Clark likewise noted an 'offensive smell' (1763: 1) in Spanish cities
and noted that the Spanish were great 'devourers of garlic' who lacked delicacy
because of it (1763: 341). More importantly, however, he argues:

> If our senses were more acute, in cafes where some men appear much
> alike, we should find them very different ... [effluvia of human bodies,
> which dogs perceive] is a sufficient proof to convince you of the difference
> of constitutions.
>
> (1763: 63–64)

One anonymous author, who the publisher names 'X Y Z', wrote of his travels around the Iberian Peninsula in 1840. When he arrived in Madrid, he
found a place where the aroma (and taste) of food finally seemed acceptable.
On his entire trip it appears that the only decent meal he enjoyed was in
Madrid. The reason for this, he informs us, was due to the owner of the inn at
which he stayed identifying himself as a French cook and restaurateur. This
liberator from distaste had 'saved us from the infliction of the national con-
diments, except in so far as our olfactory nerves have suffered ...' (1845: 102).
But, despite this respite in the inn, he could not escape assault by noxious
aromas that engulfed the entire Spanish capital city. In our author's estima-
tion, the air in Madrid was composed of the usual oxygen, hydrogen and
nitrogen but here there were also equal parts of rancid olive oil and garlic.

Concerns over air quality and odour frequently merged with broader cultural attitudes towards cleanliness. One example of this is found in the writing of Henry Swinburne. In his travelogue of 1779, he pointedly stated that the Spanish were both 'dirty in their person' and 'over-run with vermin' (1779: 196). Traveler George Downing Whittington added in 1808 that the city of Tarragona was 'every where dirty and ill built' (1808: 68) and that the towns of Valencia 'are more dirty than those of Catalonia' (1808: 74). This lack of hygiene greatly concerned middle and upper-class English and American travellers during the second half of the eighteenth century and well into the nineteenth century. New scientific advancements in England and France fit into larger cultural shifts towards the 'delicacy of the senses' (Corbin, 1986; Roche, 1987). A growing discrimination towards odours and the sense of smell in general reflected newly emerging social and cultural hierarchies.

The regulation of body odour, through an increased practice of washing and of using perfumes, signalled the emerging genteel class of citizens. The restricted upper-class culture diffused down through a middle class who ruptured into two distinct identities: the working class and the bourgeoisie. Against the backdrop of capitalism and industrialisation, the bourgeoisie constructed their identity around concepts of respectability and a growing refinement as a way to further distance themselves from the classes below (Bushman, 1992). The division resided between those who 'laboured' and those who did not, and this difference between the two was perceptible by those who smelled, and the virtuous people whose self-regulation and behaviour was as contained as was their scent (Smith, 2002).

The connection between cleanliness, labour and behaviour appears frequently in travelogues on Spain, yet reveal a moral complexity between odorous workers and dirty beggars. In the latter part of the eighteenth century, a good number of travel writers to Spain focused on topics of agriculture and industry. The Reverend Joseph Townsend is probably best known for his 1786 treatise, *A Dissertation on the Poor Laws*, in which he criticised poor relief, stating, 'it is only hunger which can spur and goad them on to labour' (1817: 15). A couple of years later, the fruits of his observational labour appeared in *A Journey Through Spain in the Years 1786 and 1787*. His perception of the country and the countrymen is very much wrapped in his moral inclinations. In the industrial city of Málaga, he saw plenty of beggars who were 'clothed in rags, and half devoured by vermin', and while they wait for a charitable serving of meat and broth, they 'employ themselves in the most disgusting occupation' of de-licing (1791: 16). It was not only the lice but the multitude of beggars themselves who, according to Townsend, 'infected every street' (1791: 17). Even though most inhabitants of Málaga bathed frequently, 'diseases of a relaxed fibre are most prevalent' (1791: 23). In Madrid, the necessity of constructing multi-storied buildings meant that there was a want of sun and air. Likewise, in Salamanca, it was only in the town square, after leaving the narrow streets, which 'gives particular expansion to the lungs, when you find yourself at liberty to breathe' (1791: 83). Cities, with the exception of Barcelona, in which he delights, tended to be described as dirty and disease-ridden. The people and the pathology – hungry and dirty, both of which translated as odorous – merged for the traveller and the reader, whose sensibility, morality and even biology were understood along national, racial and class lines.

This was not to suggest that the writers found the entire country of Spain dirty and smelly. The judgmental Townsend (1791) did greatly like the bustling city of Vélez, whose trade was based on agricultural goods. Townsend's party went out for a stroll among the poplar trees, which he found quite pleasant: 'Here, in a cool and refreshing shade, where through the whole year the nightingale sings, and lemon trees diffuse their fragrance, the inhabitants of Velez assemble every evening' (1791: 45). Thus it was 'with reluctance that I quitted this cultivated spot, where all nature seemed to wear a smile' (1791: 45). Moreover, there, even the peasants' manners are 'soft' and their 'salutations benevolent' (1791: 36). The stark difference between the inherent nature of the urban beggars and these bucolic peasants, for Townsend, was palpable, yet critique of either form served to judge place and people and supported the discourse of 'othering'.

Similarly, William Clark wrote in *Gazpacho* that the market in Madrid had 'a fresh sweet smell of the country' (1763: 60). The writer whose *nom de plume* was 'X Y Z', likewise found that the best fragrance in Spain would be found outside the city. On the outskirts of Seville were the *Delicias*, gardens where one could enjoy the shade and be in full comfort. Yet even then, this paradise could not compete with Kensington Gardens, according to the author. For English writers in the first half of the nineteenth century, rural images represented the English nation. By having positive experiences of similar environments in Spain but by repeatedly comparing them to a similar aspect of home, the travellers reinforced the collective understanding of Spain by inviting the reader to recall their own sensorial past, while simultaneously positioning England as superior (Helsinger, 1997). There was no chance of confusing the two nations, even if they might, at times, appear similar: 'Gibraltar … lies before us and now a cooler, fresher air, as if direct from England, makes every brown cheek redder and cheerier; our steps grow firmer, faster and longer. We feel the home air, and are ourselves again' (Thornbury, 1859: 215).

The comparison between England and Spain, of place and people, was evident in many passages on Spanish industry. In *Travels Through Spain in the Years 1775–1776*, Swinburne seems to compliment the Spanish culture and nation, but he frequently undercuts such favourable reviews by suggesting adulteration or an outside influence that has improved the situation, furthering the trope that the Spanish were not only different but inferior. For example: 'a good deal of strong wine is made[... but it is said to be medicated with lime, and mahogany chips, to give it spirit and color' (1779: 47). And while the Catalans were all that was 'honesty, steadiness, and sobriety' and good wine came from the region, if it were not for imports of staple goods from

America, Sicily and northern Europe, there would be a great risk of hunger and famine (1779: 65). Spain was inferior, only to be improved through intervention.

Townsend, too, thought that Spanish industry had some room for improvement. On one journey, he came across peasants pulling up oats, labour that believed would have been easier with 'a simple machine' (invented back in 1689, according to Townsend). He thought this simple adoption of technology would also solve the problem of their 'very foul' feed corn (1791: 31). But in other places, in particular in the areas around Cartagena and Valencia, he reports that the land is extraordinary fertile, and he praises the natural environment with great frequency. It is also in the countryside where he finds that the peasants working in the vineyards near Málaga in Spain are superlative in their patient attitude towards ' heat, of hunger, and of thirst' as well as 'hard work' (1791: 28). He concluded that there, the high rate of unemployment was due neither to the climate nor to their constitutions, but rather the neglectful government, a problematic assertion when buttressed against growing concerns around political economy and national hierarchies. In these narratives, because of a perceived work ethic, these peasants are framed in a positive context. Indeed, George Whittington, in 1808, connected industry and morality. When he came across a town that prospered from cloth manufacturing, he found it 'rather neat' with a 'fine race of clean and industrious people' (1808: 61), which explicitly ties together blood, body and morality.

Other writers were not so benevolent in their assessment of the Spanish work ethic. Thomas Salmon, the well-travelled English historian, sharply criticised the entire nation:

> To the pride and vanity of the Spaniards are added many other vices, as their wretched indolence and laziness, their revenge, avarice, lust, and credulity in believing the feigned miracles and fabulous stories of their monks without examination ... Their neglecting to apply themselves to agriculture and husbandry, is generally looked upon as the effect of idleness; whereas it is certainly to be imputed to their pride, or other the custom of their country, where a man is looked upon with the utmost contempt who submits to these vile employments, as they suffer them to plough their lands, or plant their vineyard.
>
> (1745: 373–374)

This perceived laziness might explain why there seemed such a number of peasants in Spain. Whether this national character stemmed from their Islamic roots or the Spanish Catholic decadence, Spanish pride (or as we saw in Ford's writing, shame) frequently appears in travelogues allowing authors to suggest cultural deficits through affect. Authors repeatedly frame the Spanish people as lacking a refined aesthetic, a *coarseness*, and the inability, by the Spanish themselves, to recognise their inferior status. What began as commentaries on disgusting smells in Spain evolved into framing the Spanish as laggards. Such attitudes suffuse late eighteenth and nineteenth-century travel narratives and serve to actualise a backwards country and culture. The rankness of the Spanish as experienced by the traveller revealed a far more consequential nature.

Tasting Spain

For many travellers to Spain, though, it was through food that one's aesthetic sensibilities and true character could be fully appreciated. At a monastery in Torrelles de Llobregat, where Swinburne lodged with a 'polite, sensible ecclesiastic': 'I cannot say much in favor of the cookery; it cost us some wry faces to get down the saffron soup and spiced ragouts' (1779: 52). Later in the book, in a lengthy, but telling passage he continues with a discussion on the very nature of the people:

> Most of the Spanish ... are sparing in diet, perhaps more from a sense of habitual indigence, than from any aversion to gluttony; whenever they can riot in the plenty of another man's table, they will gormandize to excess, and not content with eating their fill, will carry off whatever they can stuff into their pockets. I have more than once been a witness to the pillage of a supper, by the numerous beaux and admirers which the ladies lead after them in triumph, wherever they are invited. They are fond of spices, and scarce eat any thing without saffron, pimento, or garlic; they delight in wine that tastes strong of the pitched skin, and of oil that has a rank smell and taste; indeed, the same oil feeds their lamp, swims in their pottage, and dresses their salled [sic]: in inns the lighted lamp is frequently handed down to the table, that each many may take the quantity he chooses ... All these hot, drying kinds of food, co-operating with the parching qualities of the atmosphere, are assigned as causes of the spare make of the common people in Spain, where the priests and the inn-keepers are almost the only well-fed, portly figures to be met with.
>
> (1779: 194–195)

The cuisine and the people had thus become signifier and sign. The anonymous author, X Y Z, of *Spain, Tangier, etc: Visited in 1840 and 1841* did not seem to think much better of the food:

> Oh! For the pen of Cervantes, to depict you what that supper was! Vegetables swimming in oil sufficiently rank to suit the palate of an Esquimaux; animal messes redolent of garlic; boiled meat as succulent as might be a stew of tow; and fowls utterly unimpressible by human teeth ...
>
> (1845: 31)

According to him, dinner also included 'Capzicum [sic] in oil: (N.B. A Spaniard informed us this last article was in butter ... Alas! For the man if ever
his life should depend on his senses of taste or smell!)' (1845: 32). There were
also 'dry, impracticable roast fowl'; 'indifferent grapes' and 'offensive cheese'.
Not even the bread could save the meal, and despite the flour being of
'excellent' quality, it had such a heavy, dense consistency as to be felt 'as lead'
on the tongue (1845: 32). Further, the oil tasted rancid, due to the unfortu-
nate circumstance that, in Spain, there were not enough oil presses to keep
pace with the harvested olives. This sad situation clearly illustrated a 'tale of
inertness and apathy ... [and thus] tastes and dispositions are both disputable
and important' (1845: 33).[1]

Richard Ford spent some chapters discussing the food and wine in his
exceptionally popular travelogue *Gatherings from Spain* (1846), a collection of
essays gleaned from his *Hand-Book for Travellers in Spain* (1845). Although
he was ambivalent about Spanish cuisine, both praising it and complaining
about it, he certainly felt it was an important topic for discussion, and that it
had great implications for the nation. Ford went straight to the crux of the
matter, declaring that Spain was a 'hungry, thirsty, tealess, beerless, beefless
land'[2] (1846: 169). Moreover, 'Scarcity of food is implied in the very name of
Spain, which means poverty and destitution', a situation which he saw as
affecting the character of a country and people (1846: 121). Still, while Ford
is not entirely negative about food in his descriptions, this one declaration
reveals the rich understanding that he had of the profound differences
between England and Spain. It also declared that Spain was the opposite of
having the qualities of a nation being self-sufficient and satisfied, respectable,
hard working and powerful (Rogers, 2003).

Ford seems to be entranced by the country. Part of the reason for this
reaction is that he very much looks to a romanticised past in understanding
place, as did many other travellers to Spain during the nineteenth century.
When writing about lodgings for travellers he emphasises such differences
between countries and the people, and that for the traveller in Spain, where
'the everyday occurrences ... are so strange' it can seem as if one is
experiencing:

> a dream or at a play, that one scarcely can believe it to be actually taking
> place, and true. The man of the note-book and the artist almost forget
> that there is nothing to eat; meanwhile all this food for the mind and
> portfolio, all this local colour and oddness, is lost upon your Spanish
> companion, if he be one of the better classes; he is ashamed, where you
> are enchanted; he blushes at the sad want of civilization, clean table-
> cloth, and beef-steaks, and perhaps he is right ... [he believes that you]
> are laughing at him in your sleeve, and considering his country as
> Roman, African, or in a word, as un-European, which is what he particularly
> dislikes and resents.
>
> (1846: 174)

Yet by framing Spain as a pastoral, pre-industrialised nation, that was not only shaped but restrained by its past, the construction of Spanish identity becomes a powerful, cultural and political discourse. For example, when Ford noted it was 'the whole duty of a good pig ... to get as fat and as soon as he can, and then die for the good of this country' (1847: 128) he was most certainly nodding towards the role of pork vis-à-vis Spain's religious past. By doing so, he conjures images of both the Islamic legacy and the long-lasting Inquisition. Indeed, the Spanish themselves express a self-conscious shame at who they are, as understood by Ford.

By connecting cuisine, culture and politics, food and the senses had become a symbol of and a reason for national determinism. Simply put, 'the destinies of nations depend on the manner of their nourishment' according to Ford as he quotes Brillat-Savarin (1846: 119–120). But because Ford declares that Spanish cuisine is 'for the most part Oriental' (1846: 120) one is left to question just how Spain was different from other 'oriental' nations, and if it is fated any differently from nations in the east. By the end of the book, Ford suggests that an agricultural peasant society, noble yet hungry, best fits Spain. It is a country whereby gazpacho best sustained the natives, 'whose souls are more parched and dried up and who perspire less' (1846: 134) and whose few good cooks '[must] be able to make something out of nothing' (1846: 119). Whether it be rank, rancid, foul, hungry or thirsty, such affective language acts as a marker of power and a xenophobic superiority. These attitudes sustained imperial rule in the second half of the nineteenth century.

Conclusion

Traveling to a 'foreign' land is, by its very nature, an exercise where the senses reintegrate cultural meanings and social explanations, where every experience highlights different*ness* in the most personal, and affected, ways (Billig, 1995). Because travel narratives tend to richly describe the sensate world, they not only 'invite the reader to accompany the traveler and gaze through his or her eyes' but to also experience all of the emotions felt and embodied by the author-traveller when describing any sensorial scene (Bracewell, 2015: 215). Therefore, travel narratives can provide a rich case study to consider the affective nature of 'Othering' through sensual descriptors of disgust, whether it be aroma or taste, for the senses are not apolitical.

Ultimately, it was a perceived Spanish decadence and Spain's Islamic past that was understood to have created its body politic and individual bodies into the nineteenth century. Contemporary travelogues presented Spain through a convergence of diet and history that played out through aesthetics and affect. Spain's unique position – of Islamic occupation and a failed empire – allowed outsiders to reify the stagnant status of Spain, supported by economic and political evidence, and experienced first hand by travellers. By portraying Spain as romantic and savage, but also hungry and thirsty, nineteenth-century writers reduced its cultural identity as inert and unprogressive.

Spain's rancid air and unrefined cuisine reflected a national character of stunted development and misplaced pride tempered by moments of visible shame. Travel writers adopted Hume's philosophical model of knowledge based on 'delicacy of taste' which 'enables us [them] to judge of the characters of men' (Hume, 1777: 6) not restricted to a limited understanding of aesthetics, but to daily interactions with the banal. Readers of travel narratives likewise based their knowledge of Spain on a Kantian model whereby, 'it is always historical, if he who possesses it knows only so much of it as he has been given to him from outside, whether through immediate experience, or through narration, or by instruction ...' (Kant, 1922: 670). Thus, affective experiences in travel literature crossed Hume's fork, while historical developments of Spain converged with sensorial experiences. Together, the body and the senses created Spanish identity; it was a simple matter of digestion for both the traveller and the reader.

Notes

1 Charles Dickens repeats the sentiment that in Spain, olives are not pressed quickly enough after harvest, resulting in oil that is 'violently rancid' (1863: 262).
2 Tea was both the civilising beverage as well as the marker of imperial notions. The developing institution of afternoon tea became the social sphere in which manners were taught and the art of conversation was practised (Bickham, 2008; Ketabgian, 2010: 125–140).

References

Anon. (1837). *Scenes in Spain*. New York: G. Dearborn.
Batten, C. (1978). *Pleasurable Instruction: Form and Convention in Eighteenth-Century Travel Literature*. Berkeley: University of California Press.
Bickham, T. (2008). Eating the Empire: Intersections of Food, Cookery and Imperialism of the Eighteenth-Century. *Past and Present*, 198 (1), 71–109.
Billig, M. (1995). *Banal Nationalism*. New York: Sage.
Bracewell, W. (2015). The Traveler's Eye: Reading European Travel Writing, 1750–1850. In: Smethurst, P., and Kuehn, J. (Eds.) *New Directions in Travel Writing Studies*. New York: Palgrave Macmillan, 215–227.
Bushman, R. (1992). *The Refinement of America: Persons, Houses, Cities*. New York: Vintage.
Clark, E. (1763). *Letters Concerning the Spanish Nation*. London: T. Becket.
Clark, W. (1851). *Gazpacho or, Summer Months in Spain*, Second edition. London: John W. Parker and Son.
Corbin, A. (1986). *The Foul and the Fragrant: Odor and the French Social Imagination*. Cambridge, MA: Harvard University Press.
Dickens, C. (1863, May 9). "Our Oil Flasks". *All the Year Round, Vol. 9* London: Messrs. Chapman and Hall, 260–264.
Elliot, F. (1884). *Diary of an Idle Woman in Spain, Vol.* II. Leipzig: Berhard Tauchnitz.
Ford, R. (1845). *A Hand-Book for Travellers in Spain*. London: J. Murray.

Ford, R. (1846). *Gatherings from Spain*. London: John Murray.

Ford, R. (1847). *The Spaniards & their Country*. New York: Wiley and Putnam.

Helsinger, E. (1997). *Rural Scenes and National Representation: Britain, 1815–1850*. Princeton, NJ: Princeton University Press.

Highmore, B. (2010). Bitter after Taste; Affect, Food, and Social Aesthetics. In: Gregg, M., and Seigworth, G. (Eds) *The Affect Theory Reader*. Durham, NC: Duke University Press, 118–137.

Hume, D. (1777). *Essays and Treatises on Several Subjects*. London: A. Millar.

Hontanilla, A. (2008). Images of Barbaric Spain in Eighteenth-Century British Travel Writing. *Studies in Eighteenth-Century Culture*, 37 (1), 119–143.

Howes, D. and Classen, C. (2013). *Ways of Sensing: Understanding the Senses in Society*. New York: Routledge.

Kant, I. (1922). *Critique of Pure Reason*, Second edition (F. Müller, Trans.). New York: The Macmillan Company.

Ketabgian, T. (2010). Foreign Tastes and 'Manchester Tea-Parties:' Eating and Drinking with the Victorian Lower Orders. In: Wagner, T., and Hassan, N. (Eds) *Consumimg Culture in the Long Nineteenth Century*. New York: Lexington Books, 125–140.

Kisoo, K. (2005). Kant and the Fate of Aesthetic Experience: A Deconstructive Reading, PhD Dissertation, SUNY Binghamton.

Roche, D. (1987). *The People of Paris: An Essay in Popular Culture of the 18th Century*. Berkeley: University of California Press.

Rogers, B. (2003). *Beef and Liberty*. London: Chatto & Windus.

Salmon, T. (1745). *Modern History or the Present State of All Nations, Vol. 1*. London: T. Longman.

Smith, W. (2002). *Consumption and the Making of Respectability, 1600–1800*. New York: Routledge.

Swinburne, H. (1779). *Travels Through Spain in the Years 1775–1776*. London: P. Elmsly.

Thornbury, W. (1859). *Life in Spain: Past and Present, Vol. II*. London: Smith, Elder and Co.

Turner, K. (2001). *British Travel Writers in Europe, 1750–1800: Authorship, Gender, and National Identity*. Aldershot: Ashgate.

Townsend, J. (1791). *A Journey through Spain in the Years 1786 and 1787, Vols 2 and 3*. London: C. Dilly.

Townsend, J. (1817). *A Dissertation of the Poor Laws*. London: Ridgeways.

Twiss, R. (1775). *Travels through Portugal and Spain in 1772 and 1773*. London: Twiss.

Whittington, G. (1808). *Travels Through Spain and Part of Portugal. Vol. 1*. Boston: White, Burditt and Co.

X Y Z. (1845). *Spain, Tangier, etc: Visited in 1840 and 1841*. London: Samuel Clarke.

Part III
Taste, affect and the lifecourse

7 Tastes of reflection, food memories and the temporal affects of sedimented personal histories on everyday foodways

Julie Parsons

In this chapter, I draw upon written auto/biographical narratives received from 75 respondents who engaged in asynchronous in-depth online interviews on the topic of food over the lifecourse in 2011. These rich and evocative food (his)stories are reminiscent of Proust's ([1913] 2006) *Remembrance of Things Past*, in that respondent's food memories simultaneously capture both the personal and the social, as well as past and present foodscapes. Thus whilst respondents develop personal tastes and dis-tastes, these are embedded in 'common vocabularies' (Mills, 1959) that detail a transformation in middle-class values towards 'good' foodways (ways of doing food), prevalent within westernised neo-liberal societies. Mostly, this centres on a critique of the excessive industrialisation of food production from the 1970s (Mennell, 1985) and convenience foodways in favour of a kind of 'noshtalgia' (Beckett et al, 2002) infused with temporal cultural markers of class status, such as preparing home cooked meals from scratch (Pollan, 2013), 'healthy' eating (Parsons, 2015a, 2015b), a preference for fresh seasonal fruit and vegetables, as well as knowledge of what counts as good or bad 'taste' (Naccarato and LeBesco, 2012; Coles and Crang, 2011; Taylor and Falconer, 2015). Further, as Bourdieu (1984) reminds us when arguing against a Kantian (innate) sense of taste, in favour of a taste of reflection, taste is inculcated over time. Thus memories of everyday foodways become narratives of relational affectation, how we learn to know food, with our food preferences embedded, produced, reproduced and maintained through the practice of doing taste over and over again (Carolan, 2011: 6). These food memories bind together the gustatory experiences of taste, smell, touch, sight and sound, but also provide a significant commentary on contemporary foodscapes and changing taste. They are temporal in terms of capturing an essence of the past through a contemporary lens.

Sociologists, anthropologists and food studies scholars have explored individual and collective relationships with food through memory (Lupton, 1996; Sutton, 2001; Belasco, 2008), what Arendt (1996: 15) refers to as 'the storehouse of time'. Indeed, time is significant for Bourdieu (1984) in terms of cultural capital and habitus; the disposition and embodiment of taste sediments over time, with tastes in food imbued with a kind of 'temporal power' (Bourdieu, 1984: 315). Further, Morgan (1996: 166) argues that 'food represents a particularly strong form of anchorage in the past [and] serves as one of the links between historical time, individual time and household time'. The purpose of this chapter therefore is to demonstrate how 'taste', following Bourdieu (1984), is inculcated over time, and how reflections on everyday foodways from the past viewed through a modern-day lens reify and legitimise contemporary middle-class values and tastes through powerful affects of disgust.

'Taste' in food draws upon what Mills (1959) refers to as 'common vocabularies' that position our autobiographical accounts of everyday life within time and space. When referring to changing 'taste' in everyday foodways the majority of UK born respondents in my study reflected on the past through a modern day lens that demonstrated an awareness of what might be considered contemporary 'culinary capital' using food and food practices as markers of social status (Naccarato and LeBesco, 2012: 2). This was especially pertinent when considering shifts in everyday foodways from the 1970s to the present day. Hence, respondents' tastes of reflection focus on changing cultural norms and values and what counts as 'good' or 'legitimate' food/foodways. Notably respondents eschew convenience food in favour of 'home-cooked meals prepared from scratch'[1] (Pollan, 2013; Parsons, 2014b, 2016), express preferences for fresh fruit, vegetables, brown bread over white and demonstrate an awareness of culinary trends. Together they form symbolic cultural markers of distinction and taste in a culinary field that values 'time' or the temporal affects of personal histories, sedimented, like limescale fixing itself to the bottom of a kettle. It is the awareness of what has become to be known as 'good' food that enables the retrospective narratives inherent in foodways to evoke powerful affects of disgust and pleasurable temptation.

Background and definitions

Throughout this chapter I use the term 'foodways', which usually refers to the production and distribution of food at a macro level. Although it is used in anthropology when exploring food cultures or shared common beliefs, behaviours and practices relating to the production and consumption of food (Counihan, 1999), here, foodways is considered at a micro level, to reflect the multiplicity of ways of 'doing' food that incorporates all aspects of everyday food practices. This incorporates the notion of foodways as an essential aspect of an individual's cultural habitus (Bourdieu, 1984), which is cultivated and inculcated over time. Thus foodways are 'affective practices' (Wetherell, 2012: 96), because they are ongoing emotional, socially constructed, embodied, situated performances infused with sedimented social and personal history.

Further, 'foodways' has multiple meanings; it highlights the significance of modes of practice or ways of 'doing' food, as well as movement and direction across time (history) and space (culture). Consequently, foodways connect the individual with the social through everyday practices (action/habit). The significance of foodways or ways of doing food is reminiscent of West and Zimmerman's (1987) notion of 'doing' gender, Butler's (1999) conceptualisation of gender as performance and Morgan's (1996) theories on 'family practices' as significant in distinguishing between what families 'are' and what families 'do', in contrast to the institution of 'the' family (Morgan, 2011). A focus on foodways therefore emphasises the embodied, affective, everyday food performances, and the interactions and temporal ways of doing food that connect past, present and future. It is notable therefore that foodways (like gender and class) works within three interconnecting domains: (1) on an 'individual' level, through socialisation, internalisation, identity work and the construction of the self, (2) through interactional 'cultural' expectations and 'othering' of practices and (3) via 'institutions' that control access to resources, as well as ideologies and discourses (Risman, 2004). Thus performances of everyday foodways are validated, constrained and facilitated by reference to wider institutional contexts that *may* include gender (patriarchy), class (economics), culture (capital) and 'the' family (discourse). Accordingly, everyday foodways inculcate a cultural habitus through the repetition, reproduction and reinforcement of values and tastes.

The research study

The primary aim was to investigate the relationship between individuals and their food choice, using an auto/biographical approach. This included four interrelated objectives, to explore how an individual's relationship with food may have changed over time, to consider how useful it is to see food choice as a gendered experience, to contribute to current sociological understanding of 'food culture(s)' and the impact of health discourse(s) upon food choice and to consider the extent to which individual food histories are related to issues of weight management, if at all. There was an explicit auto/biographical focus in order to explore the sameness and difference across 'our food stories', and to highlight the interconnectedness of the individual with the social, the autobiographical and biographical (Morgan, 1998), the micro and the macro, the private and the public. This enables an exploration of the private troubles and public issues around everyday foodways (Mills, 1959), whilst demonstrating the inter-textuality of auto/biographical accounts. The study made use of asynchronous online interviewing techniques, which produced written texts from respondents. These texts are considered social products, not unproblematic reflections of reality, but constrained by structural influences beyond their own free will (Stanley and Morgan, 1993). The use of asynchronous in depth online interviews as a technique for gathering data is part of a repertoire of computer-mediated communication (CMC) (Illingworth, 2006; Kozinets, 2010). Although considered an 'interview' it shares attributes with correspondence techniques (Letherby and Zdrodowski, 1995; Kralik, Koch and Brady , 2002). One of the benefits of this particular method is the time respondents have to reflect upon and articulate their narratives. It also means 'interviews' can be conducted across time and space. I therefore engaged in a series of (mostly) asynchronous in-depth online interviews utilising an opportunity sample, drawing initially from my social network. I interviewed 75 respondents across the UK over 9 months in 2011, contacting between 5 and 10 people per week, to ask if they wanted to participate. I gained full ethical approval from the University of Plymouth and all respondents were given or chose their own pseudonyms. The focus of the inquiry was food over the lifecourse, and respondents were invited to write their own autobiographical food narratives. Once they had agreed to participate, I sent the following instructions:

> What I'm really after is your 'food story'. Perhaps, this will include your earliest food memories, favourite foods, memorable food occasions, whether your eating habits have changed over time and why this may be. Also, absolutely anything food related that you'd like to share ....

For some, if this proved difficult, I sent a series of questions along the same lines that centred on eating and cooking. I did not set out to question respondents about any specific tastes or memories; it was very much open for respondents to tell their own stories in their own words and on their own terms. The narratives I received varied in length from a paragraph to 12 pages of text and the interviews took from a day to several months to complete. This approach resulted in rich narratives and 'thick descriptions' (Geertz, 1973) that incorporated a range of food memories from the 1940s in the UK and beyond.

In terms of demographics (please see the table at the end of the chapter, identifying all respondents whose narratives have been used here), I interviewed 49 women and 26 men and most respondents had occupations from National Statistics-Social Economic Classification (NS-SEC) classes 1–4, although for some this marked upward mobility in class position from more 'modest' or 'working class' backgrounds.[2] The age range of respondents was 27 to 76 years of age, though the majority were born in the 1950s and 1960s and predominantly in the UK (although some were born outside the UK and others were living abroad at the time of the study). There was a geographical spread of respondents across the UK from southwest England to northern Scotland. The majority were living with partners or married, and two-thirds were parents (though not all with dependent children). After several levels of analysis running concurrently with data collection and beyond, five broad themes were identified and verified within the data. These were family, maternal, embodiment, health and epicurean foodways (Parsons, 2015b). These themes have been discussed in detail elsewhere (Parsons, 2014a, 2014b, 2015a, 2015b, 2015c). In this chapter the importance of affective reflection in understanding contemporary foodways is explored.

A (dis)taste of reflection

Almost without exception respondents made some reference to the 'food revolution' that occurred in the UK from the 1970s, with the expansion of supermarkets, frozen, tinned, pre-packaged, processed and fast food. In reflecting on the past respondents showed distaste for the 'fast food prepared by corporations' (Pollan, 2013: 9). Instead, they favoured home cooking from scratch as *the* legitimate means of performing a middle-class cultural habitus (Parsons, 2014b, 2015b, 2016). Therefore, supporting broader arguments that link culinary capital with elite status (Naccarato and LeBesco, 2012) and a politics of disgust that uses everyday foodways as a means of drawing distinctions between social groups, which then becomes symptomatic of wider social power relationships (Tyler, 2013).

Hence, reflections on everyday foodways experienced during childhood in the 1970s tended to be described in derogatory terms or written in order to illicit disgust, they are loaded with socially stigmatising meanings and values (Tyler, 2013). Ophelia for example writes:

> Later in the early 70s the frozen food revolution hit and marmite sandwiches were overtaken by cheesy balls and fish bites in batter that sort of exploded fatly in your mouth. I hated them. Frey Bentos Steak Pies also made a short visit to our house but were universally loathed.

Ophelia's distaste and hatred of this type of food is evident, the notion that it 'exploded' in your mouth, adds to the alien quality of it, as somehow not quite real food. The reference to 'fatly' is also used here to signify disgust. Indeed, notions of disgust are part of a repertoire of affective responses to foodways identified by anthropologists such as Douglass (1966) to indicate pollution and/or taboo. Here, the strength of hatred for 'cheesy balls and fish bites' is a form of social abjection, they are polluting and symbolise a kind of inadequacy and/or lack of cultural approbation (Tyler, 2013). Hence, not preparing home cooked meals from scratch symbolises lack on many levels and fuels a classed disgust that masks wider social inequalities related to class and power (Fox and Smith, 2011; Meah and Watson, 2011).

In Magenta's account she notes:

> Food at home was pretty gross too [as well as school dinners]. Lots of stodge and grease ... a common Saturday dinner was bacon, canned tomatoes heated up and fried bread – no veg included. Frey Bentos Steak and Kidney Pies – which came in a can – was also a regular ...

In this account, whilst Magenta considers this type of food as 'pretty gross', emphasising the grease/fat elements of it to illicit disgust, these are served on a regular basis, unlike in Ophelia's narrative where she claims they only made a 'short visit'. In Magenta's example, the lack of vegetables relates to contemporary middle-class cultural norms that value and reify a 'five-a-day' 'healthy' eating mantra (Parsons, 2015a, 2015b). This again is linked to the wrong sort of eating and highlights the deeply embedded symbolic values attached to what are considered appropriate everyday foodways (Taylor and Falconer, 2015: 49).

Zoe similarly reflects on a typical lunch from her childhood in light of contemporary goverment discourses around healthy eating, she writes: '[We had] white bread sandwiches, crisps and chocolate, meat and fish pastes ... in other words what we seemed to get as our school packed lunch as a balanced meal!' The exclamation mark here is indicative of a distinct shift in terms of what is considered appropriate food for children (Parsons, 2014b; James, Kjorholt and Tingstad, 2009; Wills et al., 2009). In Ophelia's account she continues: 'I don't remember eating any salad (apart from ice berg lettuce) and potatoes, which we grew ourselves and frozen peas were about the only vegetable we regularly ate ... Everything suddenly became "easy care and pre packed" ...'. Ophelia's reference to *'salad'* is a specific contemporary concern for middle-class families. Indeed, UK government discourses on healthy family foodways reify the family as a site for inculcating appropriate healthy family values (Parsons, 2015b). Hence a 'Pre-occupation with achieving a "healthy diet" reflects a middle class disposition for being "health conscious" and for taking on board "authentic" health and dietary messages, that are sanctioned by (government) experts (Wills et al., 2009: 65). Drew on the other hand is slightly less disparaging of the convenience 'food revolution' of the 1970s and instead sees it as part of an evolving culinary field, he notes: 'Then things started to change – it started with boil in a bag curry, as I remember served with deep fried curly noodles – much like a quaver ...'. Indeed, Drew positions himself as a 'foodie' with an understanding and knowledge of food history (Parsons, 2015c) and an interest in authentic culinary practices (Naccarato and LeBesco, 2012). In Stephen's account, on the other hand, he refers to these as 'Dreadful Vesta curries or meals in a tin – London Grill; pale sausages mixed with baked beans', whilst Paula finds some of the eating norms from the 1970s less disgusting and notes:

> I do recall there being curry in a can. It had sultanas in it for sure, but we all thought it OK ... I had a passion for Chunky Chicken Supreme; – a tin of chicken in thick sauce that I would spread on toast and grill ....

It is notable that Paula expresses a kind of 'noshtalgia' (Beckett et al, 2002) for the 'dirty' food of the past, the curry in a can, was 'OK'. This is a classed history that marks a temporal shift in terms of social attitudes, but also reflects a sense of longing and/or belonging to another time and place (Taylor and Falconer, 2015).

Alternatively, Dalia considers the lack of convenience food in her childhood an unintended blessing, a consequence of her mother cooking for a big family (six children) on a limited budget, she writes: 'The big upside to her cooking is that it was home-made and probably healthy (in part) and not just reheated processed ready meals'. Generally, though references to a 'lack' of fresh vegetables and fruit in childhood diets was common, reflecting contemporary campaigns such as the '5-a-day' (fruit and vegetable) government initiative launched on the back of the Jamie Oliver television programme developed to reform school dinners in 2005 (James and Curtis, 2010). Hence, in Imogen's account she says:

> The earliest memories of food are that of Ready Brek on cold mornings with lots of white sugar, plates of beef mince with peas and carrots made into a smiley face, and brown sugar sandwiches on white bread. Sundays were always a big roast dinner with crumble or pie and custard for pudding. Teatime would be jam sandwiches and cake. Fruit would always go rotten in the fruit bowl!

Again, the emphasis on 'white' sugar and bread, is reminiscent of changes in taste, as Mennell (1985) highlights there has been a shift in preferences for less industrialised processed 'white' bread in favour of brown. There are also UK government proposals to introduce a sugar tax on soft drinks, in response to a Public Health England report on 'Sugar Reduction' (Tedstone et al., 2015). Here, Imogen is highlighting how fruit was ignored in favour of a high fat, sugar and highly processed carbohydrate diet.

In Ophelia's narrative she comments: 'Bowls of tangerines sat on the sideboard with the strict instruction not to eat them all or they would have to buy more. No one ate any.' However, this is more indicative of the expense of seasonal fruit in the past and Ophelia's overall critique of her stepmother's parenting skills, following the death of her mother at the age of 12. Earlier in the account, Ophelia writes about the fruit trees that grew in her childhood garden:

> We had an orchard full of plum trees and apple trees though and helped ourselves to these. The plums were delicious, warmed by the sun with great globs of sticky amber resin where their flesh had burst as they hit the ground ....

Also, how as a family they went on lots of picnics, when she notes:

> A great hunk of Spam would be un-tinned and slices cut and put onto Mother's Pride [white bread]. In the summer we had warm strawberries in little straw pallets for pudding and I don't think I have ever tasted such delicious strawberries in my life since.

Indeed, there was an emphasis on seasonality that punctuated respondents' food memories, as Stephen writes, (capital letters in the original), 'the

FIRST CHERRIES OF THE SEASON eaten out of a brown paper bag on the walk back to the house (guilty – not allowed to eat in the street)'. It is notable that, despite the acquired cultural knowledge that fresh seasonal fruit is now a classifier of 'good' taste, this memory plays with a notion of shame; as a respectable middle-class boy it was for Stephen considered bad manners to eat in the street, i.e. outside of formal dining around the table. This shame is consciously overturned in Stephen's retrospective narrative, where he is confident that past recollections of eating fresh cherries on the street are sure to be met with less affective disgust than the descriptions of processed hydrogenated fat balls. However, this is also reminiscent of a kind of 'noshtalgia' (Beckett et al., 2002) for a time when fruit was only available in season and as Ophelia notes, the summer strawberries she ate at that time were the best she has ever tasted. Again, reflections on foodways from the past are tinged with contemporary markers of what counts as good taste, such as local and seasonal eating practices (Naccarato and LeBesco, 2012). Moreover, in a contemporary foodscape, 'good' food is linked to the key domains of cultural omnivorousness, notably; aesthetic appreciation (taste), authenticity (participation) and knowledge acquisition (Peterson and Kern, 1996; Warde et al, 2007). Hence, Ophelia is identifying her appreciation and knowledge of what counts as good taste.

Continuing the fruit and vegetable theme, in Drew's account of childhood dis-taste he writes:

> I hated carrots, soft, not sweet, fury … that was because the only carrots I was made to eat came from tins either sliced or chunked into mixed veg. I now know it is not carrots I hate / hated but the tinned variety where all the sweetness and crunch had been sucked out.

Again, this is an obvious reference to the 'lack' of flavour/taste in tinned and frozen vegetables or convenience foods. He continues with a comment on beetroot:

> School dinners, my memory is that each one included beetroot, every meal beetroot, spam, mash and beetroot, boiled fish and beetroot and the only value this vinegary pink thing added was colour - to everything, hands, potatoes in fact anything that touched it.

Beetroot here is described as contaminating and discolours everything it touches, in contrast to the beetroot he eats now as he notes:

> It took me 19 years to grow to like it / even try it again - then one day at Borough Market I had a eureka moment, feta, beetroot, mint and lemon pasta - I now grow it, bake it - eat it raw and the Borough recipe is a strong family favourite.

It is notable that his new found, acquired taste in beetroot is also shared with his family. He is responsible for inculcating 'taste' and cultural capital. It is a taste from Borough Market (come to be known as the most gourmet food market in London, selling high end specialised and artisan food produce), which is a significant cultural marker, related to culinary capital and a foodie identity (Naccarato and LeBesco, 2012; Parsons, 2015b, 2015c). Hence, the place where Drew has his 'eureka moment' highlights his knowledge, engagement and expertise (Peterson and Kern, 1996; Warde, Wright, and Gayo-Cal, 2007; Parsons, 2015c) in terms of foodie practices/ places to eat, and sources of 'good' food (Coles and Crang, 2011; Coles, 2014).

In Ophelia's account she similarly identifies a shift in her contemporary everyday foodways:

> As time has passed and after 15 years of daily cooking for my family I have become much more confident and proficient in food and what it really means. Today I balance the weekly meals between vegetarian, pasta, fish and meat and we have a lot of salad.

The reference to salad links back to Ophelia's childhood reflections, as this was something they never ate and now they have 'a lot'. In Magenta's account she says that now: 'I don't eat processed food on the whole and I make everything from scratch myself, so I would never buy a pasta sauce for example …'. Again, this is a clear culinary shift in taste that eschews convenience in favour of taking 'time' to prepare food from scratch. Imogen also refers to shifts in dietary practices from her childhood, she writes: 'I think there is a lot more information available to kids now regarding a healthy lifestyle. I don't remember ever being told about healthy diets at school or at home for that matter.' Indeed, most respondents' rejected convenience food as Carly notes:

> I see a healthy diet as pretty much everything in moderation. No banned foods, just being sensible about not eating too much, and avoiding processed foods as far as possible, and not drinking too much (loads of empty calories). Also loads of veg and fruit of as many colours as possible – I try to do at least the 5 a day and often many more … The main thing for me is eating as little processed stuff as possible – packed with salt and trans fats and sugar. I would choose to eat a couple of squares of good chocolate rather than a piece of cake or something (mostly). We virtually never eat ready meals of any kind ….

Likewise, Ursula writes: 'I live to eat rather than the other way around. The food in our fridge is, in the main, fresh rather than convenient and I have never thought of cooking as a chore ….'

Similarly, Olivia claims, 'I don't like food that is over processed (ready meals, pick and mix sweets, shop bought cakes etc.)', and Regan notes: 'I dislike processed, overcooked, tasteless food ... I avoid processed and E numbered foods as much as possible ... conscious of a balanced diet ... proper food cooked from scratch so I know what's gone into it ...'. Annie writes that she hasn't 'been to a McDonalds for years and find[s] fast food toxic', whilst Ralph says 'I am very conscious of food fashions and trends, especially home grown produce and eating healthily', Nadia comments 'I try and keep junk food to a minimum', whilst Magenta notes that: 'I can't imagine just going through life and continuously filling my body with things that I have no idea what the contents or origin of them is ...'. The association therefore between convenience or processed food and lack in terms of 'taste' is strong. The language used to describe the processed food is highly affective, and elicits distaste, disgust and loathing. It is alien and contaminating, of unknown provenance and not 'proper' food.

Conclusion

Overall respondents' narratives demonstrate that 'taste' is not an objective or fixed measure but dependent on an interplay of past and present, status and desire (Parsons, 2015b). It is linked to the politics of disgust (Tyler, 2013), which enables respondents to draw symbolic boundaries between appropriate and inappropriate everyday foodways. In some instances, this elicits a form of 'noshtalgia' (Beckett et al., 2002) or a longing for what might be considered 'dirty' foodways from the past (Taylor and Falconer, 2015). Mostly, respondents position themselves as knowledgeable participants in a contemporary foodscape that values 'taste' in good food/foodways, whether forms of culinary capital (Naccarato and LeBesco, 2012) are expressed in terms of a commitment to preparing home cooked meals from scratch (Pollan, 2013; Parsons, 2016), healthy eating, purchasing seasonal vegetables/fruit or shopping at places with a high degree of culinary capital, such as Borough Market (Coles and Crang, 2011; Coles, 2014).

Indeed, what counts as 'culinary capital' (Naccarato and LeBesco, 2012) or legitimate taste in a culinary field is continuously assigned and re-assigned through time and space. As noted previously, in Bourdieu's (1984) thesis there is no innate aesthetic or pure taste only that which is inculcated over time. This centres on a disposition for considering the future rather than living in the present that acknowledges a 'temporal power' (Bourdieu, 1984: 315). Indeed, the best measure of cultural capital is the amount of time devoted to acquiring it, because the 'transformation of economic capital into cultural [social and symbolic] capital presupposes an expenditure of time that is made possible by possession of economic capital' (Bourdieu, 1986: 214–258).

Culinary capital is therefore an investment of time in the present that involves labour/work and an eye to the future. Convenience foodways on the other hand are associated with instant gratification and 'lack' on many levels, which adds to its symbolic power and a politics of disgust (Tyler, 2013). Further, Bourdieu (1984: 176) identifies hedonism and being in the present as a quality associated with a working-class habitus, whilst investing in the future and abstaining from having a good time is associated with the petite bourgeoisie. In a secular age, at a time of heightened neo-liberalism, self-love/care or technologies of the self (Foucault, 1988) are ways of practising responsible individualism. These techniques of care, consumption and leisure are forms of cultural capital. Hence everyday foodways act as cultural artefacts that shape the dynamics of cultural reproduction; they become a means of performing/ displaying appropriate and/or legitimate subjective identities and social practices. Finally, 'food stories' have an affective symbolic power that can be used to elicit both pleasure and disgust. It is a preconceived cultural and classed knowledge of 'good' taste that allows the reader to feel repulsed by exploding fat balls and hunks of slimy spam, whilst imagining the sweet warmth of home-grown plums instantly appealing.

Table 7.1 Demographics

Pseudonym	A	Occupation	Quals	Living Arrangements
Carly	46	Consultant	Degree	Co-habiting
Dalia	50	Painter	P/G	Co-habiting
Ophelia	53	Author	GCSE*	Married +2 children
Olivia	37	PR manager	Degree	Co-habiting
Regan	43	Stay at home mum	A level	Married +2 children
Zoe	44	Recruiter	Degree	Married +2 children
Annie	50	Life coach	A level	Single +5 children
Imogen	36	P/T housekeeper	NVQ	Married +4 children
Magenta	39	Academic	P/G	Single
Nadia	40	Stay at home mum	GCSE*	Co-habiting +2 children
Paula	55	Food writer	GCSE*	Married + 2 children
Ursula	52	Stay at home mum	A level	Married +3 children
Drew	42	Senior manager	P/G	Married +1 child
Stephen	55	General practitioner	Degree	Married (+2 independent)
Ralph	55	Writer	HND	Single

Key: A = Age; Quals = Highest qualification; GCSE* = GCSE equivalent; P/G = Post-graduate qualification.

Notes

1 Pollan (2013) discusses cooking from scratch at some length, this is either 'to prepare a main dish that requires some assemblage of ingredients' or 'real scratch cooking', which is the kind of cooking that 'requires chopping onions ...' (129–130). Respondents' narratives can be located somewhere between these two extremes; mostly they did not engage in making all ingredients from scratch. They may have bought bread or vegetable stock, for example.
2 https://www.ons.gov.uk/methodology/classificationsandstandards/otherclassifications /thenationalstatisticssocioeconomicclassificationnssecrebasedonsoc2010.

References

Books and articles

Arendt, H. ([1929] 1996). *Love and Saint Augustine.* Chicago and London: The University of Chicago Press.

Belasco, W. (2008). *Food, The Key Concepts.* Oxford: Berg.

Bourdieu, P. (1984). *Distinction, a Social Critique of the Judgement of Taste.* London: Routledge.

Bourdieu, P. (1986). The Forms of Capital. In: Richardson, J. (Ed.) *Handbook of Theory and Research for the Sociology of Education.* New York: Greenwood, 241–258.

Butler, J. (1999). *Gender Trouble.* New York: Routledge.

Carolan, M. (2011). *Embodied Food Politics.* Farnham: Ashgate.

Coles, B. (2014). Making the Market Place, a Topography of Borough Market, London. *Cultural Geographies,* 21(3), 515–523.

Coles, B., and Crang, P. (2011). Placing Alternative Consumption: Commodity Fetishism in Borough Fine Foods Market, London. In: Lewis, T., and Potter, E. (Eds) *Ethical Consumption: A Critical Introduction.* London: Routledge, 87–102.

Counihan, M. (1999). *The Anthropology of Food and Body, Gender, Meaning and Power.* London: Routledge.

Douglass, M. (1966). *Purity and Danger, an Analysis of Pollution and Taboo,* London: Routledge.

Fox, R., and Smith, G., (2011). Sinner Ladies and the Gospel of Good Taste: Geographies of Food, Class and Care. *Health and Place,* 17(2), 403–412.

Foucault, M. (1988). Technologies of the Self. In: Martin, L. H., Gutman, H., and Hutton, P. H. (Eds) *Technologies of the Self: A Seminar with Michael Foucault.* London: Tavistock, 3–63.

Geertz, C. (1973). *The Interpretation of Cultures.* New York: Perseus Books.

Illingworth, N. (2006). Content, Context, Reflexivity and the Qualitative Research Encounter: Telling Stories in the Virtual Realm. *Sociological Research Online,* 11(1).

James, A., Kjorholt, A. T., and Tingstad, V. (2009). *Children, Food and Identity in Everyday Life.* London: Palgrave Macmillan.

James, A., and Curtis, P. (2010). Family Displays and Personal Lives. *Sociology,* 44(6), 1163–1180.

Kozinets, R. V. (2010). *Netnography, Doing Ethnographic Research Online.* London: SAGE.

Kralik, D., Koch, T., and Brady, B. (2000). Pen Pals: Correspondence as a Method for Data Generation in Qualitative Research. *Journal of Advanced Nursing,* 31(4), 909–917.

Letherby, G., and Zdrodowski, D. (1995). "Dear Researcher", the Use of Correspondence as a Method within Feminist Qualitative Research, *Gender & Society*, 9(5), 576–593.

Lupton, D. (1996). *Food, the Body and the Self.* London: SAGE.

Meah, A., and Watson, W. (2011). Saints and Slackers: Challenging Discourses about the Decline of Domestic Cooking. *Sociological Research Online*, 16(2), www.socre sonline.org.uk/16/2/6.html.

Mennell, S. (1985). *All Manners of Food.* Blackwell: Oxford.

Mills, C. W. (1959). *The Sociological Imagination.* London: Penguin.

Morgan, D. (1996). *An Introduction to Family Studies.* Cambridge: Polity Press.

Morgan, D. (2011). *Rethinking Family Practices.* Basingstoke: Palgrave Macmillan.

Morgan, D. (1998). Sociological Imaginations and Imagining Sociologies: Bodies, Auto/biographies and Other Mysteries. *Sociology*, 32(4), 647–663.

Naccarato, P., and LeBesco, K. (2012). *Culinary Capital.* London: Berg.

Parsons, J. M. (2014a). Cheese and Chips out of Styrofoam Containers: An Exploration of Taste and Cultural Symbols of Appropriate Family Foodways. *A Journal of Media and Culture*, 17(1), http://journal.media-culture.org.au/index.php/mcjournal/a rticle/viewArticle/766.

Parsons, J. M. (2014b). When Convenience is Inconvenient, 'Healthy' Family Foodways and the Persistent Intersectionalities of Gender and Class. *Journal of Gender Studies*, published online 20 December. doi:10.1080/09589236.2014.987656.

Parsons, J. M. (2015a). "Good" Food as Family Medicine: Problems of Dualist and Absolutist Approaches to "Healthy" Family Foodways. *Food Studies: An Interdisciplinary Journal*, 4(2), 1–13.

Parsons, J. M. (2015b). *Gender, Class and Food; Families, Bodies and Health.* Basingstoke: Palgrave Macmillan.

Parsons, J. M. (2015c). The Joy of Food Play – an Exploration of the Continued Intersectionalities of Gender and Class in Men's Auto/biographical Accounts of Everyday Foodways, Special Issue on Food. *Women, Gender and Research*, 24(4), 35–47.

Parsons, J. M. (2016). When Convenience is Inconvenient, 'Healthy' Family Foodways and the Persistent Intersectionalities of Gender and Class. *Journal of Gender Studies*, 25(4), 382–397.

Peterson, R. A., and Kern, R. M. (1996). Changing Highbrow Taste: From Snob to Omnivore. *American Sociological Review*, 61(5), 900–909.

Pollan, M. (2013). *Cooked, a Natural History of Transformation.* New York: Penguin.

Proust, M. ([1913] 2006). *Remembrance of Things Past, Volume 1.* Ware: Wordsworth Editions.

Risman, B. J. (2004). Gender as Social Structure: Theory Wrestling with Activism. *Gender and Society*, 18, 429–450.

Stanley, L., and Morgan, D. (1993). On Auto/biography in Sociology. *Sociology*, 27(1): 41–52.

Sutton, D. (2001). *Remembrance of Repasts, an Anthropology of Food and Memory.* Oxford: Berg.

Taylor, Y., and Falconer, E. (2015). Seedy Bars and Grotty Pints: Close Encounters in Queer Leisure Spaces. *Social and Cultural Geography*, 16(1), 43–57.

Tyler, I. (2013). *Revolting Subjects: Social Abjection and Resistance in Neoliberal Britain.* London: Zed Books.

Warde, A., Wright, D., and Gayo-Cal, M. (2007). Understanding Cultural Omnivorousness: Or the Myth of the Cultural Omnivore. *Cultural Sociology*, 1(2), 143–164.

West, C., and Zimmerman, D. H. (1987). Doing Gender. *Gender and Society*, 1(2), 125–151.

Wetherell, M. (2012). *Affect and Emotion, a New Social Science Understanding*. London: SAGE.

Wills, W., Backett-Milburn, K., Lawton, J., and Roberts M. L. (2009). Consuming Fast Food: The Perceptions and Practices of Middle Class Teenagers. In: James, A., Kjorholt, A. T., and Tingstad, V. (Eds) *Children, Food and Identity in Everyday Life*. London: Palgrave Macmillan, 52–68.

Archival

Beckett, F., Blythman, J., Ehrlich, R., Fort, M., Gluck, M., and Protz, R. (2002). Noshtalgia, *The Guardian*. Available from www.theguardian.com/ Beckettlifea ndstyle/2002/jun/29/foodanddrink.shopping1 [Accessed 5 February 2015].

Tedstone, A., Targett, V., Allen, R., and staff at Public Health England (PHE). (2015). Sugar Reduction, The Evidence for Action. Public Health England. Available from https://www.gov.uk/government/uploads/system/uploads/attachment_data/file/470179/ Sugar_reduction_The_evidence_for_action.pdf [Accessed 31 August 2016].

8 Our daily bread and onions

Negotiating tastes in family mealtime interaction

Sally Wiggins and Eric Laurier

Introduction: taste as twofold

Broadening the tastes of young children is a potential lifetime family project, a collaborative enterprise that shapes the domestic sensory world of food consumption. Expanding children's menus situates the act of tasting within a complex dance of testing, persuading, resisting, requesting and arguing; the building of a repertoire of foods that can be shared together. Eating and tasting new things is a central practice by which the family *becomes family* through orienting to current and previous shared experiences and displays of knowledge of its members' tastes. David Morgan, in his classic work on *doing* family, picks out knowledge of the food preferences of its members as central to producing and maintaining the family (Morgan, 2011).

Taste is itself a potentially confusing term because it can be used to refer to both the food preferences of the individual and family and, at the same time, the flavours of food. Within the family, food preferences are not routinely talked about as 'tastes' but instead as what the children (and parents) 'like' or 'don't like' and are built out of the 'taste' of the foods they are served. Children's preferences and the experience of flavours are as much a consolation and comfort as they are a source of discord and frustration (DeVault, 1991). Maintaining knowledge of family members' preferences involves monitoring, remembering and challenging what each likes and doesn't like, typically during the mealtime itself (Ochs and Shohet, 2006).

The family's shared tastes in combination with the individual favourites of each member are the central resources for the providers of the meal in determining what can be eaten and enjoyed together (DeVault, 1991; Moisio, Arnould and Price, 2004). As Ochs and Shohet (2006) argued, part of the moral expectations of family is that parents guide and establish children's tastes in a way that incorporates a variety of foodstuffs, textures and tastes (in the sense of flavour). Yet at the same time, parents are also guiding their children's food preferences as part of their cultural recognition of foods that are enjoyable or disgusting, healthy or unhealthy and so on (Parsons, 2015). Nowhere is the family's collective constructions of its tastes more clearly seen than at the point of consumption.

In this chapter we examine how children's tastes, in both senses of the word, become topicalised, investigated and occasionally contested by children and parents during the daily routine of family mealtimes. We focus on how children's tastes are formulated, made relevant and enacted in different ways. As such, we theorise taste as a sense-making device as much as a sense, to be examined for how it is collaboratively produced in family practices (Wiggins, 2014). Our aim in this chapter is not to begin with an assumption of what taste is and how it is affected by different contexts, but rather to end with an understanding of how tastes come to be established and used as part of the routine mealtime activities of families.

Our perspective on understanding taste arises out of ethnomethodological conversation analysis (EMCA) and discursive psychology. EMCA is an approach that seeks to understand members' methodical practices for organising their local affairs. It has examined sites, such as cheese shops, wine courses and cafes, where tasting foods is a central practice. Of most direct relevance to this chapter have been studies of family mealtimes through the central role that language has in constructing taste (Wiggins, 2002). What we now build on, however, is the turn towards the embodied, material aspects of the act of tasting. A shift that does not abandon language, but examines how language and non-verbal practices are intertwined in making sense of taste. For example, existing case studies have explored how cheese and coffee tasters rely upon and use the bodily and material practices of tasting (in its flavour sense) in making objective determinations about the coffee or cheese they are considering purchasing (on coffee – Liberman, 2013; on cheese – Mondada, 2018, Das and Plender, this volume, Chapter 10). For coffee, with taste descriptors on the tips of their tongues, they explore the flavours in the cup, remaining open to the poetry of flavours that they are encountering. For cheese, there are specific ways in which consumption is expected to take place during the sales process– where the customer is encouraged to feel the cheese before they eat and then the texture as it moves through the mouth and teeth as part of a performative ritual. This chewing is monitored and responded to by the seller while it unfolds moment by moment, the monitoring is then used to comment on flavour, texture and other qualities. Liberman (2013) and Mondada's (2018) work examines tasting as a collective enterprise where flavours are ventured, assessed, monitored, rejected and accepted through talking and tasting together.

In a similar vein, discursive psychology (DP) is an approach that examines how psychological constructs (such as food preferences) are invoked and made consequential in discursive practices and social actions (Edwards and Potter, 1992; Wiggins, 2017). For example, DP has identified the practices by which 'taste' is orientated towards and constructed as being a physiological or cognitive reaction, as something personal or cultural, and as within, or outside of, conscious control. With DP the focus is on taste as it is enacted within social interactions, rather than starting with an assumption that taste 'exists' in a particular form. DP scholars do not make claims about what people are individually 'experiencing' but instead examine how people themselves make taste relevant and how it is always already embroiled in other social actions, such as making an offer or a rejection of food. In examining a family meal-time in this chapter, we will consider how family members claim knowledge of each other's tastes, knowledge of the food they have eaten and whether and how experiences of flavour and taste preferences are responded to. Answering this question turns first to how children access and justify their tastes – despite their parents' objections – which diverge from those of adults (Wiggins, 2014). Secondly, how children's tastes become the focus of conversation: for inquir-ing into what is being eaten, what has and will be eaten now, in the past and on future occasions.

Collecting tastes

Our research involves documenting, on video, the everyday practices of eating in family homes. Over a number of years, we have recruited participants in England and Scotland to self-record their family meals using two video cam-eras; each positioned to record different angles around a dinner table (Laurier and Wiggins, 2011; Wiggins, 2014). Families record their meals over a period of around two weeks to become accustomed to the recording process and to include a range of different meals and discussions around the table. The video recordings are then transcribed and analysed using the approaches of DP and ethnomethodology. In this chapter, we will include two extracts from one family, recorded in the UK circa 2011. These were chosen because they exemplify the different ways in which taste can be invoked by parents and children, with two very different outcomes. The family comprises a mother, father and three children (here denoted by pseudonyms): Joseph (9 years old), Samuel (7 years old) and Emma (5 years old).

Negotiating tastes

In this section we present our empirical material, in graphic transcripts, for analyses and to demonstrate how, and when, children's preferences and experiences of flavour are negotiated at the dinner table. We will examine the turn-by-turn unfolding of tasting and eating practices, and provide the begin-nings of an inquiry into the intricate choreography of food, utensils and people. The two episodes each focus on a different child within the family. With the first, the child's negotiation of taste seems initially unproblematic though then evolves, whereas the second begins with a disagreement between the parents and child and we see how that is resolved.

Using 'different' to establish a taste

In our first episode, we demonstrate how the child's sampling of one parti-cular food item is collaboratively produced as acceptable by both the child

Figure 8.1 The first mention of the naan bread

and her mother. Over a series of turns, parent and child are involved in question and response paired actions that enable the shift from apparent uncertainty about the food to a definitive answer. Significantly, the establishment of the food assessment, and then potentially a new preference for the child, is based on the entitlement to do so by the act of having tried the food.

The family members are eating a range of dishes that have been prepared and cooked by the parents, and include dishes of curry, rice and naan bread. Our focus in this example is on 5-year-old Emma, sitting beside her Mum. Also present are Emma's Dad and her two older brothers. They have not long started eating, and Emma has been nibbling on a piece of naan bread that she took from the centre of the table. It is at this point that our extract begins, shown in Figure 8.1.

Emma's first mention of the naan bread follows a pattern of pre-announcement of 'news' (Terasaki, 2004): 'Mum see this naan bread' then announcement 'there's something different about it' about the food. She thus first nominates the recipient of her news (Mum) and the object (the naan bread), and *then* the news 'there's something different about it'. While it might seem to be a discovery about the naan bread it can also be heard as prefiguring an assessment of it. While Mum glances at Emma to show she has heard, she is busy at this point with a conversation that she is having with Dad about a different topic. It is only after an extended (three second) pause in her parent's conversation that Emma re-starts her report on the naan bread (see Figure 8.2).

On this occasion, Emma speaks but waits for a response from her Mum, who then responds verbally showing she is ready for whatever follows. Emma recycles her earlier statement – 'there's something different about the naan

Figure 8.2 The second mention of the naan bread

bread' – and looks directly at Mum with a slightly furrowed brow and a questioning expression on her face. What Emma repeats here is rather clever. Not only does her news focus attention on the bread as an independent object (rather than, say, her experience of it or how it tastes), she also frames this in a suitably vague manner: there is just 'something different' about it. It is not produced as her subjective 'like' or 'dislike', but as a statement of fact. Moreover, in producing her description Emma is claiming a right to be able to comment on the food and its objective character rather than as whether she likes it or not (Pomerantz, 1984).

The ingenuity of this report is in both how it is sequentially organised ahead of a next move, where she declares whether she likes or dislikes the taste of the bread, and how it removes Emma from being implicated in any problem that might arise as a result of this tentative assessment. She is neither beginning with a complaint, nor commenting on her own food preferences. Nor does she produce a negative assessment; at this stage in the conversation, the naan bread's character is merely raised as being noteworthy, as not yet decided upon. Even when Mum follows up the discussion with an 'Is there?' affirmation check (see Figure 8.3), Emma provides only a minimal 'Mhm' response to confirm the point. It is then the mother, not the child, who introduces the polar assessments of 'Good different or bad different?' The mother, consequently, did not have to begin by responding to a personal dislike expressed before, or during, the abandonment of eating the food.

Like the skilled moderators of focus groups (Puchta and Potter, 2002), Mum steers Emma's responses towards the identification of a clear assessment. Up until this point in the conversation, the food was treated according to its objective characteristics. It might not be out of place in a more formal environment, such as in product-testing at a food manufacturing plant or the judging in a baking contest. The introduction of the good/bad dichotomy by Mum, however, shifts the focus onto the implications of this assessment: if the difference is a positive one, then it could be a future staple of the family's food repertoire, if a 'bad' difference then it may never be purchased again. In directing the question to Emma, Mum also confers on Emma the authority to make the judgement on the bread. Or, at least, to provide *her* judgement. It is at this point, then, that Emma responds to Mum with not only a verbal

Figure 8.3 The good/bad question

Figure 8.4 Emma's response (first time)

response 'Bad different', but also an embodied display of a grimace and small shudder (see Figure 8.4).

While the embodied movements of Emma might appear pre-cognitive, they are clearly not direct physiological reactions or visceral sensations given they are offered post hoc. Indeed these gestures are sequentially positioned within this discussion about 'different' food where they make bodily assessment relevant. The focus on the naan bread could have ended at this point because soon after Emma's turn, Mum's attention moves to other matters at the table. However, Mum does not leave the topic of the naan entirely; she returns to it soon after (see Figure 8.5), and it is at this point that we get to the crux of the issue. The question is no longer whether it is 'good different or bad different', but rather 'Do you like it?'.

Again, despite the question slanted towards liking the bread from Mum, there is a second embodied negative assessment from Emma. Her delivery is skilful once more because she recycles Mum's question perhaps marking it as inattentive by doing so (given Emma had already shuddered). After her recycling she re-does the shudder. The shudder is then verbally formulated

Figure 8.5 Do you like it? Emma's response (second time)

here by Mum as a blunt 'No'. Perhaps surprisingly, this expression of Emma's dislike ends with a 'fair enough' comment from Mum, treating the dislike as a *fait accompli*. Despite Emma having begun with an objective characterisation of her tasting of the naan, it ends with her individual expression of taste. Not of the value of the food, or of its distinctiveness, but instead how this has relevance for Emma as a member of the family. Here perhaps we see the core of family's everyday concerns with taste and can begin to understand the domestic organisation of trying different foods. As we noted earlier, tasting and assessing foods within the family mealtime is a central resource for selecting the ingredients for future meals. Moreover, for Emma this new kind of naan has been established as a food dis-preference, one of which she may expect her parents to be aware.

Deconstructing risotto into likes and dislikes

In the first episode we examined how the tasting and experience of eating a food was initiated by the child as part of trying the food in question, and orienting to the food's qualities and individual preference was dealt with at the end of the sequence. In the second example, we will examine food preferences being raised by the parents as part of 'encouraging work' and a child's dismantling of his food to identify one of the ingredients that he dislikes (i.e. an established food preference); and the child's performance of struggling to eat the food in complying with his parents' requests. This second episode is thus a useful comparison to shed light on the different domestic trajectories within which tastes can feature within family mealtimes. We return to the same family during a different mealtime; this time they are concluding their main course of risotto. In the interaction below, Mum is seated to the right of the table, with her younger son and daughter seated either side of her. Her older son, Joseph, who will be our focus, sits beside his brother. Dad is seated next to his daughter with his back to the camera.

The plates on the table provide for the continuing mutual visibility of each family member's progress through their meal. They also allow for the mutual visibility of food left on the plate down to the detail of just what has not been eaten and by how much. They are not, of course, seen only once but rather glanced at by parents throughout meals to see quite how and what each child is eating, for example: 'you haven't touched your peas'. We begin our examination of this extract with a consideration of the immediately preceding context to the discussion of Joseph's taste preferences. In our case study, the continuing presence of risotto on Joseph's plate is a potential indicator of dislike (though it could also be taken by the parents to be an indication that their child is distracted or not hungry). Meanwhile, the rest of the family, apart from Dad, have all finished eating. Pursuing Joseph to eat his food when everyone is finished provides a different temporal context from pursuing him at the outset. In this part of the meal's temporal trajectory, the shared orientation is towards him finishing his food, rather than an initial

Figure 8.6 Mum makes two requests

appreciation of its taste (as was the case in the first episode). It is at this point in the meal that Mum makes a minimal request to Joseph (for example: 'Could you eat a bit more please') (see Figure 8.6) that attends to quantity of food to be eaten and inferentially to allow him to then have acceptably finished his main course. Attached to the request is a formulation of his problem as a behavioural one: the mildly sanctionable tuning out of dinner (staring into space) rather than, say, being distracted by telling stories of his day at school.

Joseph's response is a short, direct refusal 'Nah: I don't like it', made as a subject-side assessment (Wiggins and Potter, 2003), using the indexical 'it' rather than formulating what quality or ingredient of the food he does not like. Given Joseph is entitled to his likes and dislikes – just as Emma was in the previous example – there appears to be nothing directly challengeable, were it not, as we noted from the outset, that the ongoing work of parents is to widen the tastes of their children. While a food assessment like this can be challenged by parents (Wiggins, 2014), here, over two turns of talk, Mum pursues the food as something he should eat enough of, to count as having finished his food. What then becomes the concern is the 'more' that would be the criterion for him being finished.

Following the second request, Joseph upgrades his refusal, elongating the 'no' while shaking his head. The completion of Joseph's meal appears to be at a stalemate, with one person requesting (twice) and one person refusing (twice). Were Joseph and Mum to continue along this line, it might easily escalate into both sides becoming ever more entrenched in their positions. What happens instead is that Dad joins in with a response 'I'm surprised' and shifts the focus onto what Joseph has already been eating 'Have you had all the bacon?' (see Figure 8.7) A shift which might then also adjust Joseph's sense of what is left on the plate. It is at this point that Mum and Dad then begin to make claims about Joseph's food tastes and their relevance for the current meal.

Joseph's known tastes – and particularly, what 'he likes' – are then used as a way of trying to get him to reassess the remaining risotto. Mum lists out the various ingredients that are both in the risotto and liked by Joseph (bacon, peas and rice), and turns to Dad who confirms this summary of their son's food preferences. This pursuit of likes is a clear example of the way in which

Figure 8.7 What Joseph likes

parents invoke their knowledge of a child's tastes at just the right point in the meal, one where it is relevant for their local task of encouraging eating. In this episode, it is artfully produced as a dialogue between the parents about what Joseph likes rather than addressed directly to Joseph.

Their dialogue appears to succeed; after Dad mentions the bacon Joseph picks up his fork and begins a prolonged demonstration of his struggle by laboriously chewing and swallowing small morsels of food. His struggle with the risotto is accompanied by a negotiation between the parents and Joseph over the criterion for his completion: specifically, they request 'three more forkfuls' (additional dialogue). In his ensuing response, we see the careful attention from Joseph as to exactly what might count as a forkful and what contents of the fork need to be eaten to comply with the request. In Figure 8.8, we can see how Joseph re-examines the food and in response to his parents' deconstruction of the risotto into foods he likes, then raises his own ingredient dislike 'I don't like the onion bits' (see Figure 8.8). In contrast with gastronomic and professional tasting settings such as those in Fele and Giglioli (this volume, Chapter 3), or the studies into cheese and coffee referred to earlier, families typically do not draw upon detailed taste descriptors, for example, 'plum fruits' or 'tobacco', during the family meal. In part, this absence of specific descriptors may be because the family are not exploring new tastes or foods every day, nor are they consciously involved in the promotion of food consumption as a commodity or experience to be sold to discerning customers. What is noticeable about family talk about food is the formulations of its taste tend to be through ingredients – having nuts in, having onions in – rather than flavours, for example: 'nutty', 'oniony' or even more vague, as we documented earlier, for example, 'bad different'.

Figure 8.8 Negotiating units to succeed in finishing

Joseph's reference to 'the onion bits' neatly provides a reason for his apparent reluctance to eat the risotto and one that has the benefit of a commonly known challenging ingredient: onion. It also side-steps his apparent irrationality in declining the three liked ingredients that his parents used to challenge his dislike of risotto. In selecting the onion bits, he doesn't challenge his parents' claims about his tastes, nor does he contradict his earlier statement to 'not like it'. Instead, he reformulates and specifies the source of the trouble – the onion bits – that are present throughout the risotto. Just before Figure 8.8, Joseph had been playing around with his food, amusing his siblings and tipping food off his fork so that the smallest possible amount might be considered a 'forkful'. Just as Joseph is clearly focused on monitoring the food on his fork, so too are his parents. The skirmishes around the fork as a unit of the completion – as seen in Figure 8.8 – involve his parents calling out when the forkful is ready to be eaten 'right' or when it contains a sufficient amount 'full'. Joseph, however, calls attention to the 'onion bits' just as the fork is raised to his mouth. He then begins to micro-manage the fork's contents with his fingers, picking out certain pieces, and thereby embodying his dislike through his own actions. Dad continues to challenge Joseph on the amount that should be eaten, with another 'full!', while Mum quietly recognises the abiding problem in sighing before saying quietly the 'onion bits' (last panel of Figure 8.8).

At this point in the onion episode, then, the focus has shifted from a child not finishing his meal because of his dislike of the risotto to a more specific target. It is a particular food item (onion bits) within the risotto that has now been established as the source of the problem, and onions as a challenging taste for children also provides a stronger reason for why Joseph has not finished his plate. In the dialogue over likes and dislikes there is a marked difference from the first (naan bread) example, where the younger child is exploring a new food without stating whether it tasted good or bad. She was asked directly if she liked the food, and the negative response accepted this 'Fair enough' without further comment or negotiation. By contrast, the issue in this example is the centrality of the food to the main part of the meal and its recognisable and acceptable completion: risotto is the family's main source of nutrition in this meal, not an optional side dish (as with a new variety of naan bread). The stakes are therefore higher, and the parent's reaction of a more intense and exasperated manner. If Joseph is allowed to not like – and by implication, not have to eat the risotto – then he is exempt from the communal meal and may also seek different food later on. Understanding how tastes are invoked at the table, then, is not simply whether people like or do not like food. It is about how tastes are invoked by either parents or children as part of trying or completing, of main dishes or side dishes and how accepting any member's dislike of a dish or ingredient shapes what the family will dine on in future meals.

We will finish by examining what happens in the moments immediately following the forking of the risotto and the claimed dislike of the onion bits. There are continued efforts on Joseph's part to remove the pieces of onion and to negotiate with his parents about exactly how much more should be eaten. In a reversal of the norm of parents setting the measure for completion (Orrell-Valente et al., 2007), Joseph suggests that he has 'three more forkfuls'. He then proceeds to display a dramatic enactment of the effort involved in completing the task. Joseph engages in a prolonged performance of chewing each forkful of food, fixed eye gaze towards Mum and holding up fingers to visibly count each forkful as it is eaten (second panel, Figure 8.9).

Figure 8.9 The imperception of onions and counting forkfuls

In the face of Joseph's forensic inspection of his risotto, which will pre-sumably find fragments of onion, Mum further points out onion figures in the dish as an un-noticeable, and essential, element. Mum also has the cook's knowledge of how often she has served dishes to Joseph where he has not noticed onions present. Joseph reports no additional food flavours nor does he comment again on his tastes, but his embodied display of oral labour – the prolonged and exaggerated chewing – does the work for him. For a dish that barely requires chewing (it contains small pieces of food, typically cooked until soft or *al dente*), it is a wonderfully absurd display of effort. While Dad does not appear to be watching directly, Mum gazes attentively at Joseph's act of defiance, verging on irritation. It is notable that Joseph directs his perfor-mance and his counting to Mum, even though Dad has been involved in enforcing the fork-units earlier (his 'right' in Figure 8.8).

After Figure 8.8 ends, the conversation about Joseph's noticing of onions and their status in a number of dishes is again picked up by Mum and Dad – in overlap with Joseph's continued display of chewing and swallowing the risotto. They proceed to inform Joseph of the many times that onions have formed the basis of some of their regular meals (for example: spaghetti bolognese, curries) that he has eaten on previous occasions. Dad notes that, not only has Joseph consumed these dishes (and by implication, the ingredients therein), but he also 'likes' them. Claims by the children themselves, and by their parents, as to what they like (perhaps more than what they dislike) maintain and transform what is eaten. They are central in the reasoning over what and how much children should and do eat. What we begin to see in these episodes of a family eating together is therefore how children's tastes and the qualities of distinct categories of food (for example, exotic bread, common onions) are further refined to justify their consumption (or lack of consumption) on a continual basis. In the family meal's daily repetition there are always more opportunities for parents or children to make taste relevant and to use this as a resource in shaping what, how much and how foods are consumed at mealtimes.

Conclusion

Our approach to the affective nature of taste is one that situates it firmly within the domestic space and event that is the family meal, where the act of both providing and eating food is at the heart of the occasion. Taste is therefore understood here as a collaboratively produced social phenomenon, one that emerges in a close reading of shuddering and of forking risotto and how these actions are closely monitored and responded to. The public and unfolding dis-play of taste by children and parents echoes what happens during the chewing of artisan cheese by customers in Mondada's (2018) study of the multi-sensoriality of tasting. It is the complexity and vibrancy of food's flavours and textures that makes it a source of pleasure and dread (Mol, 2009). Our analysis has pursued how and when both the food preferences of the individual and the sensory qualities of the food are invoked in the course of the family meal, and how assessing food and establishing likes and dislikes are reflexively tied to the unfolding dynamics of the family's shared and differentiated eating practices. As we argued from the outset, EMCA and DP do not start with an assumption about what 'taste' is and how it is affected by situation or environment, but rather how tastes are inescapably shaping and shaped by social interactions (Ochs and Shohet, 2006; Mondada, 2018; Wiggins, 2014). Shifting away from taste as a fixed individual preference, we examined likes and dislikes as they are produced, shared, contested and drawn upon by other persons in the midst of activities such as trying new foods or finishing the main course.

Shifting from an object-side focus on the sensual qualities of particular flavours, to the changing preferences of children, their likes and dislikes, as they are discussed and disputed by children and parents, this shift has ongoing implications for what gets eaten and by whom. We have examined just two brief events in the mealtimes of the same family in which the particular preferences of children become a topic of discussion and conflict. In our first episode, we saw how one child's 'dislike' of a food was produced as a consequence of a sequence of question and answer responses involving embodied assessments which begin and end in a certain format. Child and mother establish Emma doesn't like that *type* of naan bread. In the second example, the parents repeatedly made claims using the preferences and past actions of Joseph that they know as his parents. The claims made by both the parents and the child are in the midst of establishing the amount of food that should be eaten and encouraging him to eat. In Joseph's case, we saw how the tasting and deconstruction of risotto with his fork are inextricably bound up with how the dish itself is being constructed as a 'flavour', yet also a rejection of onions, a rejection which his parents are not prepared to straightforwardly allow. It is one occasion amongst many where his personal preferences connect and clash with shared cultural knowledge of onion's utility in many staple family dishes; to allow it to be rejected entirely would have grave limitations on the future of their mealtimes.

It is important, then, to consider these familiar episodes as not exceptional nor anecdotal, but as the occasions where we can begin to understand how 'likes' and 'dislikes' are produced, maintained and transformed within social interactions (Ochs and Shohet, 2006; Mondada, 2018; Wiggins, 2014). As DeVault (1991) argued, the business of feeding the family on a daily basis rests on gaining and using knowledge of the family's changing and, at times, unpredictable tastes. Discovering what its members like and dislike is central to feeding the family without throwing unwanted food away (Cappellini and Parsons, 2013) while, at the same time, retaining the enjoyment and desirability of eating together as a family. Taste as flavour, then, becomes dependent on taste as a culturally meaningful preference rather than a private inaccessible experience. Each conversation with its accompanying shudders and chewing is then used to help shape current and future meals of the family, and also frame past 'likes'. Through recognising and demonstrating knowledge of our family members' tastes, we also display family membership: as Morgan (2011) would say, we 'do' being a family through these very practices.

References

Cappellini, B., and Parsons, E. (2013). Practising thrift at dinnertime: Mealtime leftovers, sacrifice and family membership. *Sociological Review*, 60, 121–134.

DeVault, M. (1991). *Feeding the Family*. London: University of Chicago Press.

Edwards, D., and Potter, J. (1992). *Discursive Psychology*. London: SAGE.

Laurier, E., and Wiggins, S. (2011). Finishing the family meal. The interactional organisation of satiety. *Appetite*, 56(1), 53–64.

Liberman, K. (2013). *More Studies in Ethnomethodology*. Albany, NY: SUNY Press.

Moisio, R., Arnould, E. J., and Price, L. L. (2004). Between mothers and markets: Constructing family identity through homemade food. *Journal of Consumer Culture*, 4(3), 361–384.

Mol, A. (2009). Good taste. *Journal of Cultural Economy*, 2(3), 269–283.

Mondada, L. (2018). The multimodal interactional organization of tasting: Practices of tasting cheese in gourmet shops. *Discourse Studies*, 20(6), 743–769.

Morgan, D. (2011). *Rethinking Family Practices*. Basingstoke: Palgrave Macmillan.

Ochs, E., and Shohet, M. (2006). The cultural structuring of mealtime socialization. *New Directions for Child and Adolescent Development*; Special Issue: Family Mealtime as a Context of Development and Socialization, 111, 35–49.

Orrell-Valente, J. K., Hill, L. G., Brechwald, W. A., Dodge, K. A., Pettit, G. S., and Bates, J. E. (2007). "Just three more bites": An observational analysis of parents' socialization of children's eating at mealtime. *Appetite*, 48(1), 37–45.

Parsons, J. M. (2015). "Good" food as family medicine: Problems of dualist and absolutist approaches to "healthy" family foodways. *Food Studies: An Interdisciplinary Journal*, 4(2), 1–13.

Pomerantz, A. (1984). Agreeing and disagreeing with assessments: Some features of preferred/dispreferred turn shapes. In: Atkinson, J. and Heritage, J. (Eds) *Structures of Social Action*. Cambridge: Cambridge University Press, 57–101.

Puchta, C., and Potter, J. (2002). Manufacturing individual opinions: Market research focus groups and the discursive psychology of evaluation. *British Journal of Social Psychology*, 41(3), 345–363.

Terasaki, A. K. (2004). Pre-announcement sequences in conversation. In: Lerner, G. H. (Ed.) *Conversation Analysis: Studies from the First Generation*. Online: John Benjamins Publishing, https://doi.org/10.1075/pbns.125.11ter, 171–223.

Wiggins, S. (2002). Talking with your mouth full: Gustatory mmms and the embodiment of pleasure. *Research on Language and Social Interaction*, 35(3), 311–336.

Wiggins, S. (2017). *Discursive Psychology: Theory, Method and Applications*. London: SAGE.

Wiggins, S. (2014). Adult and child use of love, like, don't like and hate during family mealtimes. Subjective category assessments as food preference talk. *Appetite*, 80, 7–15.

Wiggins, S., and Potter, J. (2003). Attitudes and evaluative practices: Category vs. item and subjective vs. objective constructions in everyday food assessments. *British Journal of Social Psychology*, 42(4), 513–531.

Part IV

Atmospheric tastes

Affect, design and creative space

9 Curating pop-up street food markets in London

Paz Concha

Pop-up street food markets, which have seen a surge in popularity in the city of London, UK, are a distinctive case study in which to demonstrate how cultural intermediaries use their understanding of taste, culture and aesthetics to create an experience of place and a particular identity for a cultural scene. In this chapter, I analyse how market organisers design pop-up street food markets; I refer to the idea of curation to describe how their job entails defining a set of preferable qualities in order to produce the 'right' atmosphere for the markets. Curation of street food markets usually entails organising and administering different forms of cultural knowledge and managing different aspects and actors in the organisation of markets across the city. Market organisers have developed a vision about what these places are supposed to be and feel; and draw upon specific markers of taste (Bourdieu, 1984) and affective atmospheres to curate places mainly for eating and socialising, creating festive environments for people to spend many more hours consuming.

Market organisers draw upon specific markers of taste and embodied knowledge- – both economic and cultural – to conduct various curatorial designs and make business decisions. Economic knowledge entails understanding consumer's choice and creating atmospheres from a marketing perspective as 'the quality of space "around" … described in sensory terms' (De Farias, Aguiar, and Melo, 2014: 88); using aesthetic and sensorial elements to enhance the experience of consumption and, ultimately, a sense of identity and belonging. Additionally, their social and cultural embodied knowledge involves curating markets as similar to 'staging atmospheres' (Bille, Bjerregaard and Sørensen, 2015), or as a way of 'place-making' by creating social experiences in which certain boundaries are drawn to include or exclude a specific classed audience (Benson and Jackson, 2013).

The findings of this chapter originate from an ethnography conducted in 2014 and 2015, as part of my PhD thesis (Concha, 2017), to describe the work of Vibes Feast,[1] a company that organises night markets in different areas in London, namely Dalston, Lewisham and Battersea. During ethnographic fieldwork, I have conducted observation at these markets and participant observation during four months in 2014 working with a food trader at the Dalston and Lewisham site. I have also conducted seven interviews with market organisers at Vibes Feast and other similar companies. I use this case study to illustrate how market organisers practically curate these markets to achieve the desired affective experience, using taste distinctions and economic and cultural knowledge. Focusing on the case study of Vibes Feast, I follow the decision-making process needed to curate such a market, considering factors such as the location, aesthetics, picking particular food traders, creating the 'right' atmosphere and defining and facilitating the inclusion of the desired clientele. I begin by defining what I term 'tasted places'. This description is twofold: first, it examines the sensorial dimension of the culinary experience on offer – the innovative, hybridised and exciting cuisines, the smells and sounds of cooking and the embodied experience of eating alongside the carefully crafted décor of the market – which amalgamates a romanticised notion of past (often working-class) market traders with a chic, urban aesthetic to create 'character'. Here the concept of taste moves beyond the culinary appeal of the food and drink on offer, to incorporate Bourdieu's (1984) theories of taste and distinction, where what is 'tasteful' is often predetermined by the powerful classes and is in continuous flux. Examining the curation of pop-up street food markets in London contributes to a far broader understanding of the complex practice of generating tasted places of consumption, those that have been purposefully curated to exclude a non-middle-class or non-upper-middle-class audience.

Night markets as tasted places

This market in Lewisham dates from the 1950s when a diverse selection of local traders used to sell everyday food products, flowers, records and offer TV repairs and hairdressing in a semi-covered space near Lewisham Station. The market used to have two entrances and a path in the middle serving as a shortcut between Lewisham High Street and the shopping centre. Shops such as card and poster shops; Hungry Tums Bistro, J and M Flowers, Kidsworld, Morps Music, Romarc Shipping and Travel, Black Beauty Cosmetics and Hair Accessories closed in 2011 when the place was bought by the urban development company Land Securities, also owner of next-door Lewisham Shopping Centre. In 2014, Vibes Feast, a company that organises night markets in London, signed a short-term lease with the developers to refurbish and re-open the space as a street food market. They refurbished, cleaned and re-built part of the setting to create a main bar area and seating area and added fittings and equipment in the old shop units to transform them into food stalls. The market maintains its layout with two paths that lead to a central patio; the stores are still placed in the paths closed with roll up doors where graffiti and old paintings remain. These paths, food units, seating spaces and other micro-dining areas create a labyrinth that customers can explore, while adding a new aesthetic element to the Lewisham Market.

In the summer of 2014, I travelled to Lewisham every weekend to work with a food trader – Marcy – selling Malaysian burgers. The stall is located inside the old Morp's Music record store, right next to the Market entrance. We share the unit space with another trader selling Mexican vegetarian food. Next to our unit is the old Jerk chicken shop, now occupied by a young jerk chicken entrepreneur. The Brownie Bar is in front of us inside the TV repairs store and writes in the window front 'Installation, wholesaler, digital receivers, repairs, TV, video, DVD, brownies and coffee'. The lightning signs and the stalls' names combine the names of the old stores creating a multiplicity of writing, fonts and messages at a first glance. Each stall incorporates an aesthetic from the original market set up, branding and decor. A 'staged authenticity' (MacCannell, 1973) of times gone past is preserved, capitalising on an atmosphere of nostalgia, exemplified in the Italian micro-diner which has been decorated with different olive' jars, ham legs and kitchen utensils.

When the market opens at 5pm, customers begin to arrive to get their hands stamped by a hostess. First to arrive are young families; parents with one or two small children. Background music is sounding, bars are open and most traders are ready to serve. Before 7pm the entrance is free, after that time there is an entry charge of £4 per person. At the beginning of the evening the place is quieter and it's easier to find a seat. After a few hours people start queuing to get in and security limits the amount of people coming in. Soon the area is packed, and customers stand in crowds in both paths, queuing to buy food and drinks from the various stalls and bars. Traders are now cooking and serving rapidly; the air smells of fried chicken, spices and smoke, and the noise of sizzling pans reverberates around the market. Customers wander past perusing the stalls and bars, and reading the signs and hanging menus with the steep prices. Marcy's offer of mini Malaysian burgers seems attractive: three for £10. Customers stop and enquire about the food: 'What is it? What is in it? Or what's the taste like?' Marcy attempts to explain the flavour without words, pointing in a friendly way to the little sample burgers prepared, located at the front of the stall. Most traders sell small portions of their own take on street food or ethnic food, like Korean or vegan tacos, mac and cheese, grilled sandwiches, organic steak and chips and bao buns among others. Although the food offering is diverse, the quality of ingredients and high price for small samples is a commonality. The place is pounding with loud music, customers chatting and laughing, the sounds from the kitchen, traders shouting orders and the same music playlist, which can be heard every weekend, repeats the melodies of 'Red, Red wine' from UB40. People take pictures of their food and drinks, of the crowds and selfies for their Instagram accounts. The party atmosphere continues into the night, and the crowds walk, talk and eat standing in groups and huddles.

How to curate pop-up street food markets

The idea of curation – a term commonly used by market organisers when describing their work – is an interesting analytical tool to understand how market organisers create affective spaces of consumption. When curating street food markets, their job is to conceptualise and create places with particular qualities, where the atmospherics or sensorial aspects of place are highlighted to create a unique consumption experience (Concha, 2017). Curation (Joosse and Hracs, 2015) in these markets usually involves calculating or defining a set of preferable qualities (Callon, Méadel, and Rabeharisoa, 2002; Entwistle, 2009) that they would like to promote at their markets by using different kinds of economic, aesthetic and socio-cultural knowledge. For example, economic knowledge is required to evaluate the practicalities and cost of finding the right urban space and venue, capitalising on knowledge of experiential marketing to transform the atmosphere of such spaces and using the concept of taste to define the aesthetics and target audience they wish to attract to their markets.

Market organisers develop a vision about what these spaces are supposed to be and feel like to consumers. In this case, organisers reflect on the particular aesthetic of taste and taste making (Bourdieu, 1984) to curate spaces designed for eating artisan and global-fusion style cooked foods and socialising, creating festive atmospheres that contribute to relaxation and enjoyment, with the intention that people will spend many more hours in the place consuming. Through this curatorial work, market organisers are constantly defining the street food scene as a particular kind of consumption experience. They define the scene interpreting how street food markets should be, and how to differentiate them from other commercial or retail places. These places need to have distinguishable characteristics in order to create a brand and to replicate this style or concept in various locations running simultaneously. In this sense, an important aspect of their curatorial work is to use material and immaterial or sensorial elements to create a distinguishable atmosphere of consumption. In this sense, curators work as cultural intermediaries by 'generating and legitimating new taste regimes' (Smith Maguire and Matthews, 2012: 23). As *taste makers* (Bourdieu, 1984), they 'perform the tasks of gentle manipulation' of taste (Bourdieu, 1984: 365). By following the practices of these curators, this research contributes to understanding how taste is developed and expressed and how cultural capital and subjective dispositions are linked with their jobs or occupations (Nixon, 2006) and cultivated in their everyday life as 'aesthetic dispositions' (Bourdieu, 1984: 141).

In the marketing literature, concepts like store atmospherics, sensory marketing or experiential marketing as well as brand experience (Kotler, 1973; Brakus, Méadel, and Rabeharisoa, 2009; Holbrook and Hirschman, 1982) are used to describe the idea of stimulating consumer's senses. This objective is achieved through organising material elements in retail spaces (architecture, decoration, aesthetics) and other immaterial elements that enhance the experience of consumption (light, colours, music, smells, movement through place or the relationship between staff and customers) in order to create a memorable and pleasant atmosphere. In this literature, the concept of atmosphere is understood as 'quality of space' (De Farias et al.,

2014) and described through sensory elements like smell, touch, vision and sound; retail spaces are designed to ignite consumers' cognitive, emotional and sensual levels of engagement. De Farias et al. (2014) claim that creating atmospheres in retail spaces should not be done informally or intuitively, but as a serious marketing strategy and careful design, and should not be 'relegated to secondary discussions, as a result of choices made by architects and decorators' (De Farias et al., 2014: 88). In this sense, creative retail professionals are essential for the design of retail spaces; in this process their personal involvement in the creation of these spaces implies using their past experience and cultural capital, as well as their participation in social networks in different fields (Kent, 2007) to incorporate new or innovative elements to retail spaces.

However, curating pop-up street food markets is also a way of 'staging atmospheres', in terms of purposively using these material, aesthetics and sensorial elements to design social experiences for an intended audience. Bille et al. (2015) discuss the idea of atmosphere and its role in shaping social life, as a 'fundamental aspect of the human experience of the world ... an important part of the identities and conceptualisations of landscapes, architecture and homes' (Bille et al., 2015: 31). Besides the ontological and philosophical discussions on the concept of 'atmosphere' and its definitional vagueness, these authors draw on Böhme (1995) to define atmosphere as the 'in between' of experiences and environments, as the connection between 'people, places and things' (Bille et al., 2015: 33). More specifically, these authors highlight the importance of understanding the process of 'staging atmospheres' as a mechanism to direct social interaction in particular living environments. This raises the issue that a 'feel of a place', or a 'tasted place' can be purposively created, manipulated, orchestrated, designed or produced by organising its different constituent elements (people, place and things), aiming to create particular social situations which, for example, invite or exclude certain audiences. In the case of the Lewisham Market and Vibes Feast, these audiences appeal to a particular cohort of Londoners and visitors, often those young, middle-class professionals who possess a high degree of economic and cultural capital, and who have been the focus of countless critiques of urban gentrification; how the middle classes make use of space and displacement of working-class communities (Benson and Jackson, 2013).

Suggesting that atmospheres can be staged shifts the focus from an abstract, perceived vagueness to an analysis of design and intentional performativity. Here we focus on how atmospheres are carefully created and subsequently experienced, and for what purpose. Preconceived and deep rooted social and economic assumptions (Sloane, 2014) play out in the work of designers, marketers or producers to create a sense of place. The design of the new Lewisham Market is an example of how market organisers as curators use different kinds of knowledge and assumptions to make business decisions, navigating a complex network of actors and interests to set up successful pop-up street food markets.

Location and character

There are multiple elements to curating successful pop-up street food markets. A crucial start is to secure the right kind of venue. Organisers identify the right venue as an ideal combination of location (preferably non-residential, easy access to public transport, footfall), infrastructure (electricity, water, covered spaces, enough square feet), aesthetic elements and 'character'. All these elements combined make this search for appropriate places a complex process; the curatorial process begins by making economic calculations, to run a less expensive operation and bringing in enough customers to their markets, and also cultural calculations to develop their market concept or brand.

In terms of location, market organisers need to find spaces where a short-term lease would allow them to cover the cost of refurbishing the place and get profit during the planned season, usually four or five months during the summer. They also need to evaluate places beyond the practicalities of location and infrastructure for service. To create a festive atmosphere, something that these organisers call 'Vibes', Vibes Feast recognise the necessity of having a place with atmospheric 'character'. This often seems to be a place with a sense of history, abandoned and unoccupied spaces with what they call 'residual features' of occupation, like exposed pipes or old fittings. They use these aesthetic features as foundational elements to build the market around; an empty space with the right infrastructure, size or location is not necessarily suitable unless it holds these multiple elements of 'character' and 'vibes'. In an interview, Alan – one of Vibes Feast's organisers – says 'character' needs to feel 'not like purposed built', but as a new environment that customers can feel curious about and want to explore. He explains:

> It's cool, because there's lots of people kind of exploring and there's lots of, most places you go to you have that kind of feeling that it's kind of purpose built for what they're doing, these building that we occupy they are places that you can't go most of the time, it's a new environment I think where you really get to explore empty warehouses, that kind of thing, there's a feeling that you're in a forgotten place, it's kind of cool, it's exciting, you're exploring the hidden archaeology of the city.
>
> (Alan, Vibes Feast)

Traders

Besides location and 'character', picking traders that offer good food and service is another essential task to curate successful markets. Market organisers are interested in bringing in quality traders that can deliver creative preparations, special or limited versions of their dishes or test new recipes at their markets. According to Alan 'it can't be just stuck in buns', it has to be something innovative like seafood or vegetarian dishes. The quality of traders includes their personality and ability to serve and sell the pitch of their business and the market. Organisers are looking for traders who can perform this form of affective labour (Hochschild, 1983; Entwistle and Wissinger, 2006), engaging customers with a smile and a story. In the case of a market in Lewisham, Vibes Feast was consciously aware of the need to bring local traders to the market; this was their first market south of the river and curating for the local people of Lewisham meant bringing local traders as well.

Alan comments on the process of selecting traders for their night markets, starting by choosing 'the big hitters first' and then local traders to finally incorporate some 'new talent coming up', meaning bringing new traders to trial their product at their markets. The company creates an A, B and C list of traders 'based on how Vibes Feast they are'; those in list A or 'Premier League traders' as they call them are those with 'good food and good people'; for example, Alan mentions a trader with a 'cool' brand that has been making an effort to fit in with their night markets operation and bought a very expensive neon sign; they prefer this kind of trader, those who want to stand out, fit in and be seen. In this sense, assessing food traders' vision or 'entrepreneurial flair' is important to find the right fit for their markets. Market organisers look for traders with similar working practices, or what Alan calls same kind of *'mentality'*, meaning someone who wants to keep improving and modernising their business. In this case, the selection of mainly young and educated traders has a significant impact in generating a familiar and comfortable atmosphere for an upper-middle-class, cosmopolitan audience. It becomes increasingly clear that creating the right 'vibes' becomes code for an atmospheric design that is attuned to the desires of this particular urban demographic.

Atmosphere

To focus on the generation of atmospheres is to explore the connection between 'subjectivity and place' (Gandy, 2017). In the theoretical literature on affect, atmospheres are considered an 'indeterminate affective "excess" through which intensive space-times can be created' (Anderson, 2009: 80). This has been conceptualised as our 'body's capacity to act, to engage, and to connect' (Ticineto Clough, 2007: 2) with place. A focus on affective atmospheres allows us to examine how our agency impacts the world surrounding us and also how we are impacted by it, looking not only at cognitive reasoning but to bodily dispositions (Leys, 2011) and emotions. Affective atmospheres are an experience that has a role in the formation of subjectivity (Gandy, 2017; Seigworth and Gregg, 2010) because it connects with belonging and non-belonging (Seigworth and Gregg, 2010) to particular places. As evidenced in our discussion of the Lewisham Market thus far, affective qualities of place can be orchestrated to attract certain subjectivities, and therefore to prevent others from participating in them. As mentioned by Anderson (2009), atmospheres are dynamic and continually forming and changing. For this reason, the work of professionals in fields such as interior design, landscaping or architecture are important in how atmospheres: 'Are circumvented and circulate. By creating and arranging light, sounds, symbols, texts and much more, atmospheres are "enhanced", "transformed", "intensified", "shaped", and otherwise intervened' (Anderson, 2009: 80).

Therefore, the role of market curators is important in maintaining and reinforcing certain qualities of place to preserve atmospheric qualities and audiences in their street food markets.

In the case of Vibes Feast, Alan claims that their market's key concept is to create a festive atmosphere through the combination of different activities, aesthetics and 'vibes' in one place. They design the layout of their places by creating 'micro-spaces', like different kinds of bars (rum bar, wine bar, whisky bar and beer bar), micro-diners (small places with seating at some traders' stalls) or special lighting and music to differentiate spaces within the market. The curation of multiple and juxtaposed atmospheres in street food markets can be described as a form of place making; in this case, they create places that (certain) customers can explore and discover, making their visit more fun and enjoyable, which also contributes to the length of stay and maximises the possibilities of consumption. They lay out the place in a way that facilitates socialising, such as the use of communal tables and chairs, props on which to place plates and drinks while standing or booths for four or five people that serve as private dining spaces.

Organisers ensure the aesthetic of the market, and the different areas reflect each traders' design elements: utensils hanging around, jars with raw ingredients and lit up signs, some of them in neon with bright colours. There are also immaterial, non-visual elements that market organisers curate: for example, they pay special attention to the music, having DJs and speakers in different areas playing different playlists at different volumes to customise the micro-spaces in the market. The music amalgamates with other elements like lighting, from bulbs to candles, to create the desired affects. In open areas, fires inside oil drums provide improvised heating, and customers usually gather around if the night is cold. As for the sensorial qualities of the food, these night markets are usually filled with the fumes and smells from barbecuing meat and the cooking and frying food; customers can explore the market by watching the preparation of the dishes and try the samples that most traders provide. Customers can experience the cooking process and evaluate close hand size, colour, smell and service.

To achieve the intended 'vibe' in their markets, curators make constant changes and adjustments according to consumer response, like rotating traders every month to keep the offers fresh and enticing, or re-converting some of their micro-spaces for a different purpose – for example, allowing a sponsored brand to dedicate a particular section of the market to advertise their products. For instance, in 2015 when Lewisham Market opened for a second season, a new open terrace, the 'Lewisham Highline', (a take on New York City's highly fashionable 'Highline') was built with a seating space and artificial grass, with a dedicated bar selling buckets of Sol beer. For these markets, organisers create a particular 'vibe' which includes the festive and socialising 'character' of place; this role requires their particular curatorial skills to create this central combination in a consistent way when opening new markets in different locations. Most summers they run markets simultaneously in two or more areas. Although the different places are not identical to one another, they share a similar atmosphere that gives Vibes Feast its recognised identity as a market organiser. Alan comments that they were once asked to provide some sole traders for a night market next to Battersea Power Station, but refused on the premise that their brand 'isn't just a franchise, it's a kind of vibe, it's gotta have a certain kind of atmosphere ... it has to feel kind of festival atmosphere, has to be done our way and have our signature on everything'.

Audience

Vibes Feast makes subtle adaptations when curating night markets in different locations for their imagined customers: more 'sophisticated' for the West End crowd in the case of their site in Battersea Power Station, where they added a Champagne Bar, or more 'local' for the people in the Lewisham Market. They also mention that they would like to create a place that they themselves would want to frequent, using their own markers of taste and networks as a point of reference for the kind of clientele that is expected in these markets. In places like Dalston (Hackney, East London), they know that given its more central location people might come from different parts of the city, but in Lewisham, they curate the place as a 'local'. However on closer inspection, in the interview narrative during Alan's interview there is not a clear definition of what the 'local' means or an explicit description of 'what kind' of local customers they are expecting to bring. According to Lewisham Council:

> The Indices of Multiple Deprivation 2011 show that the area covering Lewisham town centre is among the 20% most deprived areas within England ... The borough is the 15th most ethnically diverse local authority in England, with the overall population from a black and/or minority ethnic origin at 47%.
>
> (Lewisham Council, 2014: 10)

These particular 'local' groups or general considerations about the deprivation of the borough are not mentioned by Alan during the interview when describing Lewisham and its 'locals'. In this sense, their curatorial work defines contained places with distinguishable qualities, and serves to demarcate clear boundaries which only particular 'kinds' of people are welcome to cross; namely younger customers with disposable income in each area. A focus on largely white, upper-middle-class consumption reinforces the 'right' atmospheric qualities and 'vibe' of this market, and like many areas of

London's redevelopment sets symbolic boundaries that work to exclude other customers (Benson and Jackson, 2013).

Conclusion

In this chapter I have analysed the curatorial practices of market organisers when arranging night markets with a specific atmosphere. In the case of the curation of Vibes Feast night market, organisers have put together different elements to create carefully designed affects that give Vibes Feast its identity and feel; as well as curating for a specific clientele, meaning re-branding some of the original aesthetic elements of the place (capitalising on a sense of nostalgia and 'character'), bringing in food traders and staff from the local area or setting up special themed bars. Assumptions about their imagined customers are integral to this curated atmosphere, and are used to create a space where both culinary and aesthetic tastes are designed to attract a very specific audience to each area. These 'tasted places' are equally, if not more so, as effective at filtering the 'correct' clientele as the material boundaries of Lewisham Market, such as setting prices and controlling the entrance to the site. Their curatorial focuses on designing consumption experiences as in sensorial marketing, but also in 'staging atmospheres' (Bille et al., 2015) in built environments, where their cultural and social knowledge about the area are crucial to the decision-making process. The process of curating pop-up street food markets is an interesting case study to illustrate how cultural and economic decisions are intertwined with concepts of 'taste' in cultural economies. This chapter focuses on how markets are carefully designed to shape the experience of place; transforming local spaces according to the market organisers' perceptions of culinary and aesthetic taste. It is fair to say that the curation of street food markets exposes a process of value generation that creates a particular cultural scene that continues to transform places in a context of rapid urban change in London.

Note

1   The names of the companies and research participants have been changed to protect their anonymity.

References

Anderson, B. (2009). Affective Atmospheres. *Emotion, Space and Society*, 2, 77–81.

Benson, M., and Jackson, E. (2013). Place-making and Place Maintenance: Performativity, Place and Belonging among the Middle Classes. *Sociology*, 47(4), 793–809.

Bille, M., Bjerregaard, P., and Sørensen, T. F. (2015). Staging Atmospheres: Materiality, Culture, and the Texture of the In-between. *Emotion, Space and Society*, 15, 31–38.

Bourdieu, P. (1984). *Distinction: A Social Critique of the Judgement of Taste*. London: Routledge and Kegan Paul.

Brakus, J., Schmitt, B., and Zarantonello, L. (2009). Brand Experience: What Is It? How Is It Measured? Does It Affect Loyalty? *Journal of Marketing*, 73(3), 52–68.

Callon, M., Méadel, C., and Rabeharisoa, V. (2002). The Economy of Qualities. *Economy and Society*, 31(2), 194–217.

Concha, P. (2017). The Curation of the Street Food Scene in London. PhD thesis, London School of Economics and Political Science (LSE).

De Farias, S., Aguiar, E., and Melo, F. (2014). Store Atmospherics and Experiential Marketing: A Conceptual Framework and Research Propositions for an Extraordinary Customer Experience. *International Business Research*, 7(2), 87–99.

Entwistle, J. (2009). *The Aesthetic Economy of Fashion: Markets and Value in Clothing and Modelling*. Oxford: Berg.

Entwistle, J., and Wissinger, E. (2006). Keeping Up Appearances: Aesthetic Labour in the Fashion Modelling Industries of London and New York. *The Sociological Review*, 54(4), 774–795.

Gandy, M. (2017). Urban Atmospheres. *Cultural Geographies*, 24(3), 353–374.

Hochschild, A. (1983). *The Managed Heart*. Berkeley: University of California Press.

Holbrook, M. B., and Hirschman, E. C. (1982). The Experiential Aspects of Consumption: Consumer Fantasies, Feelings, and Fun. *Journal of Consumer Research*, 9(2), 132–140.

Joosse, S., and Hracs, B. J. (2015). Curating the Quest for 'Good Food': The Practices, Spatial Dynamics and Influence of Food-related Curation in Sweden. *Geoforum*, 64, 205–216.

Kent, T. (2007). Creative Space: Design and the Retail Environment. *International Journal of Retail and Distribution Management*, 35(9), 734–745.

Kotler, P. (1973). Atmospherics as a Marketing Tool. *Journal of Retailing*, 49(4), 48–64.

Lewisham Council. (2014). Lewisham Town Centre Local Plan. Available from www.l ewisham.gov.uk/myservices/planning/policy/LDF/lewisham/Documents/Lewisham% 20Town%20Centre%20Local%20Plan.pdf [Accessed 9 August 2016].

Leys, R. (2011). The Turn to Affect: A Critique. *Critical Inquiry*, 37, 434–472.

MacCannell, D. (1973). Staged Authenticity: Arrangements of Social Space in Tourist Settings. *American Journal of Sociology*, 79(3), 589–603.

Nixon, S. (2006). The Pursuit of Newness: Advertising, Creativity and the 'Narcissism of Minor Differences'. *Cultural Studies*, 20(1), 89–106.

Seigworth, G., and Gregg, M. (2010). An Inventory of Shimmers. In: Gregg M., and Seigworth, G. (Eds) *The Affect Theory Reader*. Durham, NC and London: Duke University Press, 1–25.

Sloane, M. (2014). Tuning the Space: Investigating the Making of Atmospheres through Interior Design Practices. *Interiors: Design, Architecture and Culture*, 5(3), 297–314.

Smith Maguire, J., and Matthews, J. (2012). Are We All Cultural Intermediaries Now? An Introduction to Cultural Intermediaries in Context. *European Journal of Cultural Studies*, 15(5), 551–562.

Ticineto Clough, P. (2007). Introduction. In: Ticineto Clough, P., and Halley, J. (Eds) *The Affective Turn*. Durham, NC and London: Duke University Press, 1–33.

10 Tales from the cheese counter

Taskscape and taste at Neal's Yard Dairy

Mukta Das and Celia Plender

At Neal's Yard Dairy in Covent Garden, London, the shop counter is long, stretching almost the entire length of the premises. The brick base has a worktop of thick black slate, on top of which sits a vast array of cheeses. The darkness of the slate contrasts sharply with their pale hues. There is order to the abundance; whole wheels, wedges and logs of the same cheese are piled together, and sheep and goat cheeses sit side by side. Each cluster is accompanied by a label – black with white writing, laminated and inserted into a wood block to hold it up and straight. The labels are straightforward: 'Kirkham's Mature Lancashire. Made by Graham Kirkham near Goosnargh, Lancashire, England. Raw Cow's Milk, Animal Rennet. £28.50/kg' or 'Lincolnshire Poacher. Made by Simon and Tim Jones near Alford, Lincolnshire, England. Raw Milk, Holstein Cows, Animal Rennet. £25.45/kg'. The labels continue all the way down the line as cheddars give way to blues and blues to soft cheeses.

The smell of cheese is deep and long thanks to the humid air, which is churned out by a sprinkling humidifier and, in part, by glistening, wet floors. The shop's high humidity (between 70 and 80 per cent) and cellar temperatures (between 10 and 14 degrees centigrade) are, on the whole, the optimal conditions for tasting cheese, and for maturing some. The counter is only one source of the smell; the custom-made shelves filled with wheels of cheddar and stilton that hug the walls are another. In combination, the shop is cheese in surround-aroma.

To a large extent, this space has been shaped by Bob Coleman, the Dairy's designer-carpenter, enacting the vision of Randolph Hodgson, the Dairy's owner, and one-time carpenter's helper to Bob back in the 1970s. 'We just want it to smell of cheese and be like a [farmhouse] cheese store', Bob explains:

> And so you keep the cheese in cold, cool damp conditions, and the atmosphere ... I suppose part of our ethos is that we want to be authentic and that's a key word in our ethos. You know, we want to sell it as it is, as it's matured. It's farmhouse cheese.

Neal's Yard Dairy's preoccupation with authentically evoking a farmhouse cheese store is built into the very wood, stone, concrete, stainless steel knives and tasting irons; into the social environment that shapes the Dairy; and the tastes that are generated within it. Bob is aware that balancing the feel and taste of an authentic farmhouse with the practicalities of a retail business is an ongoing and often contested process. Talking of the legitimacy of certain cuisines anthropologist Arjun Appadurai suggests a definition of authenticity that gestures at its perpetually unfinished state. 'Authenticity measures the degree to which something is more or less what it ought to be' (1986: 25). But how it comes to conform to this norm is highly contextual, and reliant on many different actors.

Much like the Dairy, this chapter approaches authenticity as something not quite at hand, but made imaginable through the work demanded of its physical and social materiality, in other words, its taskscape. In her study of the growth of America's artisanal cheese movement, Heather Paxson suggests that a taskscape is a 'working landscape' of connected everyday practices which attract tourists but are also laden with the 'true values of dairy farming' (2013: 202); values which are used to craft an identity among artisanal cheese makers. Paxson's taskscape is, for the most part, farm-based, nearer the production of milk than the market. In this chapter we relocate the taskscape to the urban shop floor and within certain intersubjectivities that flavour the shopping environment and inform how the cheeses taste and are tasted. Much of this comes down to the craft practices apparent at the Dairy.

Bob, now a director of the Dairy, has worked with Randolph for more than 30 years to shape the materials and the ethos of the business. Although not

Figure 10.1 Setting up at Shorts Gardens
Source: Tricia de Courcy Ling: www.triciadecourcyling.co.uk.

formally trained in design or carpentry, over time and through practice, he has built up his skills designing and building for the Dairy and other Neal's Yard businesses. Evidence of people practising craft skills is also present in other aspects of the shop. The most obvious is the farmhouse cheeses themselves and the time, techniques and knowledge required to produce them. Cheese does not stop changing once it leaves the farmhouse though, and it is the cheesemonger's job to maintain its integrity between the store, the counter and the customer's home. As Paxson puts it, 'Call it crafty, call it craft: skilled, reputable cheesemongers move cheese in varying states of decomposition to trusting customers' (Paxson, 2014).

Indebted to ethnographic work of Paxson on cheese and craft (2013, 2014), as well as Ingold (2001) and West (2013) on taskscape, knowledge and environment, we argue that the process of cheese making continues here among the teak and stone, and that the tasks related to judging 'when a cheese is most itself' (Paxson, 2014) form part of an apprenticeship in taste, in which the cheesemongers and customers are both implicated. Looking at and out from the counter, we explore the craft practices that have shaped the Dairy and its cheeses. And, in turn, how the practical and affective qualities of the ethos, sensual materiality and taskscape that these practices have created inform how the taste of the cheese is experienced.

This in-depth case study of the Dairy is based on several walking interviews with Bob Coleman at the Dairy's shops in Covent Garden and Borough Market in 2015, as well as oral history interviews conducted with managers,

Figure 10.2 Cutting cheese
Source: Tricia de Courcy Ling: www.triciadecourcyling.co.uk.

staff and customers of the Dairy in 2014, and engagement with the Dairy as intermittent customers.

The making of Neal's Yard Dairy

A small number of early important decisions have come to define why the shop space looks as it does. In 1979 Nicholas Saunders, the alternative entrepreneur and countercultural figure responsible for setting up a wholefoods shop and many other businesses in Neal's Yard, invited Randolph Hodgson to run the Dairy in the Yard. In the beginning, the small store was dedicated to making and selling its own cheese, yoghurt and ice cream. Within months of opening, Nicholas had sold the Dairy to Randolph Hodgson, soon writing off Randolph's debt for the sale as neither believed the Dairy would become profitable enough for him to pay it back (Albery and Mills, 1987: 46). By the second winter Randolph had decided to start selling other people's cheeses. Although he had turned to a few wholesalers to populate the shop, it was farmhouse cheese maker Hilary Charnley who ignited in Randolph a desire to seek out others like her after she sent the Dairy a sample of her Devon Garland. Randolph toured British farms (sometimes with Bob), and soon direct contact with the few surviving English and Irish cheese makers replaced buying through uninspiring wholesalers. When more and more boxes of diverse, non-uniform cheeses of varying ripeness were collected or delivered to the Dairy, the physical nature of the shop had to change. As Bob recalls:

> Cheeses that were presented in [other] shops were presented in cold cabinets, wrapped in cling film which wasn't exciting … we had what was essentially a dairy and we felt that it would be much more interesting to present cheeses on the shelves like we saw them when we went and visited the farms. We'd go into the cheese stores and you'd see all the cheese on the shelves and there was a terrific atmosphere … so, more or less, we agreed that we wanted to put cheese on the shelves in the shop … to let the product sell itself fill it full of cheese, and the only way we can fill it full of cheese without ruining the cheese, is to use it as a place for storing or maturing cheese.

A decision based on a desire to present an 'authentic' experience would quickly come to define the business. Maturing and storing cheese is an intensive and highly skilled process of temperature and humidity control, of washing rinds, brushing and turning cheeses and scraping clean their cut faces. It also demands certain types of spaces – counters, shelves, cabinets and cold rooms, and a number of skilled and knowledgeable workers with a deep understanding of space, time and taste.

Having earned his stripes on the earlier, successful redesign and refit of the bakery in Neal's Yard, and finding regular work on the interior of the Yard's wholefoods shop, Bob was asked to remodel the Dairy. Under the guidance

Figure 10.3 The counter
Source: Tricia de Courcy Ling: www.triciadecourcyling.co.uk.

and leadership of Randolph, Bob returned to the lessons learned from experiments with time and motion at the bakery to turn the miniscule Dairy into a maturing/storing site and retail space; and he turned to the farmhouse in his choice of material – wood. On a shoestring budget, Bob made do with found materials from skips and local reclamation yards, and built the shop fixtures in his workshop above Monmouth Coffee Shop, where his drilling would send a regular dusting of ceiling plaster over the baristas. Randolph and Bob worked together, iteratively, and sometimes separately; Randolph on the plumbing and Bob the carpentry. Long-standing customers, including Jason Hinds, who became a Neal's Yard Dairy cheesemonger and eventually a director, recalls the results of Randolph and Bob's work. An overladen L-shaped counter, rows of shelves against the walls and an early version in Bob's series of quirky humidifiers, built from buckets and pans, which all gave the shop the look of informal, experimental, overflowing abundance. 'You did kind of feel like the cheese was coming in on you, I liked that feeling … you really felt immersed in cheese' (Hinds, 2014).

Relocations and the spread to more sites, Shorts Garden in 1992, Park Street in Borough Market in 1997 and on Dockley Road in Bermondsey in 2014 required more of Bob's design work, but buildings are never complete. On one of our walking interviews we asked a long-standing shop manager for an explanation of Bob's design process. 'Bob stands in a corner, watching for a while. Then in a few weeks, something about the counter will have changed and our lives are a little bit easier', he answers.

Observations and non-verbal communication are not unusual among crafts people. As Marchand notes of the experienced masons in Mali, 'spatial configurations exist in the mind's eye of the master mason' (2009: 85), but the mind's eye is a social space, filled with human interactions; there are 'ways of knowing and thinking that can be best expressed in action and skilled performance'(Marchand, 2009: 85). Bob's silent observations and subsequent adjustments of the counter are partly his approach to time-motion configuration, but are also a recognition that much of the knowledge and skill required at the Dairy is embodied by the cheesemongers and the customers. They are, in fact, both highly skilled. The cheesemongers' and customers' everyday activities and routines, as an embodiment of this knowledge, need to be more proficient, more discernible – these farmhouse taskscapes rendered more understandable to managers, staff and customers.

The farmhouse and shop — a continuum in taste

The farmhouse is a powerful symbol. It is often evoked as a place of artisanal rather than factory-produced foods, where people close to the land and its harvest churn, age, cure and pickle, following timeless traditions. Who evokes the symbol of the farmhouse and to what end are important questions? As anthropologist Harry West highlights, the romanticisation and heritagisation of the 'authentic farmhouse' can mummify places and processes even when producers see their cheese making as a dynamic, 'living tradition' (2014: 74).

Despite the changes to the materials of and in farmhouses over the years, their importance as artisanal places continues to be reinforced and regenerated in opposition to industrial food-making's faceless non-places (Coles, 2013). Cheese maker Joe Schneider is co-reinventor of Stichelton cheese. Randolph Hodgson, founder of the Dairy, and one of Stichelton's most important distributors is equally credited with its revival. In interviews with West, Schneider describes a taskscape at his farm where it is possible to actively respond to the environment in which he makes it. Schneider (2013) works with the principle of holism to produce cheeses that taste within a certain bandwidth, not by eliminating variables, which is the goal of industrial cheese-making processes, but rather by intimately understanding and anticipating the future needs of the milk produced by his Holstein cows. Maintaining this bandwidth links the milk and the maturing cheese with a variety of tasks that veer between waiting and handling, and comes with risks and rewards that are also a cheesemonger's lot.

As Paxson suggests, cheesemongering can be a craft in its own right, which has an equally 'marginal status, [is] financially tenuous and prone to romanticization' (2014). Skilled, intensive labour – a number of people working in a coordinated way, but each fulfilling specialist and discrete tasks – can convey much about the risks and romantic characteristics of the cheese-making process, which continues here. Sales have been buoyant at every site where Neal's

Yard Dairy has combined the work of maturing, storing and retailing, in essence collapsing the psycho-geographic distance between the farmhouse and the urban grocer and producing the resultant taskscape. Bob understands that this insight into the taskscapes of cheese's ecology increases curiosity and enhances appetite: 'If you've got a lot of activity, people turning cheeses, cutting them, this sort of thing, that affects your taste buds, it makes you fascinated and … you can't just taste things in isolation, it's everything associated with that'. Tasting the practices and social values that go into making artisanal cheese can help to make the cheese taste good (Paxson, 2013: 195).

The task of storing farmhouse cheese

Being both a storehouse and a retailer of farmhouse cheese, the Dairy demands its own particular approach to ergonomics and environmental controls with materials. This is by no means an easy process. Wooden shelves, a tried and tested farmhouse technology that the Dairy has adopted, have come under particular scrutiny from the health and safety inspectorate. As Bob recalls:

> Bare wood was the best material [for keeping cheese], but you'd always be fighting with the health and safety brigade with this kind of thing. They say you should use stainless steel or plastic … if you use something like stainless steel or plastic … the cheese tends to stick to it and you get a syrupy wetness under the cheese. It's sort of the perfect place for developing the wrong kind of bugs really, and we found … that just using, well it was old knowledge really, but just forgotten knowledge, that you just put it on sawn wood — it's got a slightly rough surface — and the cheese keeps perfectly well on it. And these cheese shelves that we designed, we have sold them to farms and things that produce cheese.

Contemporary farmhouse cheeses have become increasingly moist, and the biggest challenge lies in drying the cheese at a steady pace, which requires controlled dampness in shops that need to keep their doors open to entice customers. Controlling dampness has been a challenge. The original plywood used for the counter in Shorts Garden rotted and almost collapsed through the floor after several years of use. It has been replaced by brick in more recent iterations. But at the Dairy, function never completely dictates form, although it is hard to identify whether form or function most animates Bob. Bob selected an engineering brick which has far less water absorption; but it is also a handsome blue-black. He has made wooden inserts which slot into the space under the counter, the treated wood and blue-black brick forming a beautiful contrast. These inserts hold cheese-wrapping paper of different sizes; the most popular sizes are the most easily to hand. A thicker hand crafted Welsh slate now covers the counter, built into which are wire cheese cutters that can be pulled and extended over any sized wheel without damaging the rock. The shelves are still made from rich, honey-coloured spruce, sourced from Comte in France or the UK. But because spruce also has an inclination to rot Bob now lines the bottoms of the shelf posts with more hardy teak or iroko.

How does Bob know his work makes the cheese taste good? Bob does not taste cheese as a task to determine the quality or success of his designs. He prefers to interact with the Dairy as a customer, buying the cheeses he loves. He leaves the tasting of the cheese as it matures to the cheesemongers. It is they who give him the vital feedback he needs to assess the efficacy of his work – observations on tasting cheese with customers; the progress of pre-servation and degradation measured on charts and in tasting notes; logs of daily temperature and humidity checks; or sales analyses shared in key meetings.

The task of tasting

On the wall column behind the counter on magnetised strips are rows of cheese knives. It is with these that some of the toughest work happens at the Dairy's shops. If industrially produced cheeses are made to be consistent farmhouse cheeses are not. The flavour and feel of a cheese can vary from batch to batch, season to season or year to year. Each day the Dairy's cheesemongers spend a great deal of their time tasting cheese to determine whether the levels of salt, acidity and moisture are at peak condition. Hard cheeses are ordered on a Monday and soft cheeses on a Wednesday. When they are delivered the same or next day, the cheesemongers taste them straight away and make flavour notes that determine which are ready for the counter and where the others should be kept. Cheeses in the batch are ordered according to ripeness – the ripest, runniest cheeses are sometimes left in the cold room before being placed on the counter to stop the cheese from taking on an overly harsh ammonia flavour. Softer, smaller and more bloomy-rinded cheeses tend to last better in cooler conditions, and they are packed into plastic trays and returned to the cold store as soon as the day is done.

Scholars who study craft practices often highlight the significance of learning through doing. In his work on food and memory in Greece, for example, anthropologist David Sutton suggests that learning to cook, is an 'embodied apprenticeship'. Rather than following an easily replicable set of written rules it involves, 'images, tastes, smells and experiences' (2001: 135), leading to embodied knowledge built up through time and practice. Becoming part of the Dairy's taskscape is a similarly sensual process.

David Lockwood, one of the directors of the Dairy, recalls that his apprenticeship in taste started from his first day as a cheesemonger in the Neal's Yard shop. Presented with around 30 Stilton cheeses he was tasked with deciding the order in which to sell them. Rather than judge by batch or date, this was done by tasting every single one. As David explains,

Figure 10.4 Tasting knives
Source; Tricia de Courcy Ling: www.triciadecourcyling.co.uk.

> That's how you learn about cheese, you eat it, that hasn't changed. It's inward looking. And so that's what we try to do in the shops, we try and teach people to eat the cheese … the work that we do is to taste the cheese and to taste it with other people and if we do our work well, they the customers'll buy.
>
> (Lockwood, 2014)

If the process of judging when the cheese is ready is a task shared by both cheesemonger and customer, then these encounters have the power to reconfigure the spaces of the Dairy. In such times of judgement, the fridge, shelves and counter become a continuum rather than fixed as places of storage and selling. Shop manager Martin articulates how the porousness of these spaces is a through interactions with the customer.

> Then we need to know that if a customer wants a Tunworth, that we ask them, is it for today, in which case I have something super ripe that you might like in the cold room or do you want something for this weekend?
>
> (Matheson, 2014)

Customers are invited to learn to taste as soon as they enter the shop. The cheesemonger will offer a sample of cheese but through bodily gestures will indicate that no verbal exchange on its taste is required, unlike the analogical language demanded in oenology or fine chocolate tasting (Terrio, 1996: 71).

The Dairy's cheesemongers are dissuaded from offering 'foodie chat' (Matheson, 2014) or expecting it from the customer. With near silence at the counter, it takes a practised observer to understand what other information to impart, or what cheese the monger should offer next. It may be three or four tastings in before the customer offers more or any structured feedback – more often than not, this takes the form of a purchasing decision.

Silent, sensual apprenticeships need a social context in which people can understand that learning is taking place, and their subjective experiences of tasting is their main teaching device. This is something that West has observed at every stage of cheese making. Even when cheesemongers or producers taste among themselves, the language used to describe the cheese and the science behind the taste and texture is less developed than he had expected, almost sublinguistic.

Allowing this process to permeate a social space that is usually fraught with judgement and expectation is to understand what retail space the Dairy occupies in opposition to other elite shopping experiences. Usually in high-end shops or boutiques, the shop floor is stage managed by a group of experts and the space is socially organised into knowers and buyers. In contrast, the bustle of the Dairy's taskscape – staff otherwise preoccupied with work, washing rinds, turning cheeses – and the act of silent tasting draw customers in towards the cheeses' taskscape as co-producers of the final product. As the Dairy's owner Randolph puts it, 'a cheese must be good on the customer's palate to be a good cheese' (West, 2013: 340).

Figure 10.5 Cheese labels
Source: Tricia de Courcy Ling: www.triciadecourcyling.co.uk.

Conclusion

West describes the Dairy as 'the most important cheesemonger in the United Kingdom' (Ibid: 323) due to the work it has done to support and successfully promote farmhouse cheeses in the UK. On its busiest days, nearing Christmas, up to 15 cheesemongers work the counter at Shorts Garden, and sales have sometimes reached a record £26,000 a day.

Can such a space full of related activities – a taskscape – be considered tasty? Of course environments have an impact on taste. At the Dairy, the design of the shops feeds into a taskscape that is focused almost entirely on shepherding a cheese to its optimum taste point. A good taskscape is tasty because it resonates with the type and level of craft and of value generated by the holistic, thoughtful actions of farmhouse cheese making – by the producers, cheesemongers and the customers who help to determine what is good and when it is at its best. A busy day at the shop is also a tasty day. The interplay between craft, task and taste, between subjective experiences of taste and bodily knowledge are understood empirically (Paxson, 2013). The Dairy is a practical, yet affective retail space in which customers are not just buying cheese, but also engaging in 'the adventure and pleasure of taste, the status of connoisseurship, the pride of supporting a local business or the institution of small-scale farming' (Ibid: 154).

As Marchand notes, craftwork 'entails continual improvisation and problem solving in response to an evolving and changing context'. As a consequence, the 'final plan or design' is often the 'result, and not the generator, of the work' (2009: 96). Ingold agrees that taskscapes are dynamic, transforming and transformative, ever responding to their environment (2001). Bob has observed this as the Dairy has grown to occupy more sites, resulting in a split between retail, wholesale and maturing spaces and tasks. This has been felt most keenly at Park Street in Borough Market, since the Dairy's wholesaling and maturing moved to a neighbouring site in Bermondsey. For the first time in the Dairy's history at that site, sales have levelled off. The Dairy now faces a choice about how to refill the space, which has drawn Bob back to his and Randolph's original idea, to recreate a tasty taskscape. The last words are Bob's, musing on his preferred option,

> I don't know if I can get people into this, if we are going to keep the premises large, which we'll probably have to for a while … [we could] use it to mature cheese even if we can't sell it all across the counter. We'd send it back to wholesale or whatever and so you'd actually use it as a cheese-maturing place just to get that kind of activity and ambience back into the site.

References

Books and articles

Albery, N., and Mills, C. (1987). *The Neal's Yard Story*. London: Institute for Social Invention.

Appadurai, A. (1986). Introduction: Commodities and the Politics of Value. In: Appadurai, A. (Ed.) *The Social Life of Things: Commodities in Cultural Perspective.* Cambridge: Cambridge University Press, 3–63.

Coles, B. (2013). Ingesting Places: Embodied Geographies of Coffee. In: Abbots, E. J., and Lavis, A. (Eds.) *Why We Eat How We Eat: Contemporary Encounters Between Foods and Bodies.* Ashgate, Oxen and Burlington, MA: Ashgate, 255–270.

Ingold, T. (2001). From the Transmission of Representations to the Education of Attention. In: Whitehouse, H. (Ed.) *The Debated Mind: Evolutionary Psychology Versus Ethnography.* Oxford and New York: Berg, 113–153.

Matheson, A. (2014). The Stink Interviews … Martin Tkalez, Manager of Neal's Yard Dairy in Covent Garden. *Wordpress*, 7 May. Available from https://thestinklondon. wordpress.com/2014/05/07/the-stink-interviews-martin-tkalez-manager-of-neals-yard -dairy-in-covent-garden [Accessed August 2016].

Marchand, T. H. J. (2009). *The Masons of Djenné.* Bloomington and Indianapolis: Indiana University Press.

Paxson, H. (2013). *The Life of Cheese: Crafting Food and Value in America.* Berkeley: University of California Press.

Paxson, H. (2014). *The Art of the Monger.* Limn, May 2014. Available from: http://lim n.it/the-art-of-the-monger [Accessed August 2016].

Sutton, D. E. (2001). *Remembrance of Repasts: An Anthropology of Food and Memory.* Oxford and New York: Berg.

Terrio, S. (1996). Crafting Grand Cru Chocolates in Contemporary France. *American Anthropologist*, 98(1), 67–79.

West, H. G. (2013). Thinking Like a Cheese: Towards an Ecological Understanding of the Reproduction of Knowledge in Contemporary Artisan Cheese Making. In: Ellen, R., Lycett, S. J., and Johns, S. E. (Eds) *Understanding Cultural Transmission in Anthropology: A Critical Synthesis.* Oxford: Berghahn Books, 320–345.

West, H. G. (2014). Bringing It All Back Home: Reconnecting the Country and the City through Heritage Food Tourism in the French Auvergne. In Domingos, N., Sobral, J. M., and West, H. G. (Eds) *Food Between the Country and the City: Ethnographies of a Changing Global Foodscape.* London and New York: Bloomsbury, 73–88.

Archival

Hinds, J., interviewed by Celia Plender, 2 April (2014). London. *An Oral History of Neal's Yard*, British Library Sound Archive, London, C1649.

Lockwood, D., interviewed by Mukta Das, 7 March (2014). London. *An Oral History of Neal's Yard*, British Library Sound Archive, London, C1649.

11 Blackout

Blurring the boundaries between senses

Nina J. Morris, Vania Ling and Ericka Duffy

In summer 2015 Dublin-based ensemble Kirkos (led by Irish composers Sebastian Adams and Robert Coleman) – in collaboration with food-specialist Vania Ling, chef Kevin Powell and scent-technician Ericka Duffy — hosted three pairs of immersive, multi-sensory, contemporary music concerts in the Royal Irish Academy of Music under the collective title *Blackout*. Performed in near complete darkness each concert centred on music chosen for its engagement with the 'dark' themes of war — *Quartet for the End of Time* (1941) by French composer Olivier Messiaen, *Different Trains* (1988) by Jewish-American composer Steve Reich and *Harry Patch* (2015) by Sebastian Adams.[1] The concerts incorporated visual, olfactory and gustatory elements designed to enhance the audience's engagement with the music and the ideas behind it (Murray, 2015). Inspired by recent research on sensory cross-modality (Deroy, Crisinel and Spence, 2013; Spence and Wang, 2015a) and drawing on the connections between the senses of smell and taste and human emotion (Lupton, 2005), the goal was to generate a 'thick atmosphere' capable of detaching the audiences not just from their 'habitual experience of space' (Edensor, 2015: 133) but also their conventional experience of music.[2] As such, these multi-sensory performances might be described as 'affective landscapes', if we understand affect as 'something that moves, that triggers reactions, forces or intensities ... simultaneously engaging the mind and body, reason and emotions' (Berberich, Campbell and Hudson, 2013: 314).

Focusing specifically on the experience of dining in the dark, and drawing on extant work relating to sense, space and experience, this chapter will consider how taste can be influenced by the visual, auditory and olfactory qualities of an environment. The first section outlines the ambient dimensions of the performance space. Stroebele and De Castro (2004: 821) describe ambience as consisting of those 'parts of the environment that are hard to localize and that surround the organism integrally like temperature, sound, smell and so on'. Ambience is 'that which surrounds us, that which pervades. Always-on. Always by-your-side' (Jaaniste, 2010: 1). Ambience has 'potential for impinging upon human functioning at nearly all levels—physiology, motivation, mood, behavior, cognition and social interaction' (Stroebele and De Castro, 2004: 821). The second section documents the way in which Kirkos attempted to utilise people" visceral experiences of food (tastes, textures, aromas) to effect and affect the audience' in situ emotional and affective relations (Longhurst, Johnston and Ho, 2009). Food can at times connect us to the very core of ourselves (Ibid.); in facilitating a deeper connection with the self. Kirkos hoped that the audience might, as a result, connect more deeply, personally and, perhaps, more emphatically with the music. In concluding, we briefly note the impracticality (and undesirability) of trying to 'prime' affect (Edensor and Falconer, 2014) in order to elicit a *singular* emotive response from an audience. Acknowledging Kirkos' avowedly open approach to meaning-making we celebrate their attempt to sensitise the audience to the music via a stimulation of their full sensorium.

In the dark

Being in the dark is a uniquely 'reflective and bodily aware experience' (Vongsathorn, O'Hara, and Mentis 2013: 1277). For diurnal humans complete darkness can be risky, full of copious absence (Alston, 2016). We see differently in the dark and not always what we would wish to see (Morris, 2011). Loss of visual acuity can leave us literally grasping for information; in such a state of uncertainty 'matter matters more than ever [only] in the certainties of the lit world [do] material things pass beyond concern' (Welton, 2013: 14). Yet, darkness can also be a voluptuous and supportive realm replete with transformative potential (Morris, 2011); we not only 'see' differently but can *be* differently in the dark (Welton, 2013).

In the last decade, a growing number of artists, musicians and theatre groups have begun to exploit the affective possibilities of darkness in a 'move away from the representational' prioritising instead, 'the sensual and affective experience of the visitor' (Edensor, 2015: 133).[3] Spanning a wide range of interests, these works have used darkness either as a means to unsettle their audience, appeal to their imaginations or to encourage them to address their immediate sensations (Ibid.). As affective landscapes these works demand audience participation rather than their passive receptivity (Berberich, Campbell and Hudson, 2015). The *Blackout* series used darkness as a simultaneously disquieting and self-actualising entity. It eschewed the standard conventions that traditionally dictate the flow and appearance of theatrical performances and kept its audiences literally and metaphorically 'in the dark'.

Convention dictates, for example, that performances 'begin with the lowering of the houselights in the auditorium prior to the raising of the those focused on the stage', an act usually preceded by the audience waiting

> under the houselights, for their lowering [during which time] they take stock of their surroundings and of one another, and in [the] lull before the show starts begin to develop something of a sense of themselves as a collective [and prepare] for the experience to come.
>
> (Welton, 2013: 7)

In the *Blackout* concerts the auditorium lights were already off when the audience arrived. Only a brief description of the concerts was provided upon booking. Although some in the audience may have had knowledge of the musical pieces, they would have known little about what the concerts entailed.[4] The black paint strokes background detail on the pages of the concert programme became progressively denser eventually obscuring the text completely.

On arrival, following a short briefing in the foyer on the rules of participation (for example: no mobile phones, no talking, follow the guide) the audience were led swiftly away, in groups of five, through a door and down a long, semi-dark hallway by a black-clad, white-masked 'light bearer' holding a torch aloft.[5] At the end of this corridor they were ushered into a dark 'entrance room' where they paused before being led into the minimally-lit concert hall. Illuminated by a candle on each table and (periodically by) the black-clad musicians' stand-lights (Figure 11.1), the auditorium was more 'shadowy' rather than wholly dark, however, this processional had two key effects (Welton, 2013). It performed the representational work expected from a conventional 'blackout' (it signalled the start of the performance, it facilitated a blurring of time and place). It also played a key role in constructing the affective atmosphere, 'countering [the] entrenched, predefined systems of thought and feeling' that one might expect a traditional concert goer to have (Berberich et al, 2013: 313). Moving through these dimly lit and dark spaces

Figure 11.1 Musicians with stand lights
Source: Kirkos Ensemble.

the audience encountered a 'distinctive sensory immersion' (Radywyl, 2010) wherein vision was put on an equal footing with their senses of smell, touch, taste and hearing.

Attentive listening

Human attention becomes more focused in the dark. In the *Blackout* concerts the darkness had the 'effect of augmenting the audience's attention to a laser-like focus ... dehumanis[ing] the performers, making the movements and expressions that were visible even more effective, as if an intrinsic part of the music being played' (Murray, 2015). Yet we do more than re-calibrate our sight in the dark, we also re-evaluate our other senses. Humans pay more attention not just to sound per se, but to small changes in sound (Vongsa-thorn et al, 2013): texture, pitch, tone, timbre, dynamics, volume and other sonic properties (Vannini et al, 2010). Sound played a key role in transporting the audience's attention elsewhere before they had even entered the performance space. Acclimatising to the darkness of the entrance room the audience's attention was snagged by sampled sounds emanating from hidden speakers: raindrops for the *Quartet* concert, ear-piercing train whistles (accompanied by a life-size projection of a train approaching from one side and leaving via the other) for the *Trains* concert and children's' laughter interspersed with the voices of war veterans for the *Patch* concert.

During the concerts the music exercised the audience's auditory perception alternating between extremes of pitch, audibility and tempo. Written while Messiaen was interned in Stallag VIIIA prison camp in Görlitz, Germany, the *Quartet* was inspired by text from the *Book of Revelation* and symbolises an apocalyptic future when time no longer holds true. Scored for clarinet, violin, cello and piano the piece has eight movements – 1. Crystal liturgy, 2. Voca-lise, for the Angel who announces the end of time, 3. Abyss of birds, 4. Interlude, 5. Praise to the eternity of Jesus, 6. Dance of fury, for the seven trumpets, 7. Tangle of rainbows, for the Angel who announces the end of time, and 8. Praise to the immortality of Jesus. Premiered on a bitterly cold (possibly rain-soaked night, accounts vary) to an audience of inmates and guards, the music avoids the rhythmical cadence generally associated with Western music preferring rhythms that expand, contract, repeat and stop suddenly, following constantly changing (sometimes symmetrical, often unpredictable) patterns (Ross, 2004).

Reich's *Trains* references the trains that were transporting European Jews during the Holocaust at the same time that a juvenile Reich was being shut-tled by train between his separated parents in New York and Los Angeles. First performed by the Kronos Quartet at the Queen Elizabeth Hall in London, and one of Reich's best-known compositions, the piece is scored for a string quartet in three movements – 1. America before the war, 2. Europe during the war, and 3. After the war. Alongside the physically present quartet the audience also hear a pre-recorded soundtrack featuring two pre-recorded string quartets, and other sounds including American and European train noises, sirens and sampled voices (from interviews with Reich's ex-governess, a retired US train porter and Holocaust survivors) describing the train journeys they took during this period. It is a complex work with multiple rhythms bound together by texture, harmony, tempo changes and repetitive elements (Haydock, n.d.). Although there is 'very little discernible dynamic change in the individual levels of the instruments or samples', Reich 'alter[s] the amplitude of a passage by increasing or decreasing the amount of texture' (Ibid.). Likewise, there is a symbiotic relationship between the voices and the instruments; the cello and viola doubling the male and female speech melodies respectively (Thacker, 2013).

Composed specifically for the *Blackout* series, *Patch* was inspired by the last surviving British veteran of World War I's emotional statement 'war is not worth one life'. Composed for a quartet of flute, horn, cello and piano, this work is stylistically similar to Messiaen's *Quartet* with an eight movement structure, whilst replicating the theatricality of Reich's *Trains* through the use of off-stage and pre-recorded music played at differing levels of audibility (Dervan, 2015). Closing the series the work aimed for the same emotional world as the *Quartet* but meditates instead on the horror, futility and dispiriting inevitability of war, the stark reality of which is laid bare in 'the final, extended repetition of a bare octave, where [Adams] seems to ask: will this never end?' (Ibid.). It is a 'restless piece' which plays with the audience's expectations, harbouring

> a core of anger, or despair, struggling to … express itself through a haze of smoke and noise, of chaos and turbulence, until it eventually gives up and fades into obscurity, repeated chords on the piano sounding like a slow, dying inhalation and exhalation.
>
> (Murray, 2015)

During the performance the off-stage elements disrupted the conventional 'performance space' weakening the stage as a focal point and making the 'soundworld of the piece seem remote where those of the [preceding] works were intimate' (Ibid). During the penultimate movement the table lights were gradually removed, leaving the pianist illuminated from above by a spotlight which slowly dimmed to nothing as the final bars of the last movement were played.

Smell sensitivities

Odours are known to influence how we think, act, feel and behave (Low, 2009) often at a subconscious or unconscious level (Lupton, 2005). The:

> Most subliminal, the least controllable, the most evocative, the least knowable, and possibly the most gendered of our senses … Smell … is

thought to get us when we are "not looking", to take us unawares and bypass conscious will.

(Jones, 2006: 13–14)

Environmental (or ambient) fragrancing has long been used to increase worker productivity and influence consumer behaviour (Damian and Damian, 2006; Paterson, 2006) and, although restaurants avoid ambient fragrancing for fear of interrupting diners' flavour experience, some do use scent in their entrances to attract people in serving 'as a transition between the hectic world outside and [the] curated gastronomic experience inside' (Spence and Piqueras-Fiszman, 2014: 289).

According to Howes (1987), there is a universal connection between olfaction and transition. This, he argues, works on three different levels: (1) the logical level, for example: one tends to notice odour most at the threshold of a room before we adapt and the smell 'disappears'; (2) the psychological level, for example: smells are said to trigger intense emotional and physiological changes; and, (3) the sociological level, for example: smells (such as incense in churches) can create an 'inter-subjective we-feeling' among participants. Kirkos utilised the affective properties of odour – their ability to draw attention to and re-attune us to the overlooked, marginal or forgotten (Berberich et al, 2013) – in several ways. For the first two concerts a nebuliser hidden in the entrance room enveloped the audience in scents inspired by the music to follow. For the *Quartet* concert oak moss with black pepper was used to elicit the sensation of a cold, damp night outdoors;[6] this was interspersed with the woody aroma of stacked crates and the earthy smell of ferns hanging from the ceiling. For the *Trains* concert the harsh metallic fabric and mechanical motion of this form of transportation was conveyed by cade oil (a species of juniper) with its very strong industrial smoky odour almost like motor oil or coal (Figure 11.2).[7] Our sense of smell is rapidly dulled (Peynaud, 2005) so the audience only needed to be in the entrance room for a short time. Just long enough to gain a sense of themselves as a collective of 'we-group individuals' (Low, 2009) going forward into the unknown.

There is extensive evidence to support the existence of a number of cross-modal correspondences between aromas and sound (Spence and Wang, 2015b). Vanilla is said to have a soft, dull timbre and is evocative of small-step intervals and a slow tempo, whereas citrus is reminiscent of bright and sharp tonality, large-step intervals and a staccato articulation. Perfumers frequently describe the composition of fragrances in terms that bear resemblance to those used by composers; they 'search for the right balance and harmony between high and low notes, they think about tones' (Deroy et al, 2013: 878). In the *Quartet* concert, the use of scent was continued into the performance space. For Ling, listening to the first movement of the *Quartet* (with songbird-like clarinet and piano *ostinato*) brought to mind an airy floral scent; iris, gardenia, neroli or blossom. It was important to wait a while. Scent dispersal is not instantaneous. The change from one scent to another must be managed

Figure 11.2 Vania Ling's notes for *Different Trains*

to avoid cross-contamination; likewise, it was important to get the strength and perceived 'naturalness' just right so as not to detract from the desired effect (Paterson, 2006). In the entrance room the nebuliser made the scents very strong. During Movements 3 and 4 an atomiser was used to spray an orange-blossom scented mist through and over the audience giving a lighter atmospheric effect.

Odour is known to be an effective retrieval cue for both recent events and past happenings (Stroebele and De Castro, 2004). After the concerts the audience were sent home with a 'clean' programme (although the scent and food components were not noted) in an envelope.[8] For the *Trains* concert the programme was sprayed with one full atomised spray of an alcohol and cade oil emulsion so that the audience might reflect on their experience beyond the concert hall.

Taste sensations

Under normal lighting conditions we rely heavily, if unconsciously, on visual cues (for example: variations in illumination and colour) to verify the edibility of food, to make choices regarding its (cultural) acceptability, to evaluate taste and flavour[9] and to monitor the amount we eat (Wansink et al., 2012; Spence and Piqueras-Fiszman, 2014). It is unsurprising then that those eating in dine-in-the-dark establishments often feel 'vulnerable' (Spence and Piqueras-Fiszman, 2014) having transferred responsibility for making these decisions to the chef. Yet, flavour is one of the most multi-sensory of our everyday experiences (Ibid.). Research has also shown that odours emanating from the environment or food itself can also affect our food intake in complex ways (Stroebele and De Castro, 2004). According to Spence (2015: 11), however, 'sound is undoubtedly the forgotten flavour sense'. Although we may not realise we all eat with our oral somatosensory ears; think about squeaky Haloumi cheese, crunchy crusty bread, crispy celery, creamy mousse and the pop of carbonated water. What we listen to while eating and drinking can also affect what we think about what we taste, with our perception of sweetness, acidity, fruitiness, astringency and length all subject to potential modification by ambient sound (Spence and Wang, 2015b).

It is not uncommon for food and wine connoisseurs to describe particular dishes or wines 'in terms of specific musical notes, musical styles, or pieces of music' (Deroy et al, 2013: 878–879) and, indeed, researchers have noted a 'number of cross-modal correspondences between music (or musical attributes) ... and the taste, aroma/bouquet, mouthfeel, and or flavours that are found in wine' (Spence and Wang, 2015a). People have been shown to match sweet and sour tastes with tinkling or reedy high-pitched sounds (for example: piano, oboe, violin), saltiness or dryness with a middle-pitch and bitter tastes with low-pitched brassy sounds (for example: trombone, clarinet, cello) (Deroy et al, 2013; Spence and Wang, 2015a). When designing the food for the *Blackout* series Ling drew heavily on the work of the Crossmodal Research Laboratory at the University of Oxford and musicologists' accounts of Messiaen and Reich's work. As a classically trained musician, Ling also had prior knowledge of these two pre-written works. This was supplemented with research on the composers and the musical inspiration for each piece.

As Moore (2013: 22) notes, we 'cannot know all the meanings given to a musical work by its creator'. By listening carefully to the music, however, and analysing it (noting the instrumentation and non-instrumental sounds used, the main intervals, dominant melodies, textures, underlying tempo, significant harmonies and repetitions), Ling was able to build a detailed sensory map for each work. The result was a set of taste notes which informed the choices made by Powell when he selected the ingredients he would use to create the final dishes (Figure 11.3). For example, the multiple elements of the *Trains* piece and its harrowing personal testimonies left Ling with an overriding sense of danger or 'the unknown' which she correlated with the intense flavours of cloves or caraway seeds (Figure 11.2). The high-pitched, dissonant beat and shocking speed of Movement 2 she associated with the sharpness of spicy hot pepper flakes. Whilst the third movement with its repeating themes, for her, had a more 'salty' middle pitch interspersed with the cello's bitterness. Using these prompts, Powell designed dishes with sharp (for example:

Table 11.1 Menus

Blackout #1	*Quartet for the End of Time*
Movement 2	Rhubarb pickled in blackberry vinegar, cider vinegar and blood orange juice, wrapped in wild garlic leaves with gorse flowers and mushroom sugar syrup
Movement 3	Nameko mushrooms marinated in pineapple sage oil topped with matcha sea salt
Movement 5	Carrot poached in vanilla sugar syrup with bean and goose Tanzania chocolate soil
Movement 7	Preserved orange choux pastry with orange and vanilla creme patisserie

Blackout #2	*Different Trains*
	Earl Grey tea tonic brew
Movement 1	Smoked jelly with woodruff sugar
Movement 2	Cider vinegar jelly with sumac sugar
Movement 3	Caraway cracker with chilli and pepper jam and preserved lemon

Blackout #3	*Harry Patch*
Movement 2	Soft caramel fudge
Movement 4	Beet tartare with radish powder and celery salt
Movement 6	12-day lactofermented veg (radish, kohlrabi)
Movement 7	Sour pickled cucumber, miso and fermented pear

vinegar) and smoky overtones which would tingle the nose and conjure up thoughts of charcoal, the smell of burnt wood or the taste of the ash on the tongue. Keeping in tune with the hopeful aspect of the piece, where possible, the ingredients for this concert reflected embracing the dark and flourishing in it, for example: mushrooms, root vegetables, forced rhubarb.

Getting the sound-taste combination right, Ling knew, had the potential to 'deliver an experience that would appear to be so much richer, or more powerful, than the sum of the individual sensory experiences' (Spence and Wang, 2015b: 10). However, there was a danger that if they tried to do too much the audience would find the experience difficult to decipher. A decision was therefore made to focus on just a few movements in each key work and to try to direct the audience's attention to only a few key elements at a time, for example: a sound, a texture or a smell. So although Ling made comprehensive notes for all the movements in Messiaen's *Quartet* (Figure 11.3) in the end the audience's attention was drawn to: the tender avian lyricism of the clarinet and efflorescent violin of Movement 1; the resonant 'sweet and sour' piano chords in the first and third parts of Movement 2 and the citrusy sweet cascading piano chords and plainchant-like violin and cello of the second

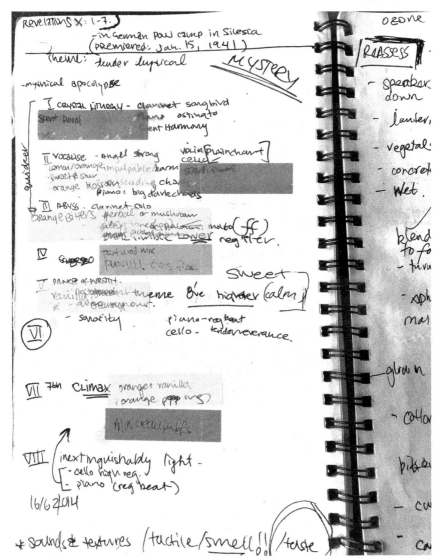

Figure 11.3 Quartet notes

section; the bitterness of the clarinet solo in Movement 3; and, the sweet climatic leap into an imagined paradise beyond time of Movement 7. This simplification of flavours is not uncommon in dine-in-the-dark establishments (Spence and Piqueras-Fiszman, 2014) as previous research has shown that diners-in-the-dark have difficulty identifying even the most commonplace foods (Edensor and Falconer, 2014). The affective role of the taste, flavour and mouth-feel of the food was to heighten and simultaneously re-set the audience's awareness 'like a shock to a wearied system of predefined and

Figure 11.4 Bento Box for *Harry Patch*

long-established expectations' (Berberich et al, 2013: 316) of what listening to a clarinet, violin, piano, etc. might involve, feel like and mean.

Careful attention was also paid to the tactility of the dishes served. Given that the audience would be eating in semi-darkness the easiest way to serve the food was in bite-sized pieces from a bento box (Figure 11.4).[10] In the West we are used to using implements (for example: knife, fork, occasionally chopsticks), to transport our food to our mouths but in some contexts using one's hand to scoop up food is thought to add flavour and a fuller appreciation of texture (Law, 2001). Tuan (2005: 75) has lamented the tendency of modern society and scholars to 'discount the importance of tactile pleasures' noting that most tactile sensations are now experienced indirectly via the eyes. Dining at *Dans le Noir*, however, Edensor and Falconer (2014: 10) noted that they paid much more attention to the 'intensity of the food, its flavours, consistencies, chewiness, smoothness or graininess', with many of their interviewees commenting on 'the intensification of flavour and texture engendered by eating in the dark'.[11] Served to co-ordinate with Movements 2, 4, 6 and 7 the texture and mouthfeel of the dishes ingested by the audience during *Patch* emulated the sensory and textural qualities of the music. In Movement 2 the smoothness of the fudge matched the extremely quiet yet high-pitched simplicity of the flute and cello. In Movement 4 the juxtaposition between the beef tartar and the rye-cracker referenced the contrasting textures of the cello at the start (long notes, expressive) and end of the movement (shorter notes, loud and powerful). In Movement 6 the lacto-fermented radish echoed the contrast between the two extremes of the flute's range. In Movement 7, described by Adams as the 'beefiest', the sour crunch of the cucumber with miso and fermented pear was designed to reflect the sense of tragic failure which imbues the whole piece (rather than the magical moment of redemption as expressed in the *Quartet*).

Conclusion

Aware that our visceral sense and experience of taste is deeply influenced by the qualities of the environment that surrounds us, Kirkos paid careful attention to gradations of light, sound and smell in their staging of the performances. Although the affective atmosphere was different each time, the overriding aim was to harness the multi-dimensional nature of taste so that the audience, through their consumption of the food, would engage with the music in a more embodied way and on a deeper psychological, physical and emotional level than they might ordinarily. Drawing on the transitional qualities associated with smell, the ability of sound to transport the imagination, and the dual sensations of corporeal uncertainty and confidence that darkness brings, Kirkos affected within the audience both a heightened sensitivity to the morsels they consumed and (swept along by the 'we-group' feeling) a willingness to experiment with flavour/mouthfeel sensations. In so doing, they encouraged the audience to become entangled within an affectual landscape comprised of various and complex layers so that they might be impelled to think and rethink, to feel, perceive and relate emotionally to the music in ways that they could not have anticipated (Berberich et al, 2013).

Not surprisingly, co-ordinating the event was not easy; layers of logistics and innumerable moving parts (for example: musicians, audience, sounds, smells, food and lights) meant that it was practically impossible to manufacture a 'universal' experience. Likewise, the audience were not a uniform group; each individual brought their own personal, social and cultural associations relating to food, sound, smell and darkness with them to the concerts (these were as diverse as assumptions about the 'proper' sequencing of a meal to connections made between high-pitched laughter, masks and Halloween). Opting to embrace the multiple variables that can influence, and the highly subjective nature of, people's sense of taste, Kirkos did little to engender within the audience any particular meanings or memories in relation to the performances. Rather, they set out to create a series of complex material, sensual and emotive atmospheres and taste combinations which, when experienced in conjunction with personal subjectivities, worked together to create a series of affective landscapes with limitless possibilities for personal meaning-making. As such, the performances offered each audience member a unique and personally meaningful route through which to contemplate (viscerally and cognitively) aspects of war which they might ordinarily ignore, avoid or be unable to relate to (loneliness, emptiness, despair, grief). In this respect, multi-sensory performances such as *Blackout* have transformative potential because in attending to the complex relationships between the senses, body and mind, they facilitate a departure from all-encompassing, accepted or habitual concepts and theories of events and experiences.

Notes

1 Each central piece was preceded by newly-commissioned 'responsive' works by young Irish composers (Kevin Volans, Raymond Deane, Roger Doyle, Ed Bennett, Seán Clancy, Tom Lane and Robert Coleman) and/or 'complimentary' pre-written works (by Gráinne Mulvey, Olivier Messiaen, Peter Sculthorpe, Roxanna Panufnik and Johann Jakob Froberger).
2 In this sense, the series presents an interesting counterpoint to recent research (Spence and Wang, 2015a, 2015b) on the effects of music on taste.
3 Notable amongst these are John Metcalfe's contemporary musical performance *A Darker Sunset* (2013); Chris Goode's theatrical performance *Who You Are* (2010) (within the darkened interior of Miroslaw Balka's installation *How It Is* at London's Tate Modern); Sound and Fury theatre company's *War Music* (1999), *The Watery Part of the World* (2003?) and *Going Dark* (2011); Complicite theatre company's co-production with Tokyo's Setagaya Public Theatre *Shun-Kin* (2008); the six plays – *The Flooded Grave* by Anthony Weigh, *He Said …* by Mike Bartlett, *Two Cigarettes* by Jack Thorne, *His Ghostly Heart* by Ben Schiffer, *Psychogeography* by Lucy Kirkwood and *Little Dolls* by Nancy Harris – written for the Bush Theatre's *What the Dark Feels Like* series staged during its 2008 *Broken Space* season; and *nacionale vita active* (NVA's) nocturnal installations including *The Storr: Unfolding Landscape* (2005).
4 Although just over a third of the audience were Kickstarter campaign supporters and other individuals intrigued by the promised theatricality of the event, the bulk of the audience was made up of middle-aged, traditional, classical music concert goers and younger contemporary and experimental music listeners. Participants were given no information about the menu prior to the event other than it would be vegetarian and would take personal dietary sensitivities into account.
5 The audience arrived around 22:30 for a 23:00 start – the corridor connecting the foyer to the 'entrance room' had large, high windows and it was necessary to wait for sunset to achieve the required light levels.
6 Alternatives such as evergreen (Balsam fir) or a combination of oak moss and patchouli were considered but discarded in favour of the pepper's pungent mustiness.
7 Also considered was the citrusy, aromatic and slightly smoky smell of bergamot, the strong scent of jonquil or the pungent, camphor-like odour of Southernwood; the cade oil triumphed due to its sulphur tones.
8 The *Patch* programme was not scented, instead it contained a paper poppy.
9 The colour red, for example, is often associated with ripeness or sweetness.

10 Small paper LED lanterns at the front of the room lit up to indicate when the audience should eat the food items.

11 Spence and Piqueras-Fiszman (2014) note that whilst removing vision definitely does allow one to concentrate more on the taste and aroma of food and drink there is, as yet, little evidence to confirm that flavours do become more intense in the absence of sight.

References

Alston, A. (2016). Theatre in the Dark: Spectatorship and Risk in Lundahl and Seitl's Pitch-Black Theatre. In: Alston, A. (Ed.) *Beyond Immersive Theatre*. London: Palgrave Macmillan, 75–107.

Berberich, C., Campbell, N., and Hudson, R. (2013). Affective Landscapes: An Introduction. *Cultural Politics*, 9(3), 313–321.

Berberich, C., Campbell, N., and Hudson, R. (2015). Introduction: Affective Landscapes. In: Berberich, C., Campbell, N., and Hudson, R. (Eds) *Affective Landscapes in Literature, Art and Everyday Life*. Farnham: Ashgate, 1–20.

Damian, P., and Damian, K. (2006). Environmental Fragrancing. In: Drobnick, J. (Ed.) *The Smell Culture Reader*. Oxford: Berg, 148–162.

Deroy, O., Crisinel, A.-S., and Spence, C. (2013). Crossmodal Correspondences Between Odours and Contingent Features: Odours, Musical Notes, and Geometrical Shapes. *Psychonomic Bulletin and Review*, 20, 878–896.

Edensor, T. (2015). Introduction: Sensing and Perceiving with Light and Dark. *The Senses and Society*, 10(2), 129–137.

Edensor, T., and Falconer, E. (2014). Dans le Noir? Eating in the Dark: Sensation and Conviviality in a Lightless Place. *Cultural Geographies*, 22(4), 601–618.

Howes, D. (1987). Olfaction and Transition: An Essay on the Ritual Uses of Smell. *Canadian Review of Sociology*, 24 (3), 398–416.

Jaaniste, L. O. (2010). The Ambience of Ambience. *M/C Journal*, 13 (2), www.journal. media-culture.org.au/index.php/mcjournal/article/view/238.

Jones, C. A. (2006). The Mediated Sensorium. In: Jones, C. A. (Ed.) *Sensorium: Embodied Experience, Technology, and Contemporary Art*. Cambridge, MA: MIT Press, 5–49.

Law, L. (2001). Home Cooking: Filipino Women and Geographies of the Senses in Hong Kong. *Cultural Geographies*, 8, 264–283.

Longhurst, R., Johnston, L., and Ho, E. (2009). A Visceral Approach: Cooking 'At Home' with Migrant Women in Hamilton, New Zealand. *Transactions*, 34(3), 333–345.

Low, K. E. Y. (2009). *Scents and Scent-sibilities*. Newcastle upon Tyne: Cambridge Scholars.

Lupton, D. (2005). *Food and Emotion*. In: Korsmeyer, C. (Ed.) *The Taste Culture Reader*. Oxford: Berg, 317–324.

Moore, S. (2013). *The Listener is the Artist*. In: Carlyle, A., and Lane, C. (Eds) *On Listening*. Axminster: Uniform Books, 22–24.

Morris, N. J. (2011). Night Walking: Darkness and Sensory Perception in a Night-time Landscape Installation. *Cultural Geographies*, 18(3), 315–342.

Murray, A. (2015). Kirkos Ensemble – Blackout #3. *The Journal of Music*, 17 August. Available from http://journalofmusic.com/focus/kirkos-ensemble-blackout-3 [Accessed 22 August 2016].

Paterson, M. W. D. (2006). Digital Scratch and Virtual Sniff: Simulating Scents. In: Drobnick, J. (Ed.) *The Smell Culture Reader*. Oxford: Berg, 358–370.

Peynaud, E. (2005). *Tasting Problems and Errors of Perception*. In: Korsmeyer, C. (Ed.) *The Taste Culture Reader*. Oxford: Berg, 272–278.

Radywyl, N. (2010). "A Little Bit More Mysterious ...": Ambience and Art in the Dark. *M/C Journal*, 13(2), http://journal.media-culture.org.au/index.php/mcjourna l/article/view/225.

Ross, A. (2004). Revelations: Messiaen's Quartet for the End of Time. *The Rest is Noise*. Available from www.therestisnoise.com/2004/04/quartet_for_the_2.html [Accessed 22 August 2016].

Spence, C. (2015). Eating with Our Ears: Assessing the Importance of the Sounds of Consumption on Our Perception and Enjoyment of Multisensory Favour Experiences. *Flavour*, 4(3), 1–14.

Spence, C., and Piqueras-Fiszman, B. (2014). *The Perfect Meal*. Oxford: John Wiley.

Spence, C., and Wang, Q. (2015a). Wine and Music (II): Can You Taste the Music? Modulating the Experience of Wine Through Music and Sound. *Flavour*, 4(33), 1–14.

Spence, C., and Wang, Q. (2015b). Wine and Music (III): So What If Music Influences the Taste of the Wine? *Flavour*, 4(36), 1–15.

Stroebele, N., and De Castro, J. M. (2004). Effect of Ambience on Food Intake and Food Choice. *Nutrition*, 20, 821–838.

Thacker, S. (2013). Steve Reich's "Different Trains" Draws Inspiration from Record- ings of Holocaust Survivors. CBC. Available from www.cbc.ca/manitoba/scene/m usic/2013/01/31/steve-reich [Accessed 22 August 2016].

Tuan, Y.-F. (2005). The Pleasures of Touch. In: Classen, C. (Ed.) *The Book of Touch*. Oxford: Berg, 74–79.

Vannini, P., Waskul, D., Gottschalk, S., and Rambo, C. (2010). Sound Acts: Elocution, Somatic Work, and the Performance of Sonic Alignment. *Journal of Contemporary Ethnography*, 39(3), 328–353.

Vongsathorn, L., O'Hara, K., and Mentis, H. M. (2013). *Bodily Interaction in the Dark*, paper presented at the Conference on Human Factors in Computing Systems, Changing Perspectives Conference, Paris, 27 April–2 May.

Wansink, B., Shimizu, M., Cardello, A. V., Wright, A. O. (2012). Dining in the Dark: How Uncertainty Influences Food Acceptance in the Absence of Light. *Food Quality and Preference*, 24, 209–212.

Welton, M. (2013). The Possibility of Darkness: Blackout and Shadow in Chris Goode's Who You Are. *Theatre Research International*, 38, 4–19.

Archival

Dervan, M. (2015). Total Recall: Musical Feats of Memory. *The Irish Times*, 22 July. Available from www.irishtimes.com/culture/music/total-recall-musical-feats-of-mem ory-1.2292315 [Accessed 22 August 2016].

Haydock, N. (n.d.) *Different Trains*. Available from www.haydockmusic.com/music_ essays/steve_reich_different_trains_part_one.html [Accessed 22 August 2016].

Index

Figures are indexed with *italic* page numbering, Tables with **bold** page numbering.

Printed in the United States
By Bookmasters